THE AMERICAN REVOLUTION IN THE LAW

The American Revolution In The Law

Anglo-American Jurisprudence before John Marshall

Shannon C. Stimson

Princeton University Press
Princeton, New Jersey

© 1990 by Shannon C. Stimson
Published by Princeton University Press
41 William Street, Princeton, New Jersey 08540

Library of Congress Cataloging-in-Publication Data

Stimson, Shannon C.
The American Revolution in the law: Anglo-American jurisprudence
before John Marshall/Shannon C. Stimson.
p.   cm.
Includes bibliographical references.
ISBN 0–691–07874–2 (alk. paper):
    1. Justice. Administration of—United States—History.   2. Jury—
United States—History.   3. Judicial review—United States—
History.   4. United States. Supreme Court—History.   5. United
States—Politics and government—1789–1815.   I. Title.
KF8700.S69   1990
347.73—dc20
[347.307]   90–35658
                                                                  CIP

Printed in Hong Kong

For Joseph and Emily

Contents

Preface   ix

Acknowledgements   xi

PART I   REVOLUTIONS AND CONCEPTUAL CHANGE

1 Political Thought and Historical Problematics   3
     Origins of Judicial Space

2 Historical Transformations and Legal Legacies   10
     The New Legal History and the 'Good Old Law'
     Legal Uncertainty and Fundamental Law
     The Problem of Judicial 'Independence'
     Juries and the Limitations of Judicial Space
     Juries and the English Constitutional Denouement

3 Juries and American Revolutionary Jurisprudence   34
     Bringing Locke Back In
     Law and Adjudication: Who Shall Judge?
     Juries and Judicial Independence in Revolutionary
     America
     Legal Uncertainty and Jural Space in Colonial Law
     Denouement on Judges and Jural Powers in Post-
     Revolutionary America

PART II   FROM JUDICIAL SPACE TO JUDICIAL REVIEW:
FOUR PERSPECTIVES ON THE POWER OF JUDGMENT
IN AMERICAN POLITICS

4 Locating the 'Voice of the People'   69
     The Power of Juries and the 'Reason' of Law
     Adams and the Wilkite Controversy
     Law, Judgment, and the Moral Sense
     Juries and the Expansion of Democratic Republics

5 Law in the Context of Continuous Revolution   86
     Jefferson and the Reconsideration of Jural Judgment
     Laws from the Nature of Men
     Reason as Will, and the Problem of Reflective Judgment

Legal Certainty and Political Utility
Politics in the Absence of Judicial Space
Denouement on Jefferson's Jurisprudence

6 The Politics of Judicial Space   106
  The New Politics and the New Law
  Reason, Will, and Judicial Independence
  Judicial Space and Judicial Review
  Judgment and the Centre of Liberalism
  Common Sense Judgment and the Democracy of
  Majority Rule
  Judgment and Democratic Self-Rule
  Juries and Democratic Self-Rule
  Judicial Review and 'Juries of the Country'

7 Government by Discussion: Continuing Debate over
  Judicial Space   137
  Rethinking the Jurisprudence of John Marshall
  Judicial Retrenchment and Judicial Space

Notes   149

Bibliography   197

Index   221

Preface

This book is about the intellectual underpinnings of that most American of political phenomena – the transformation of political questions into legal ones. As such, it treats a subject at the intersection of jurisprudence, legal history and political theory. It is an attempt by someone trained as a political theorist and historian of ideas to offer a different conceptual vantage point from which to view the development of that peculiar and perhaps most problematic of American institutions, the Supreme Court exercising the power of judicial review. This study began life in some measure as an effort to solve a puzzle proposed by Gordon Wood, taking seriously his suggestion that the development of 'what came to be called judicial review' in America 'was not simply the product of their conception of a higher law embodied in a written document'. Certainly neither the writtenness nor fundamentality of law alone provided sufficient conditions for its development. Rather, it was 'different circumstances', and equally important, 'different ideas' which ultimately must have served to make the practice of judicial review both 'possible and justifiable' in America.[1] In an effort to provide answers to the question of what circumstances and which ideas I chose to examine the locus of a particular *mentalité* prevalent among revolutionary era colonials with regard to the proper source of knowledge and judgment about law. That locus was the jury.

The trial jury in the Revolutionary era served a broader function than in either seventeenth or eighteenth-century England. Of course, from a methodological standpoint, to suggest the importance of such expansive jural powers among mid- and late eighteenth-century Americans is not to argue that either the particulars of jury practice or of commitments to them were uniform across all colonies. They were not, and each colony arrived at 1765 via its own particular experience with jural institutions. Yet, by the time the crisis engendered by the Stamp Act was in full force, the threat to jury trial stood out as a pre-eminent objection in the official and unofficial protests of revolutionary colonials in every colony but Virginia. By the 1770s, Virginia would 'catch up' and follow suit with its Declaration of Rights containing a guarantee of jury trial which would be most closely emulated by the later federal Bill of Rights.[2] Equally important from an interpretive standpoint, colonial America's perceived attachment to jural institutions should be considered more than a case of revolutionary innovation. The *mentalité* about judgment and legal control evident in the decades of the 1750s and 1760s stretched backward in time to colonial ideas about law expressed well over a half-century earlier. And, it would reach beyond the Revolution to Alexander Hamilton's recognition in *Federalist 83* that 'the friends and adversaries' of the newly proposed Constitution, 'if they agree in nothing else, concur at least in the value they set upon trial by jury; or if there is any difference between them it consists in this; the former regard it as a valuable safeguard to liberty; the latter represent it as the very palladium of free government'.[3] Its central ideas and values encapsulated colonial unwillingness to retreat from a politics of inclusion, of discussion, and even of routine challenge, where the content as well as application of law was in dispute. This *mentalité* about judgment and legal control which their earlier experience with juries had afforded them – entailing as it did demands for legal inclusion, discussion, and challenge – shaped as well the perspective of many post-revolutionary Americans to judicial power. Translated to a post-revolutionary issue of constitutional judgment, it offered the different ideas about the power of ordinary men to know and judge the law – different certainly from their English predecessors – which helped to focus and to shape the jurisprudential perspectives of several constitutional framers, among them, John Adams, Thomas Jefferson, Alexander Hamilton, and James Wilson. In following the evolution of their differing perspectives on law and courts, and ultimately on judicial review, one conclusion was consistently reasserted. Well before they had irreparably severed the political ties that bound them to their British rulers, American colonials were already waging (and winning) a revolution in their thinking about law and legal judgment. In this revolution, conducted well before John Marshall's argument in *Marbury v. Madison*, America's distinctive conception of judicial review emerged, like the late colonial jury, as a means of providing reflective and serious reconsideration of constitutional questions of law.

Acknowledgments

In the course of researching and writing this book I have relied on the generosity and assistance of many helpful teachers, institutions, colleagues, and friends, whom it is a pleasure now to acknowledge. In its original form as a dissertation, this study was supervised by Professors Judith N. Shklar and Harry N. Hirsch. Their support as well as their questions and initial reactions to my early efforts to develop a theoretical and historical perspective on early American jurisprudence contributed decisively to the shape and format of the present work.

It is a pleasure also to acknowledge the following institutions that have contributed generous financial assistance in order to facilitate research in England and America on all or part of the manuscript: the American Association of University Women, the National Endowment for the Humanities, the Fulbright Commission, the Clarke Faculty Research Fund of Harvard University, and the Mark DeWolfe Howe Research Fellowship administered by Harvard Law School. My research work at Harvard has been greatly assisted by the superior staffs of the university's Widener, Houghton, Hilles and Law School Libraries, and in particular by both David Ferris and David de'Lorenzo of the Harvard Law School Treasure Room. In the final stages, Alan Huston, Liam Lavery, and Stuart Semmel provided excellent additional research assistance.

Subsequent drafts of the manuscript have been read or discussed with friends and colleagues to whom I am especially indebted for their kindnesses as well as their critical acumen. I owe special thanks in this respect to Colin Brooks, Josh Cohen, Vivien Hart, Stephen Holmes, David Landes, James Muirhead, Patrick Riley, Beth Rubenstein, and Debra Satz. There have been those along the way, particularly Julian Franklin, J. R. Pole, and especially John Murrin, whose probing and difficult questions pushed me to rethink and reargue my position. As a teacher, colleague, and friend, Samuel H. Beer has been kind enough to read the entire manuscript with thoughtfulness and care, and to offer numerous excellent criticisms and suggestions. Two individual, Cheryl B. Welch and Murray Milgate, have read every chapter more than once, and have contributed so much of their own time, intellectual energy, and critical

xi

judgment to my work that I can scarcely begin to repay that debt. My greatest debt, however, is to Joseph and Emily Duncan, who have made all things possible and to whom this book is dedicated.

Part I
Revolutions and Conceptual Change

1 Political Thought and Historical Problematics

For the mind having in most cases, as is evident in Experience, a power to *suspend* the execution and satisfaction of any of its desires, and so all, one after another, is at liberty to consider the objects of them; examine them on all sides, and weigh them with others . . . This seems to me the source of all liberty.
(John Locke, *An Essay Concerning Human Understanding*)

The aim of this essay is to challenge the assumption of a basic unity of vision and purpose at the roots of Anglo-American jurisprudence through a study of the role of juries and judgment in revolutions. Through a comparative look at the relationship between English and American conceptions of law and judgment in the seventeenth and eighteenth centuries, the conclusion can be reached that British and American jurisprudence are separated not only historically by differing court practices which commentators have frequently observed, but correlatively by essentially different theoretical conceptions of sovereignty, the nature of law, and the extent of ordinary citizens' power to judge the legitimacy of law. This last factor has been far less frequently observed, if not implicitly denied, by legal commentators. From a theoretical perspective, this comparative analysis helps to explain why the question of the scope and limits of the judicial function in a democratic state is the overarching question of American jurisprudence, whereas in English jurisprudence it remains a question of little significance.[1] At the same time, this study aims to contribute to the contemporary debate among legal and philosophical analysts of the American judicial system, by adding to these typically limited and abstract discussions of competing theories of law and adjudication a theoretical and historically informed discussion of the evolution of judicial institutions whose nature these theories are intended to elucidate.[2] The aim is to reconstruct an intellectual and historical problematic that provoked both significant constitutional debate and innovative legal and jurisprudential responses in eighteenth-century American jurisprudence. That problematic is one of determining the proper locus of judgment about the content and 'constitutionality' of law.

3

ORIGINS OF JUDICIAL SPACE

The American revolution has been called the seminal event of the late eighteenth century and this is no less true in law than in politics. In 1773, John Adams observed that a major difficulty in the debate with England over colonial government lay in the 'different ideas' each had of the words 'legally' and 'constitutionally' – different ideas that were, as we shall see, symptomatic of deeper jurisprudential, epistemological, and political differences between the two governmental systems. This was not idle revolutionary rhetoric. Differences in the perceptions of the role of courts, judges, and particularly juries characterized the conditions of law in seventeenth-century English revolutionary contexts as compared to those of late eighteenth-century America. By examining these differing perceptions, it becomes apparent that in many instances eighteenth-century Americans and Englishmen held fundamentally dissimilar conceptions of law, of the basis of its legitimacy, and of the character of its certainty. And when one considers the nature of the tension between judges and juries during the constitutional revolutions in each of the two countries, the extent of the dissimilarity is brought sharply into focus.

Legal argument, and particularly jural argument, is informative in periods of revolutionary upheaval. Struggles over the scope and function of the jural power can serve to bring forward issues of considerable political interest, such as who controls the legal ground in claims to legitimacy as well as sovereignty. In England, throughout both seventeenth-century periods of political upheaval and after the protracted constitutional settlement, court and judges remained administrative adjuncts to government with only a tenuous 'independence'. It would seem that the controversies that developed between judges and juries during this period in political prosecutions for the seditious libel (or treason) of suggesting that either the King or his ministers had breached constitutional 'limits' embodies two jurisprudential conclusions.

First, that by acquitting defendants in cases of seditious libel, contrary to evidence and 'over the heads' of judges, juries acted as the only regularized voice 'external' to government and in this way broached the difference between the rule of law and arbitrary power. Second, that in this role, English juries of the 1650s and 1660s, and later, in the 1670s and 1680s, developed a nascent 'space' for judgment within the political sphere that judges did not have or were not trusted to employ impartially against the state. In both periods, this jural function seems to have developed in order to adjust for the widely recognized uncertainty extant in both the content and administration of law – an uncertainty that political upheaval only served to exacerbate. However, unlike their later American counterparts, seventeenth-century English juries chose in certain cases to override judicial authority and to determine law not because they questioned the judges' knowledge of it, nor even because they challenged the judges' superior claims to be the sole legitimate interpreters of law. Rather, the effort by English juries to exercise significant lawfinding powers in such cases was clearly identified with the effort to prevent political arbitrariness in the application of law, and not with the effort to challenge, or to actually control, the content of it. While developing a 'space' for potential popular legal and political reform, the claims of English juries to determine both law and fact therefore remained legally conservative despite their more politically ambitious implications. Indeed, in contrast to the radical social and political picture routinely drawn of the Levellers, their legal and jural claims for reform remained modest, and any hope of more radical legal reform foundered.

In America, the jural story is quite different. Both before and during the revolution, colonial jury practices and the vision of law that underpinned them went much further than their English counterparts of a century earlier. Implicit in colonial pamphlets and jural claims, a profoundly innovative, even instrumental, understanding of law can be seen at work. In debates with their British governors, revolutionary colonials refused to define law as an instrument of state policy which could not be judged unsuitable or even 'unconstitutional' by common men. Rather, they conceived of it as the 'reflection' and 'defender' of *their* 'community and customary authority', which ordinary men were equally capable of knowing and judging for themselves. In contrast to the dilemmas of English juries a century earlier, the basis of the tensions between colonial judges and juries, and the issue of central importance in colonial seditious libel cases, was not simply a protest against the administration of arbitrary political power. Instead, the content of the law itself and the question of 'who shall judge' in matters of law was in dispute. Unlike English juries, colonial juries did challenge whether 'lack-learned' or 'overbearing' judges knew the law, and whether they, and not the juries themselves, should be final judges of it. Where English juries limited their concerns during politically unstable times to adjusting for factors such as legal uncertainty and lack of judicial independence, revolutionary colonials went further, developing a space for judgment within law which recognized the claims of common men as jurors to know, and in so doing to challenge, the content of the laws under which they lived.

The impetus for this colonial constitutional innovation can be understood in epistemological as well as jurisprudential terms. It suggests three problematics of central concern in American revolutionary considerations of law – legal certainty, judicial independence, and judicial space – prompted juries to take the final judgment of law away from justices in colonial America. And these same three problematics can be seen to feature in the post-revolutionary decision by framers of the Constitution to move this power of final judgment into the forum of a newly conceived court, in the form of judicial review. The actual functioning of this court was less than clearly conceived of or articulated by its originators, in part because it was an innovative amelioration of their own diverse perspectives on the character and function of law and judgment in the uncertain arena of a new, national politics. Nevertheless, these diverse perspectives shared a common recognition of the continuing demands for securing that judicial space for registering citizens' 'constitutional' challenges and demands for reconsiderations of law which had been effectively occupied by revolutionary colonial juries.

A comparative study such as this one, of the interplay between political institutions such as juries and courts and ideas of law and judgment, ineluctably raises questions of approach as well as ones of methodology. And indeed, one effort of this essay is to relate political and legal theory to historical study in a manner which offers a more satisfactory reconstruction of the intellectual conditions that provoke theoretically innovative responses and conceptual change within particular historical settings. Two current approaches to the history of political thought have not proven themselves very robust in providing an explanatory net adequate for capturing the basis of conceptual innovation and change.

On the one hand, we have had an earlier approach to the history of ideas which focused on a canon of great texts of political philosophy and on an acontextual assessment of their 'influence' on actual political actors and institutions. Whatever the philosophical insights obtainable from this approach, and there are many, the obvious limitation of it from the viewpoint of its critics has been that while it constructs a chronological 'history' of ideas, it is so consciously ahistorical in approach that it tends anachronistically to insinuate elements of conceptual innovation or uniqueness in these great texts without the ability to defend such claims in historical terms. Therefore, as John Dunn has observed, not only have Locke's theories of contract and consent been generally misunderstood, but his purported relevance to either eighteenth-century or contemporary liberal political concerns has been vastly overstated by those who would wrench the *Two Treatises* from its seventeenth-century context and recast it in the 'contemporary shiboleth' of 'government by consent'.[3]

Certainly theorists and historians still have much to learn from the more recent and alternative approach, which places an intense focus on the political language or 'modes of discourse' within localized and historically narrow 'contexts' of political and social life. However, in so far as political 'discourse' is seen both to direct and to constrain the contextual parameters of political thought, such an approach appears particularly unmalleable in explaining innovations within the constraints of the 'historicity of answers' to political questions.[4] On this approach, Locke's *Two Treatises* contributes little beyond rhetoric to eighteenth-century American political or intellectual life, because neither 'the political situation to which it was addressed' nor the 'persistent intellectual preoccupations' of Locke's life that make it intelligible were of genuine concern to American colonials.

The juxtaposition of these two historical approaches with respect to Locke's relevance to American revolutionary and constitutional thought has effectively created a pendulum of interpretation swinging from earlier claims of *Locke et praterea nihil* to *omnia praeter Lockem*, in which neither extreme could possibly be right.[5] Locke's thought undoubtedly contributed to the development of American revolutionary and constitutional thought in a manner that is perhaps less than earlier, monolithic treatments of 'Lockean liberalism' have suggested, but certainly more than simply convenient 'rhetoric' or ideological window-dressing. Indeed, some of Locke's preoccupations, particularly those concerned with epistemology and the moral force of judgment, were clearly shared by a significant number of colonial religious and political thinkers. It would seem then that Locke's significance to American political thought needs to be reconsidered, and the character of any 'influence' his work may have exerted on colonial attitudes toward the establishment and maintenance of legitimate authority re-examined. Part of this task has been accomplished in Jay Fliegelman's excellent study of American colonial educational theory, *Prodigals and Pilgrims: The American revolution against patriarchal authority*. However, my effort here is to reassess the extent to which a Lockean epistemology, particularly as taken from the *Essay Concerning Human Understanding*, informed pre- and post-revolutionary debates about the certainty of law and judgment, and, in so doing, provided a framework for jurisprudential innovation in American law. By focusing on the legal arguments thrown up in the revolutionary debate and dialogue with Britain – a debate which cut across conceptual disagreements in the understanding of such terms as 'constitutional' and 'legal', as well as 'representation', 'legitimacy', and 'rights' – a logic of argument emerges in which discontinuity and innovation can be highlighted. Against the recent trend of thought minimizing Locke's importance in America, I have brought him back. But it is a different Locke, whose influence follows a different route. The effort is not so much to deny the relevance or diminish the importance of Locke's explicit commitments to natural rights, or fixed government, or toleration. Rather the intention is to bring another and important aspect of Locke's thought to bear on American political thought.

Employing the notion of 'judicial space' to characterize the problem of bringing reflective judgment to bear on expressions of legislative decision-making is in some measure an effort to remain in keeping with the spatial metaphors of 'spheres', 'arenas', 'domains', and 'centres' that, as one political theorist has recently observed, are 'essential elements of the modern understanding of freedom and individual rights'.[6] Indeed, spatial metaphors have been used by critics of America's eighteenth-century constitution such as Hannah Arendt, who argued that it 'cheated [Americans] of their proudest possession' because it 'provided a public space only for the representatives of the people, and not for the people themselves.' In Arendt's analysis, the Revolution 'had given freedom to the people' but 'failed to provide a space where this freedom could be exercised', leaving them with a political life no more demanding than casting a ballot.[7]

While not wishing to challenge the extent to which the exigencies of national government have operated to divert both the demands and benefits of direct participatory democracy into representative channels, the division of civil society under the Constitution into the larger bipolar categories of public and private spheres would seem to overlook important, if residual, arenas for – in Arendt's terms – 'expressing, discussing, and deciding'.[8] One thinks immediately of localism within federalism, which its more contemporary analysts (to say nothing of de Tocqueville) have observed remained a significant locus for making 'public use' of citizens' reason in the sense Arendt understands it until well into this century.[9] Certainly, the failure of the Constitutional framers explicitly to incorporate 'townships and town-hall meetings' in that document did not alone amount to the 'death sentence' Arendt suggests for it. More important, her view of representation as closing off 'public space' sounds distinctly more like the view of virtual representation and parliamentary sovereignty impervious to public judgment which the framers explicitly rejected than like the legislative and judicial equipoise which they actually devised. Indeed, the creation of a Court in which the laws produced by representatives might be publicly reconsidered and reversed suggests another space for judgment and 'public reason' beyond what Arendt thought to exist. Therefore, while the Constitution did not guarantee the same degree of participation as that of smaller, direct democracies, it did seek to guarantee that in certain political questions reasons and reflective judgments, rather than numbers, would carry greatest weight. In this sense, such a liberal constitution proves potentially far more demanding of its citizens' capabilities and contributions than Arendt perhaps recognized.

This study highlights the extent to which the issue of judicial power formed an issue of strategic political importance around which centred intense theoretical interest as well as practical debate both at the time of the Revolution and the founding. Some of the more recent and widely cited law school studies of constitutional thought in the revolutionary era have chosen to categorize as 'Whigs' all American thinkers who supported independence, and to treat them for convenience as holding a 'monolithic set of views'.[10] However, such blanket categories mask a significant diversity among the competing views of law and jurisprudence carried out of the Revolution by those who contributed most to structuring the constitutional framework and institutions of the post-revolutionary order. This study focuses on the theoretical basis of a supreme court responsive, in theory, to those problems of judgment and of certainty which were central to liberal politics at its origins, and which in America have remained at the centre of continuous political and constitutional controversy ever since.[11]

2 Historical Transformations and Legal Legacies

Let all men hereby take head how they
complain in words against magistrates,
  for they are gods.
(John Haywarde, *Les Reportes del Cases in Camera Stellata*, 1609)

THE NEW LEGAL HISTORY AND THE 'GOOD OLD LAW'

It has been said that in the absence of legal training, past historians have failed sufficiently to appreciate the relevance of law as a conceptual template, shaping the character of the American revolutionary project. One legal historian, John Reid, has even suggested that non-legal historians have indeed 'misunderstood the legal and constitutional history of the American Revolution'.[1] In particular, Reid pinpoints a failure to appreciate the function of law both 'in setting the stage' for rebellion and in 'formulating the conditions' under which it was to be fought.[2] By such 'conditions of law' Reid understands 'not merely substantive rules of law, but the certainty, the power, and the effectiveness of that law and whether it was directed by a unicentric or multicentric authority'.[3] Indeed, Reid argues persuasively that 'legal stagesetting' as well as constitutional concerns played a pervasive but distinguishable role in pre-revolutionary American politics. It would therefore seem particularly fruitful to consider how such conditions or legal stagesetting may have featured as well in the developing post-revolutionary American understanding of court function – particularly in decisions with regard not only to interpreting but to striking down procedurally legitimate laws.

Reid establishes what he takes to be two essential elements in the American revolutionary conditions of law. Perhaps most important to the argument to be developed here was the factual condition of an essential uncertainty within the American colonies concerning the status and character of the British constitution and the content and local applicability of English law generally. According to Reid, the very concept of a constitution was so ambiguous that its definition remained 'more a matter of personal usage than of judicial certainty'.[4] This condition was exacerbated not only by the British constitution's unwritten form, but also by the lack of a single judicial authority to settle conflictual views, leaving the 'constitution' to be less the test of good legal argument than the outcome of 'whatever could be plausibly argued and forcibly maintained'. Convincing legal briefs might be produced on both sides of many constitutional questions and even Crown lawyers could not agree on its exact nature with regard to colonial territories such as Ireland and North America.[5]

This radical uncertainty was if anything even greater with regard to the status of English laws. There was the vexed question of whether American colonists were by right entitled to all English laws, or to some, or to none. Moreover, as Jack Greene has noted, '[e]ven had every judge and lawyer in Britain agreed that the colonists were entitled to English laws . . . there remained the extremely difficult question of precisely what English laws might apply to the colonies'. The problem again lay in the imprecision of a law composed of a 'complex combination of common law practices as applied by the courts and statute law enacted by Parliament'.[6] While exacerbated by the immediate political tensions of the 1760s, such legal uncertainty had been a long-standing condition of American colonial jurisprudence, as registered in a 1734 tract by New York and New Jersey lawyer and judge, Lewis Morris:

> The Extent of the Laws of *England* into the Plantations has been a Question often Debated, but never satisfactorily resolv'd. Some thought the British common law only, some that the common and statute both, did extend; those of the first Opinion were puz[z]led to tell what period of the common Law extended; and how it could extend, without the help of those Statutes esteemed declaratory or explanatory of the common Law. . . . Those who held that both common and Statute extended were as much puz[z]led to tell, what periods of Time were to be taken in.[7]

This condition of legal as well as constitutional uncertainty within the colonies produced the possibility of alternative sources of authority over the interpretation and application of law. One principal source was colonial juries. New legal historians have noted the colonial tendency to turn to juries to 'find' law, leaving judges in many cases 'very little law-making power'. The representatives of local communities assembled as jurors often wielded effective power over control of the content of provincial substantive laws, and were empowered under these conditions to 'reject common law' and 'permit local custom to prevail over clear common law'.[8] As well as posing a recognizable challenge to British legal and political authority, such jury practices signalled a radical departure from their British contemporaries in the colonial legal understanding of the power of ordinary men to judge the legitimacy of law. This, however, is not a conclusion reached by new legal historians. Instead, most of the new legal scholarship assumes that the source of colonial interpretation and understanding of law – that is, the other, and theoretical element in Reid's 'conditions' of colonial law which led colonial juries to challenge law – was simply the British understanding of an earlier time. Simply put, American colonials essentially shared an 'old constitutionalism', revealed in the appeals of colonial resistance leaders to 'the seventeenth-century English constitution of customary restraints on arbitrary power'. The legal mentality of colonial revolutionaries, it is argued, was firmly grounded in the 'old constitutionalism' of Sir Edward Coke, John Hampden, and John Pym in which the constitution was a bundle of 'primarily common law property rights, and rights to traditional institutional arrangements and legal procedures'.[9] Thus colonial legal thought is claimed to have mirrored a view ostensibly held by Pym and Coke that the content of law is a product of 'the "right" of consent, custom or consensus'. This "older" view, it is argued, in turn led colonials to believe that through custom and consent they had developed a 'legally binding unwritten constitution that [legally] limited Parliament's authority over the colonies'.[10]

This recourse to an argument from 'old constitutionalism' by new legal historians to explain revolutionary legal thinking is unsatisfactory for several reasons. By highlighting the diversity and uncertainty of colonial legal conditions, the new scholarship has begun to provide clues to a considerably more complex view of the legal attitudes of revolutionary colonials than has been traditionally assumed. Yet there has been relatively little effort to explore the possibility that those views might signal a radical departure from British views about the power of ordinary men to judge the legitimacy of the law by which they lived. Rather, the conclusion, that in their uncertainty American colonials legally turned back the clock to a shared and somehow clearly articulated 'old constitutionalism' and became 'the heirs, not the progenitors of their constitutional world',[11] is exactly congruent with the conclusions of the 'old scholarship' they seek to displace. It has been over fifty years since Roscoe Pound described the colonial era as the 'age of Coke'.[12] More important, this conclusion implicitly suggests an Anglo-American orientation in which the point of departure for understanding American jurisprudence is tracing the transplantation of legal ideas and institutions from the mother country to her infant fragment. Unfortunately, this position lies at the heart of the non-legal scholarship which the new legal historians set out to criticize.[13]

In political and constitutional terms, this 'transit of ideas' perspective interprets the American colonists as arguing the case of 'the old English constitution' against the merits of the new British constitution of parliamentary sovereignty which had come into existence during the century after they had left the mother country. And, indeed, this characterization appears to echo in the political rhetoric of colonial revolutionaries who hounded Parliament to 'give us the good old law'. However, this view of colonials as summoning up an old constitutionalism is inherently unsatisfactory, not the least because its characterization of eighteenth-century colonial thought conflates rhetoric and reality.

It is notoriously common in revolutionary rhetoric to summon the restorative myths of history, tradition, and the 'good old law' in justification of the most sweeping and unprecedented changes. After all, appeals to Magna Carta supported a change in the line of succession and establishment of the 'new' British constitution under parliamentary sovereignty. Similarly, appeals to 'divers sundry old authentic histories and chronicles' had supported a constitutional and religious Reformation in England over a century earlier which represented an unprecedented break with the past.[14] In explaining the many, often conflicting demands of American revolutionary leaders, it is difficult to sustain the argument that they simply wished Britain to turn back the institutional clock in legal and constitutional matters. For example, when their focus turned from parliamentary impositions to the colonial judiciary, revolutionary leaders complained that judicial appointments and dismissals in the colonies were still archaically controlled by the Crown, while in England the Revolution Settlement of 1701 had severed this institutional control by creating permanent tenure (on good behaviour) with dismissal subject to parliamentary approval.[15] It seems safe to say, then, that with regard to the 'old' and 'new' constitutions, American revolutionary leaders very often seemed to want it both ways, that is to say, their way.

Although the argument that Americans appealed to an old constitutionalism follows from a close examination of colonial constitutional and legal rhetoric, it pays little attention to the actual dynamics of colonial political and legal debate. In addition, its internal logic seems flawed. It is almost certainly correct to claim, as Reid does, that the fact that 'the seventeenth-century constitution of customary rights would never be reestablished as the constitution of Great Britain does not prove that the eighteenth-century British Constitution of parliamentary supremacy had been established in the North American colonies'.[16] However, such an argument says nothing about whether the jurisprudence of eighteenth-century American colonials was in any significant sense the same as that older constitutionalism of their seventeenth-century predecessors. By and large, the leaders of the American Revolution were eighteenth-century, post-Enlightenment thinkers, politically and legally. To mistake the 'good old law' rhetoric they employed for the actual theories of politics and law taking shape at their hands has made the institutional and jurisprudential innovations derivative of their thought – innovations such as judicial review – inexplicable in other than legally anachronistic or politically simplistic terms.[17]

A second and equally important problem with the argument that the colonials went back to the 'old constitutionalism' in an effort to construct their own legal vision is the underdeveloped account of the constitutional thought of the colonials' purported seventeenth-century counterparts. Historians often assume a conceptual clarity for fundamental law which, whether one considers the seventeenth or the eighteenth centuries, simply cannot be shown to exist. The key to the argument from 'old constitutionalism' lies, of course, in its reliance on explicit colonial allusions to fundamental law. Indeed, one American legal historian has claimed that while 'during the colonial period Americans had not been much given to debate over issues of constitutional theory, their few pronouncements reflected their intellectual debt to 17th century England and its idea of fundamental law'.[18] But, in order to clarify and more accurately assess the actual degree of this putative intellectual debt, it is necessary to examine in a more systematic way the context of earlier English appeals to fundamental law, particularly in the period of English revolutionary upheaval of the 1640s and 50s from which it is suggested colonials inherited their understanding of the concept.[19]

LEGAL UNCERTAINTY AND FUNDAMENTAL LAW

While there was much discussion and rhetorical reference to fundamental law in England of the 1640s and 50s, it seems clear that there was never any single 'idea' of fundamental law, or even general agreement to be had as to which laws or customs were the fundamental ones and which were not.[20] References to fundamental law generally failed to pick out particular laws as the most essential, offering instead vague references such as John Pym's to 'that universal, that supreme law, salus populi.' Pym continues, 'This is the element of all laws out of which they are all derived, the end of all laws to which they are designed, and in which they are perfected. . . . The (fundamental) law is that which puts a difference betwixt good and evil, betwixt just and unjust'.[21] Not only did seventeenth-century Englishmen disagree about which particular laws were fundamental, but also they disputed the legitimating origins of those fundamental laws or customs, and argued over who could be said to know them authoritatively. Was Parliament the originator of the fundamental law, or equal in antiquity and status to it, as some claimed?[22] If so, how could it coherently be argued that Parliament was limited by such a law?

For others, the fundamental law was enshrined in the common law and in those common law institutions such as trial by jury that were believed to have roots in a remote Saxon and legally pure English past preceding the Norman Conquest. This view was expressed not only by the most frequently cited proponent of fundamental law in the pre-revolutionary colonies, Sir Edward Coke, but also by Leveller critics of contemporary common law.[23] Yet there are dramatic differences between the views of Coke and of Levellers such as John Lilburne, John Jones, and William Walwyn. These different views as to the character and legibility of the fundamental law only exacerbate the difficulty of postulating a unified seventeenth-century idea of 'fundamental law' which served as a foundation for eighteenth-century American theorizing.[24]

For the same reason it is particularly unsatisfactory simply to pick one thinker as 'representative' of the fundamental law perspective, such as is frequently done with Coke, and to claim that his jurisprudence reflects the origin of any clear American vision of fundamental law. It is by now a well-worn commonplace that 'few legal authorities have received such conflicting interpretation as Sir Edward Coke'.[25] He has been anachronistically called the father of judicial review by

American jurists intent on positing an English judicial root for the institution. By English jurists he has been called the author of parliamentary sovereignty. Ironically, both views turn on the same reference to Coke's comments in an ill-fated interview with James I, and to opposed readings of his reported opinion in the now infamous *Dr Bonham's Case*.[26]

Unfortunately, Coke's remarks in both instances, when taken alone, do little to establish the view that his conception of the 'fundamental law' was composed simply of those laws of England's historical past discoverable by judges such as himself. Nor do they support the Pocockian claim that Coke's thought represents an historically grounded legal continuity with the common law past starkly opposed by the radical, natural reason of law arguments made by Levellers.[27] Both claims for Coke's historical sensibilities are seriously diluted by the considerable number of other statements and opinions made by Coke over the course of a long legal lifetime.[28] Even Coke's *Commentary on Littleton* amounted to little more, in the words of one historian, than Coke saying, 'don't bother to read *Littleton*, it has all changed.' The same may be argued for his 'unhistorical' commentaries on Magna Carta.[29]

The view of Coke as defender of the known and historically grounded fundamental law against threatened change from incursions by royal prerogative has been created by fusing disparate and largely unrelated statements. It disregards Coke's own role as a conscious and creative innovator. For while Coke is recognized as the defender of the traditional rights of Englishmen, it is far less recognized that many of them were of his own invention. Nor, without considerable distortion, can Coke be made the author of the argument that fundamental law was an unchangeable law which limited or 'reviewed' parliamentary statute.[30] Coke's rules for making new law and for correcting old in the preface to the *Fourth Report* did not suggest that any form of law was unchangeable, only that it might be inconvenient, even dangerous at times, to innovate:

> The laws of England consist of three parts, the Common Law, customs, and acts of Parliament: for any fundamental point of the ancient laws and customs of the realm, it is a maxim and a policy, and a trial by experience, that the alteration of any of them is most dangerous; for that which hath been refined and perfected by all the wisest men in former succession of ages . . . cannot without great hazard and danger be altered or changed.[31]

Coke's view that fundamental law was not unchangeable in principle, but that legal reform or adjustment was dangerous in practice, rested on one paramount concern: that unless carefully controlled, change produced legal uncertainty. Indeed, Coke's writings in general prove far more coherent when organized around the central problematic which all his work appears directed to solve, the problem of legal uncertainty, than when organized around some notion of fundamental law which he never clearly articulated.

It is precisely Coke's refusal to admit that his opinions, once reached, had left any uncertainty in the law that gave to his writing a pronounced adversarial rather than judicial character.[32] His statements to James I and the dicta of *Bonham* were both made in the service of enhancing and securing judicial control over the law in order to secure its certainty. And, in this sense, Coke's words to James I simply replicated, in intention and in legal rationale, those comments of an earlier Justice – Sir John Fortescue – made to an equally legally inquisitive King, Henry VI: 'Sir, the law is what I say it is, and so it has been laid down ever since the law began, and we have several set forms which are held as law, and held and used for good reason, though we cannot remember the reason'.[33] Indeed, Coke's overwhelming desire to bring certainty to law goes a long way in helping to understand those inconsistent statements which have long been held to 'disfigure' Coke's work and to make it exceedingly hard to pin him down to any particular theory.[34] Legal certainty achieved through tight judicial control over the interpretation of law, rather than the clear articulation of fundamental law or any particular theory of the locus of sovereignty, was Coke's paramount pre-occupation.[35] In fact, Coke's desire to achieve legal certainty was shared by those radical political thinkers whose understanding of the sources and legitimacy of law have been set in sharpest opposition to him – the Levellers. That is why they repeatedly cited him. However, if what is apparent in the discussions of fundamental law by the more radical Leveller writers of this earlier period is the concern they shared with someone like Coke over the central problem of legal uncertainty, what is equally apparent is their quite differing perspectives on the sources and solutions to this problem.

For the Levellers, a principal source of uncertainty lay in the continued practice of rendering all law in 'law-french', a language inaccessible to all but the few – judges and lawyers. Calls for reform of this practice gained in intensity throughout the ill-fated reign of Charles I. 'I[t] is a miserable slavery where the law is uncertain or unknown', lamented one anonymous tract, and 'a wonder it was to all wise men, even to the ingenuous of the professors of law themselves, that the law should be so close lockt up in an unknown tongue, when the reason why the laws were first written in that brackish French, was because that language was then best understood of those who those laws most concern'd (the Normans).'[36] On this account legal 'slavery' arises not from poor or unjust laws, but rather from an 'unavoidable' ignorance of law imposed on individuals – even those of the 'meanest capacity' – who should, in principle, know it. The proffered solution of this apparently moderate pamphlet was that Parliament should act to render the laws less 'mystical', and 'so plain and obvious to every understanding, that every man might know his duty and his property', 'without', the author adds, 'Herculaean labour'. The solution to legal uncertainty should on this account be the simplification and reduction of an existing welter of laws to 'one considerable volume'.[37]

However, the proposal favoured by radicals such as the Levellers, that Parliament take steps to translate and simplify the uncertain 'mystery' of the existing law, was a direct and explicit challenge to the virtual monopoly held on the interpretation of law by common law judges such as Coke. It has been noted that the closest Coke ever came to defining the fundamental common law conceptually was to call it 'the absolute perfection of reason'.[38] Now this view was staunchly shared by both the Levellers and their judicial counterparts of the 1640s and 50s. The question at issue was, whose reason? Leveller law reformers explicitly challenged Coke's claim that only the professionally trained and artificial reason of judges could unlock the meaning of the law. The Leveller challenge, then, was directed less to common law or to its historical grounding *per se* then to the judiciary's privileged control over the actual selection of historical precedents based on the claim to superior reason. And, it is the explicit critique of the uncertainty created by judicial control over the actual ability of men to know law, as much as any historical 'inconveniences' or 'doubts' as to its content introduced by Norman conquerers, which lay at the heart of the Levellers' own references to fundamental law.[39] This can be seen most clearly in arguments raised about the reason of law and jury function in the celebrated 1649 treason trial of Leveller John Lilburne.[40]

Lilburne's trial remains a setpiece of seventeenth-century radicalism which it is unnecessary to recount in detail. What is significant for us here is that for a representative figure of a movement who has been characterized as being 'engaged in a revolt against the whole existing structure of the common law', Lilburne's arguments at his trial – indeed in all his writings – are remarkably legally conservative in character. Throughout his trials, Lilburne's tactic was to exploit the intricacies and uncertainties of the very common law which many Levellers were challenging. He refused to plead, for example, claiming that he had not seen a copy of the indictment before his trial and that in any event he could not read it, because it was in Latin. The claim that the existing common law as related by justices is one of 'snares, tricks and provocations' both unknown and unknowable in advance to common men is a staple theme of Leveller writing. Accompanying this claim is the theme highlighted in Lilburne's trial that common men can know the reason of the law because it is natural, not artificial. Lilburne claimed that his ignorance of the intricacies of his indictment did not mean that, upon hearing it, he could not employ his own reason to determine its validity. Although not a lawyer, Lilburne claimed:

> I have read the Petition of Right, I have read Magna Carta, and abundance of laws made in confirmation of it; and I have also read the 'Act that abolisheth the Star Chamber,' which was made in the year 1641. . . . In the reading of such laws I do not find a special Commission of Oyer and Terminer to be legal and warrantable.[41]

Lilburne was technically challenging the Commission under which he was being tried. He did not deny the common law legitimacy of ordinary Commissions of Oyer and Terminer; he denied only that 'extraordinary and special' Commissions could try an 'individual person or persons for a pretended or extraordinary crime'.[42] He arrived at this conclusion by 'reasoning' his way through the existing law. He would later employ the same tactics at his trial in 1653 to challenge the statute under which he was banished.[43] The logic of Lilburne's reasoning was simple. If the present government refused to recognize the legitimacy of the earlier Rump Parliament, why should the court recognize the legitimacy of the statute under which he was banished, a statute made by this same unlawful Parliament? In support of his reasoning, Lilburne frequently cited none other than Coke: 'where reason ceaseth, the law ceaseth; for seeing reason is the very spirit of the law itself'.[44] He could easily have added a reference to Coke's dictum – as he had in *The Legall Fundementall Liberties* – that 'in ambiguous things' the interpretation of law 'is always to be made, that absurdities and inconveniences be avoided', since, clearly, recognizing the legitimacy of statutes made by an 'illegitimate' Parliament might qualify as an absurdity if not, as in Lilburne's case, an 'inconvenience'.[45] However, the justices quickly quashed such obvious misreadings of Coke. 'You have done yourself no good; I thought you had understood the law better than I see you do.'[46]

In fact, Lilburne understood Coke's meaning very well, but he persisted in using Coke's words to bypass the intransigence of his judges and to appeal to the 'common reason' of his jurors – a jury composed of petty merchants and craftsmen like himself. 'Although the Jury, if they take upon them, the knowledge of the law, may give a general verdict', Lilburne quoted, carefully omitting Coke's cautionary conclusion, 'yet it is dangerous for them to do so, for if they mistake the law, they run into danger of attaint'.[47]

Indeed, Lilburne threatened to press his claims of the rights of juries to rhetorical extremes when he asserted late in his first trial that jurors were, 'by law', 'not only judges of the fact, but judges of law also: and you that call yourselves judges of the law, are no more than Norman intruders; and in deed and in truth, if the jury please, are no more but cyphers, to pronounce their verdict'. What Lilburne intended by this claim is not entirely clear, but it seems apparent that he was encouraging his jurors to find that his actions did not fit within a reasonable application of any treason statute previous to the most recent and questionably extended one. Obviously, there was no common law basis for a suggestion that jurors alone were judges of the law, and nothing in Lilburne's trial statements, nor in their later development by the radical pampheteer John Jones, suggests such an extreme interpretation.[48] However, the potential for such claims to develop into direct challenges to judicial (and therefore governmental) control over law was clearly recognized. Judge Jermin called Lilburne's claim that the jury should determine the application of the law by use of the general verdict a 'damnable blasphemous heresy'. He reiterated the standard position that judges alone 'have ever been judges of the law, from the first time that ever we can read or hear that the law was truly expressed in England; and the jury are only judges of matter of fact'.[49] By this time, both sides had cited Coke's words as support!

The seventeenth-century judicial recitation of fundamental law as the law of reason could easily be mistaken, out of context, for the Leveller claim that the fundamental law should in principle be knowable by 'all rational men'. However, Justice Keble made it clear at Lilburne's trial that his meaning was quite the opposite. 'The question is but this', Keble claimed, 'Whether the law of God, and the law of reason, and the law of man may be consonant with each other? And whether the court or John Lilburne shall be the judges thereof. That is the question'.[50]

The core of Lilburne's challenge was not then to the common law, nor to the judges' knowledge of it, but to the court's claim to sole possession of the reason necessary to apply its content. The contrast between Lilburne's and Coke's solutions to the problem of uncertainty is readily apparent. While Coke's solution had been to press the idea of a fundamental law which might indifferently limit Crown and Parliament, the content of that law remained woefully uncertain to common defendants and simply enlarged – as Coke had intended – the powers of courts and judges. What the fundamental law was – its explicit content – was, on Coke's view, a difficult and professional question that common men should accept from the bench on trust. The fundamental law was the law of reason, but not the reason of Everyman. *This* was the argument to which the Levellers took exception.

The tracts, trials, and judicial decisions of the mid-seventeenth-century confirm that no clear or shared concept of fundamental law emerged in this period – certainly not one that would automatically place all power in the hands of the judiciary to determine the law by Cokean 'artificial reason'. Reference to fundamental law was also made in order to support arguments giving common men – 'the plaine people' and 'the rude multitude' – some role in registering dissatisfaction at the tangled and uncertain web of common law applied by judges. It was registered by juries, such as the one which found John Lilburne to be 'not guilty of any crime worthy of death'.[51] Although any genuine legal challenge to the monopoly of judges over control of the content was missing, the potential threat was unmistakable. After Lilburne, when Cromwell's Council chose to try a political offender, it used the High Court of Justice, which sat without a jury.[52]

References to Lilburne's comments on the scope of jural powers reappeared during the 1660s, in the tract literature surrounding the politically and religiously motivated post-Restoration trials of Quakers such as William Mead and William Penn. However, once again jural challenges remained legally conservative.[53] That judges knew the law was never denied, nor was the act to suppress 'seditious' conventicles challenged. More importantly, the problematic of legal uncertainty which stood behind the rise of earlier jural challenges gave way to an effort to mitigate the increasingly harsh practices of a dependent judiciary.

THE PROBLEM OF JUDICIAL 'INDEPENDENCE'

The recognition that no unified understanding or shared consensus on the content of fundamental law emerged in the uncertain legal context of seventeenth-century constitutional struggles highlights the weaknesses of the 'transit of ideas' hypothesis for understanding the American colonial response to its own uncertain 'legal condition'. The same can be said of efforts to link a version of seventeenth-century fundamental law to the demands of revolutionary colonials for an unprecedented degree of judicial independence – an independence that would permit courts to challenge the very constitutionality of statutory enactments.

Appeals to 'fundamental law', whether in the hands of Coke or more radical Leveller reformers, never came close to producing such an institution as judicial review of statutory enactments within the British constitution.[54] The Levellers, as we have seen, opened the question of challenge to law in the course of arguing for legal reforms, but they never pursued this challenge, and certainly they never considered the very *judiciary* they opposed to be the proper locus of such challenges. What is perhaps as important as the observation of a lack of nexus in Britain between fundamental law and the legitimacy of any judicial review of law is the collateral observation of a lack of nexus between fundamental law and *any* British court function at all.

The great period of appeal to fundamental law was a revolutionary era in which rhetorical appeals to Magna Carta or to a royal oath to rule *sub deum et sub lege*, were extra-legal claims without any institutional mechanism to permit a legal resolution of the constitutional issue.[55] More important than the lack of a routinized external point of judgment was the political fact that any *public* appeal to fundamental law against state authority risked prosecution. That is, to claim that government had breached the fundamental law, or that the King had moved beyond his jurisdiction under law, or even that some external rule limited his prerogative was, regardless of truth or intent, an immediate seditious libel against government – perhaps treason. The courts then entered into the issue of a constitutional question or challenge, but only as the administrative arm of government prosecution in a political trial.[56]

Until 1792, the legal definiton of seditious libel was understood to include 'written censure upon any public man whatsoever for any conduct whatsoever, or upon any law or institution whatever'.[57] In such trials, courts were necessarily cast as defenders of a system under challenge. Nothing about their institutional or historical role placed them in a position to make 'independent' judgments about the legitimacy of such challenges. Their legal judgments could never be understood to be external to, or independent of, government in this way. In England the 'rule of law' was historically a promise that the sovereign would rule *by* law. It was a promise to abjure arbitrariness and was, therefore, of largely procedural significance. As a promise it was not legally enforceable because, until the Stuarts irretrievably corrupted it, it was supported by nothing more than an oath. It was a personal commitment to exercise self-restraint. In cases of his own Prerogative, that is his personal sphere, the King was his own judge. While it shrank the sphere of Prerogative judgment and consolidated the various lawmaking jurisdictions under its authority, parliamentary sovereignty did not alter the locus of final legal and political judgment in this vision of the rule of law.

Rather, as even the harshest historical critics of British eighteenth-century government recognize, in the aftermath of 1688 and the protracted political 'settlement' that followed, the inheritors of the Whig revolution and its rhetoric chose to pick up a somewhat tarnished promise regarding the rule of law and to more or less limit themselves by it.[58] Therefore, while it is now commonplace for Americans to expect the 'independent' judiciary to perform this constitutional function, it is important to recognize why for seventeenth-century Englishmen, as well as for later American colonials, this was not an obvious conclusion.

In English courts of the seventeenth century, the independence of the judiciary in our modern sense was not construed in constitutional or public law terms. Courts were 'independent' only in the sense that they were a source of rules – 'judge-made law' – for the settlement of private disputes. Judges' 'independence' from politics meant, in fact, that they had no jurisdiction to adjudicate on the merits of public challenges to the government – and such challenges progressively increased in the last third of the century, particularly in the ten years prior to 1688. One need only mention the Popish Plot, the Meal Tub

Plot, the Rye House Plot, and the trials connected with the Duke of Monmouth's Rebellion to gain a sense of the political instability and paranoia of the period. In this context, judges did not regard themselves as constitutional arbiters between the Crown and the people, or (later) between Parliament and the people.[59] Within the public sphere, the common law courts held no function independent of their role as administrators of the will of the sovereign power. James Stephen accurately, if caustically, captured the dilemma of judicial discretion in this period with his observation that any study of the state trials of the period 'leads the reader to wonder that any judge should ever have thought it worthwhile to be openly cruel or unjust to prisoners' at the bar, since the judge's position 'enabled him, as a rule, to secure whatever verdict he liked, without taking a single irregular step, or speaking a single harsh word.'[60] A degree of mechanical as well as ideological coordination suggests that judges possessed discretion, but no space for legal manoeuvrability within the political constraints of this role. Both Charles II and James II of course exploited this for all it was worth. Judges were dismissed, just as they had been appointed, for political reasons: Coke (1616), Chief Justice Crew (1626), and Heath (1634). Judges were pressured to delay justice in cases in which the government was interested.[61] This pattern continued after the Restoration, reaching scurrilous extremes in the conduct of Justices Scroggs and George Jeffries.[62]

Some have argued that under the last Stuarts, judges 'tended to become merely civil servants of the King, and not the independent expositors of the law that they had been in the Tudor period.'[63] But it is the existence of an earlier 'independence' that is more apparent than real, drawing on an image of judicial function in the absence of any internal or popular opposition to royal authority. Once again, Chief Justice Coke's judicial career illustrates the point well. Throughout the first revolutionary period, his resistance to executive pressure to administer enactments generated under the King's prerogative sphere represented no legal or 'principled' judicial determination, but a political choice to side with Parliament in a constitutional crisis. Indeed, in his subsequent parliamentary role Coke was forced to repudiate some of his earlier judicial opinions supporting Crown 'excesses' in matters touching on public and political matters.[64] Coke's removal from the bench and his subsequent move to the leadership of the parliamentary opposition are merely graphic evidence that the court justices were in no position to adjudicate a constitutional issue 'independently'. There was no third corner or independent side to be taken in a dispute between either the King and Parliament, or between the government and 'the people'.

In the revolutionary turmoil of the seventeenth century, one sees the judiciary make a final shift in a nearly century-long move from an original position as simply a facet of the King's majesty (a position in which any criticism was *lèse-majesté*) to their new but exactly analogous position as judicial administrators of a sovereign Parliament's enactments.[65] Throughout the move, the court remained an inadequate vehicle for the legal resolution of basic constitutional issues.

This weakness of the court remained even after the 1701 Act of Settlement fixed judicial salaries and made judges' tenure, in England at least, run during good behaviour rather than at royal pleasure. After 1689, the courts recognized Parliament as competent to make or change the law in any way it chose. From within the legal system, no statute could be attacked on the ground that it trespassed on a field of governmental activity reserved for another organ of state. More important, as the sole source of law in the aftermath of 1688, no power which Parliament could exercise by giving expression to it in law, could be in theory arbitrary or extra-legal. Practice was another matter. Later, astute political and legal minds among American colonials, of whom James Otis was perhaps the most perceptive, would come to recognize that 'Acts of Parliament could never be set in opposition to the adjudication and procedures of the common law courts; they were identified with them'.[66]

In the absence of competing lawmaking jurisdictions with which to side, the English judiciary receded from the politically controversial position it occupied during the Revolution, although it was not wholly unscathed. Parliament sent a clear message to the judiciary when, in the aftermath of the Revolution, it imprisoned former judges whose decisions, rendered years before, had limited the vast privilege claimed for either the Commons or the Lords.[67] The character and degree of court 'independence' must be understood in these terms when one is evaluating the often made observation that 'judicial theory has not constituted a major part of the body of political ideas in modern Britain. The law has been considered to be a world neutrally detached from the contests of political ideas and arguments'.[68] Certainly from the viewpoint of those groups or individuals challenging government both within England and later from within the American colonies, this observation fails to match the facts. Institutionally, judges were in no position to remain 'neutrally detached'. And, as trials for seditious libel of the government grew steadily more frequent in both locations during the eighteenth century, those opposing government turned increasingly to juries rather than to judges, in hopes of finding 'independent' judgment of their legal (and political) claims.

JURIES AND THE LIMITATIONS OF JUDICIAL SPACE

In a period characterized by political conspiracy and paranoia, legal uncertainty and fundamental challenges to authority, the judiciary's lack of institutional independence from Crown manipulation led those who would question governmental actions to seek alternative points of judgment. The jury was one such alternative institution. As Holdsworth writes, 'juries represented an external point of judgment', that is, an 'outside sense' or 'outside animation' not only to the 'inside technical world of common law', but potentially to the broader context of constitutional challenges as well.[69] In the early period of political upheaval and challenge to existing authority, juries of the late 1640s and 1650s maintained a certain space for judgment about the application of law by acquitting defendants (despite the facts) in cases of seditious libel or treason. It was a space which judges, as royal appointees administering the King's justice, did not have and in general were not prepared to recognize as other than a legal and political usurpation. If common law judges disapproved of acquittal verdicts as being against evidence, they retained the power in this period to overturn jury decisions and to fine or even imprison jurors for perjury.[70] Coke could be cited in support of such action.[71] After the Restoration, the common law courts actually increased the exercise of this power in order to coerce juries into support for challenged political and legal authority.[72] During the political upheaval of the revolutionary period, however, popular opinion was shifting to the view that finding verdicts contrary to the direction of the court or contrary to the evidence ought not to expose the jury to penalties.[73]

Nevertheless, given the position of the courts and judicial system as I have described it, one would not expect such a change in jural procedure to come about simply because of a shift in public opinion, and, technically at least, it did not. Rather, the incorporation into common law of the view that jurors should not be penalized came in Bushell's Case (1670), based on narrow legal grounds of the changing nature of jurors from witnesses to weighers or judges of the facts in evidence, as presented in court.[74] Once juries lost their character as witnesses, and were considered as judges of evidence previously unknown to them, perjury could not longer be an issue. On this reasoning, Chief Justice Vaughan cancelled the fines against Bushell and the other jurors who, despite brutal treatment by the court, had persisted in acquitting the Quakers William Penn and William Mead in a highly political prosecution for tumultuous assembly. The charge against the jurors was that by acquitting those indicted 'against the direction of the Court' they had challenged the law, and had attempted to determine for themselves what the law should be.[75]

While that may have been interpreted as the practical impact of their verdict, an examination of the proceedings in this trial gives no indication that the jury verdict turned on an interpretation of substantive law. Certainly the jury challenged the repressive administration of the law in the case of Penn and Mead. That is, they challenged the judges' determination that the defendants' actions transgressed the law proscribing tumultuous assembly. However, no argument was made by jurors, Commons, or Chief Justice Vaughan that might suggest that any of them believed the law itself to be oppressive or challengeable. Indeed, in confining its jury challenges to corrupted or 'dependent' application of law rather than the content of the law itself, the pamphleteers of the Restoration remained in this sense as legally conservative as their Leveller predecessors.[76] In all but the most politically controversial cases, such as the *Trial of the Seven Bishops*, juries appear to have accepted judges as the ordinary interpreters of law, and more often than not convicted those charged with seditious libel.[77] No move was made after the Glorious Revolution to alter the law of seditious libel until Fox's Libel Act in 1792. Even then, the Act took a procedural form instead of making any substantive changes in the law.[78]

Just as English juries of the mid-century had worked an active space within legal procedure for lessening the uncertainty of law – or perhaps for manipulating that uncertainty in the service of defendants – so later juries to some extent worked it to mitigate the effects of dependent judges. Yet, later jural proponents never developed the more radical implications of the Leveller critique. And, for later reform justices such as Vaughan, it remained simply 'not intelligible' to charge that a jury had decided against the direction of the Court in a matter of law, 'for no issue can be joyn'd of matter in law, no jury can be charg'd with the tryal of matter in law barely, no evidence ever was, or can be given to a jury of what is law, or not; nor no such oath can be given to, or taken by, a jury, to try a matter in law'.[79]

The problem, Vaughan concluded in a stinging chastisement of the original trial judge, was not an attempt by the jury to determine the law, but rather an attempt by the judge to intrude into the area of fact and to direct the jury to a guilty verdict by deciding for them what the facts, as well as what the law, entailed. The jury, however, had disagreed with the judge's interpretation of the facts and acquitted. Of this attempt to manipulate the jury's role – to seal completely its space for judgment – Justice Vaughan concluded:

> For if the Judge shall by his own judgment first resolve upon any tryal what the fact is, and so knowing the fact, shall then resolve what the law is, and order the jury penally to find accordingly, what either necessary or convenient use can be fancied of juries, or to continue tryals by them at all?[80]

As it stands, then, the Bushell case did not raise the legal question of whether the jury might determine for itself what the law will be. It did settle legally the political question of whether a jury might be coerced by judges to render particular verdicts. Moreover, it is instructive in other ways. It suggests that within ten years of the Restoration, some judges, such as Vaughan, were able to distance themselves from the Crown, as its actions became publicly more controversial. The Bushell decision received wide popular support. After it, judges did not cease altogether to harass and pressure juries, but the only way the Crown could effectively exercise pressure for a favourable verdict in politically motivated and unpopular seditious libel cases was by packing the jury. This was a technique which James II employed with limited success.[81] In other cases, juries shielded critics of the Crown, as the failed attempt to indict Shaftesbury for treason indicates. A message was being sent by juries – the only non-governmental institution having both the legal legitimacy and the occasion to send such a message – to the Crown that its arbitrary manipulation of the Law was approaching the limits of political acceptability.

In the *Seven Bishops' Case* (1688), a curtain-raiser to the Glorious Revolution, the limit was breached. The case arose when seven Anglican bishops refused to read publicly and support James II's proclamation dispensing Catholics from the political restraints of the

Test Acts. The bishops privately petitioned the King in order to explain their refusal of support. The petition served as the basis of their prosecution for seditious libel. In summing up for the jury, Justice Allybone tried desperately to press the Crown's case by drawing the line separating the legitimately expressible interests of the private citizen from the proper exercise of governmental power (about which the citizen could claim no interest and therefore could express no critical opinion): 'No man can take upon himself to write against the actual exercise of the government, unless he had leave of the government, but he makes a libel, be what he writes true or false'.[82]

The jury acquitted. However, the basis for their acquittal, given the arguments of the defence counsel and at least two Justices hearing the case, was new, and for the King the message was ominous. All three essentially joined with the defendants in challenging the legality of the King's dispensation. Legally, the case has been described as a 'remarkable exception', and considered sufficiently anomalous that no legal argument was later based on it in England.[83] However, the political argument was clear. Dissident judges might be dismissed, and impertinent defence attorneys disciplined, but juries, external to government and echoing a rising popular opposition, were moving beyond reach of any regular method of control. Within six months of the *Seven Bishops' Case*, the King was in flight to France, and Locke was preparing to come home.

JURIES AND THE ENGLISH CONSTITUTIONAL DENOUEMENT

In revolutionary settings, contests over the locus and legitimacy of law-determining power are eminently political. The question of who controls the legal ground, that is, who gives content and meaning to the law in such situations, transcends the boundaries of legal technicalities as the courtroom becomes an active centre for resolving contested claims of legitimacy within the state. The two political upheavals of seventeenth-century England, and the protracted constitutional settlement which followed, saw courts and judges cast in the role of administrative functionaries with only a limited and tenuous 'independence' from challenged authority. As we have seen, the controversies that developed in this period between judges and juries in prosecutions of seditious libel (and treason) suggested the perceived need to counterbalance this administrative functioning through wider claims for jural action. In this sense, the claims of juries in England to determine both law as well as fact, and to acquit (contrary to evidence) defendants in cases of seditious libel, functioned to create a regularized voice of opposition 'external' to government – a voice which might serve to accentuate the difference between rule of law and the exercise of arbitrary power. In so doing, the English juries of these two contested periods effectively occupied and developed a space for judgment over law that royal-appointed judges either were perceived to lack or distrusted to use. In both periods, the evidence suggests that this jural function developed in order to control for a recognized and politically exacerbated uncertainty in the known content as well as administration of law. However, it would not be correct to conclude from these contested cases that English juries of the seventeenth century were posing any legal challenge either to the judges' actual knowledge of the law, or to the judges' right to interpret it. The jural cry within the courtroom (particularly the one heard from the defendant's dock) for greater 'legal certainty' was identified with achieving greater clarity and popular comprehensibility in law, not with controlling the direction or content of it. Thus, while their actions served to develop a 'judicial space' for potential popular legal and political reform, the actual claims of English juries to determine both law and fact remained legally conservative, despite the ambitious political implications which later thinkers have imputed to or sought to draw from them. The modesty (and technicality) of the legal arguments and jural claims for reform of Levellers such as Lilburne, for example, contrast sharply with the more radical social and political picture routinely drawn of them. In the second period of seventeenth-century political upheaval, as prosecutions for seditious libel increased and penalties became harsher, juries functioned less to mitigate legal uncertainty than to mitigate a perceived lack of judicial independence. Thus, confronted with the problems of legal uncertainty and a lack of judicial independence, juries functioned to create a space for popular reaction to government within a political nation in which ordinary citizens without distinction had little, if any, active role to play in politics. However, even after the Revolution and the establishment of parliamentary sovereignty, English jurymen accepted a vision of law as essentially government's instrument, whose content they must rely on judges and magistrates generally to determine.

In the seventeenth century, then, charges to juries, as well as the pamphlet literature directed to jury conduct, highlight two issues of legal contention – the character of reason and knowledge of the law available to common men, as well as the issue of the certainty of law – which posed a challenge to the hierarchical structure of the existing political order. They also serve to highlight the conceptual basis of citizenship and subjection, since jury duty represented one of the very few times 'citizenship' was exercised by the common order of men. Finally, jury activity, and the literature surrounding jural obligations and practice serve as a powerful indicator of the growth of public opinion as important to political rule. Indeed, in the seventeenth century, discussions of the power of juries serve as an important precursor of popular attitudes about the possibility and character of self-rule.

The argument that the common individual is capable of knowing and understanding the law, and having understood is the best judge of its application to individual cases, is an inherently democratic claim of epistemology. In this sense, the jury argument threatened a radical, perhaps 'democratic', discussion by critics of governmental action. However, if openly critical judgments of government could not be made public without threat of prosecution for seditious libel, they could scarcely be encouraged from the jury box.

Efforts were made late in the Stuart era to routinize control over juries, short of forcibly coercing or packing them through the qualifications for selection. For example, in the 1680s selection presupposed 'estate . . . discretion and integrity.' Not surprisingly, however, the preeminent qualification was peaceability: 'the more peaceable man you have been, the more fit you are.'[84] After 1688, the established qualifications of jurors reflected the changing character of juries as judges of fact rather than as witnesses, and the growing importance of neutrality in judgment. An essay on juries written in 1722 declared that jurors must be 'good and lawful Men . . . of sufficient Freeholds, according to the Provisions of Several Acts of Parliament'. They must not, however, 'be of Kindred or Alliance of any of the Parties; And . . . not to be such as are presupposed or prejudiced before they hear the Evidence'.[85] While Bushell served to protect juries from attaint, permitting them to shelter seditious libellers in unpopular Crown prosecutions without fear of reprisal, the decision also served indirectly to give judges an added measure of control over the final disposition of cases, if not over the final verdict. As Chief Justice Vaughan noted, 'If the jury were to have no other evidence for the fact, but what is desposed in court, the judge might know their evidence and the facts from it equally as they.'[86] One solution was for judges to grant new trials if verdicts were clearly contrary to the weight of evidence, and there is pointed development of this practice in this period.

In the aftermath of the 'Glorious' Revolution juries retreated from their politically controversial checking position. The political controversy over 'arbitary power', was declared to be at an end, and the Whigs in power now employed reference to fundamental law to legitimate the unchallengeable legal sovereignty of Parliament, just as it used the maxim 'salus populi' to defend the 'status quo'.[87] In England the jurisdictional separation between law and fact, between judge and jury, held. Juries focused on the procedural; they perceived and manipulated a certain space for judgment that allowed them to adjust for the uncertainty which political upheaval had introduced into the application of the law.

More than a half century later Blackstone would fix the point at which the 'theoretical perfection' of England's public law was reached at the year 1679, although, he added, 'the years which immediately followed it were times of great political oppression'.[88] For Blackstone, law and politics were separate considerations. From the Whig perspective, the time of political oppression ended practically with the accession of William III, and theoretically with the advent of parliamentary sovereignty. However, in political and constitutional terms, the Revolution 'settlement' was not achieved in one stroke, and the increasing number of trials for seditious libel of the government after the Revolution and throughout the eighteenth century suggest considerable political and social stress.[89] Indeed, the need for Whig leaders to control or suppress post-revolutionary expressions of critical popular sentiment – expressions brought about by a public following up the logic of the Whigs' own political principles – goes a considerable way to explain the actual reduction of the franchise after 1688, and the narrowly limited and rather grudging toleration afforded Protestant dissenters. 'You are a set of narrow-minded bigots', ran the legislation, 'but we will not punish you for it'.[90] Catholics were placed under laws nominally harsher than any which were in force before.

With regard to law, the Whig leadership under Walpole was prepared to declare that the constitutional settlement and particularly the establishment of judicial independence on good behaviour rendered any effort at jury nullification of judicial direction regarding law as unnecessary and definitely unwelcome.[91] By the 1730s, judges –

anxious to reduce still further the possibility of jury mitigation in unpopular prosecutions – turned to Parliament for approval of the use of 'special', selected juries in prosecuting certain criminal offences such as seditious libel.[92] Judges additionally played a more active role in questioning defendants on the basis of evidence given in court, and apparently employed little reservation in revealing to jurors their own attitudes toward the defendants.[93] It was this disjunction between revolutionary rhetoric and post-revolutionary realities that spawned the Opposition pamphleteers who were so important to the development of American revolutionary ideology. At home in Britain, at least, these criticisms of the government, appeals to fundamental law and rights of Englishmen, continued to be prosecuted in common law courts, although defendants now garnered little jury support. Juries routinely returned guilty verdicts in cases where the seditious words were harmless and hardly intemperate. In others they at times convicted libellers of government despite the court's recommendation of acquittal.[94] In America, however, there was a growing recognition that there, both the reach and scope of jural practices, as well as the vision of law and jurisprudence underlying them, were proving to be entirely different.

3 Juries and American Revolutionary Jurisprudence

> The Colonies adopt the common Law, not as the common Law, but as the highest Reason. (Roger Sherman, 1774)

The colonial judiciary and particularly the jury system have been neglected subjects of early American law. Yet, it is common knowledge that the American colonies won their independence at a time when the jury system was being acclaimed as a fundamental guarantor of individual liberty. When colonial intractability was first displayed over the Sugar Act of 1764, the issue was not simply one of taxation, but, as Burke recognized, principally one of the power of Parliament to set aside trial by jury in an effort to enforce vastly unpopular legislation.

> By this act . . . *so construed and so applied*, almost all that is substantial and beneficial in a trial by jury is taken away from the subject in the colonies. A person is brought hither in the dungeon of a ship's hold; thence he is vomited into a dungeon on land, loaded with irons, unfurnished with money, unsupported by friends, three thousand miles from all means of calling upon or confronting evidence, where no one local circumstance that tends to detect perjury can possibly be judged of; – such a person may be executed according to form, but he can never be tried according to justice.[1]

The British insistence on trying offenders in hated Admiralty courts was precisely a heavy-handed attempt to preclude the registering of popular sentiment with regard to these laws through jury trials. Colonials held tightly to the institution of trials by jury and lashed out at any attempt to curtail or circumvent it.[2]

Even where colonial juries have been considered, they have frequently been represented as mere accessories to evasions of the revenue acts. The more basic constitutional issue which the colonial jury raised – who would exercise final judgment in matters of law – is slurred over as a mere gambit of 'opposition politics' in the contest

with Parliament.[3] Nevertheless, the issue of allocating jural power –
of who shall judge the law – warrants careful attention, since it
was basic to the colonial method of raising constitutional questions.
Indeed, there is an important sense in which the jury issue unites
not only America's pre-revolutionary period and Founding era, but
also the 'settlement' years immediately following 1789. What
emerges in the examination of discussions of jury powers in the
American context is a vision of law – not simply of lawmaking,
and of adjudication – very different from the static, quasi-medieval,
fundamental law-as-limit vision put forward both by new legal historians and Hartzian 'fragment' theorists as descriptive of American
colonial legal thought. Certainly, it is a vision of law and adjudication
different from that held in Britain either at that time or at any earlier
time. It is a vision of law and adjudication less continuous with its
English past than with its American future. The question remains,
then, of how this vision can best be understood and explained.

A more promising alternative to approaches which take the concept of fundamental law or an older (Tudor) institutional heritage
as a basic explanatory factor in American jurisprudence, is a line of
recent historiography which emphasizes the role of ideology and
contemporary eighteenth-century political culture in explaining constitutional developments in the revolutionary period. The primacy
of ideas and of the nexus between religious, political, and legal
ideology is considered the most basic factor in the work of historians
such as Bernard Bailyn and Gordon Wood. Common to Bailyn's
and Wood's characterizations of American revolutionary politics is
an image of revolutionary political ideology as shaped by the Enlightenment, and therefore as intrinsically modern. In this sense their
analyses of the ideological and political culture that shaped the
American Revolution present a sharp departure from the institutional vantage point of the 'old constitution' perspective.

Bailyn, in particular, has attempted to induce a shift in our understanding of the American Revolution by suggesting that the motivat-
ing ideological convictions sparking the revolutionary impulse were
not derived from the 'common Lockean generalities' of natural
rights, consent, and contract. Rather, they originated in certain eighteenth-century British political ideas – those of the radical publicists
and early parliamentary opposition writers.[4] Their peculiar strain of
anti-authoritarianism was bred, Bailyn claims, in the early upheavals
of the English Civil War, and was transposed to eighteenth-century
America through its colonial publicists and revolutionaries as a cre-

ative ideology of defiance to all aspects of the traditional order.
Bailyn writes:

> Faith ran high that a better world than any that had ever been
> known could be built where authority was distrusted and held in
> 'constant scrutiny . . . where the use of power over the lives of
> men was jealously guarded and severely restricted. It was only
> where there was this defiance, this refusal to truckle, this distrust
> of all authority, political or social, that institutions would express
> human aspirations, not crush them.[5]

In fact, Bailyn's argument constitutes a sustained argument that
understanding is increased when intellectual and institutional history
are not taken as discrete projects to be treated independently. But,
in his words, it is less the ideas or conceptual influence of a thinker
such as Locke than a 'peculiar bent of mind', a particular eighteenth-
century pattern of ideas and attitudes – those of paranoia and conspiratorial fear of the oppressive intentions of British rule – that
undergirds a revolutionary propensity to check all authority. It is an
argument that rejects not only a transplanted seventeenth-century
constitutionalism, but also those seventeenth-century ideas – carica-
tured Lockean generalities – often associated with it, as helpful in
understanding the basis of either the revolutionary impulse or of
later institutionalized checks on power such as judicial review.

However, Bailyn's argument, drawn as it is from the influence of
the opposition pamphleteers, threatens by turns to be both too weak
and too strong in its explanatory reach. A pervasive feeling of distrust
characterized colonial politics not only in relation to Britain but also
within indigenous and more narrowly local levels of politics as well.
One has only to look at common descriptions of the machinations
within legislatures, such as that within the Delaware legislature of
1770 over the location of a new county seat. Here, one colonial
lamented,

> What disturbances a few Ambitious designing Men may effect –
> they seem Determined at all Events, to Oppose whatsoever is
> Proposed by some other, who are not of their party . . . for let it
> be right or wrong, they will immediately cry out their Liberties
> are sinking; they are alarmed at such proceedings; they are
> oppressed, etc. – so that they make some people believe that Ruin
> is even at the door, by which means the more Ignorant sort will
> sign Petitions or do anything these Patriots shall advise.[6]

The litigiousness of colonial Americans is legendary, and evidence suggests these truculent attitudes and vociferous internal tensions within colonial politics easily existed more than a hundred years prior to the colonial revolution.[7] Yet, as Edmund Burke recognized, the internal politics of colonial America had astounded foreign observers by thriving on such disagreements while remaining politically stable.[8] Such an observation suggests that a generalized attitude of 'truculence' was too common and too diffuse within the colonies to be isolated as the cause of decisive instability in relations with Britain in the 1770s.

Indeed, other historians have sought to challenge as well as to develop Bailyn's analysis of the ideological character of American revolutionary politics as uniquely conspiratorial and paranoiac. Gordon Wood, in particular, has argued that 'revolutionary Americans may have been an especially jealous and suspicious people, but certainly they were not unique in their fears of dark malevolent plots and plotters. In the Anglo-American world at the time of the Glorious Revolution, there was scarcely a major figure, Whig or Tory, who did not explain political events in these terms.'[9] The 'paranoid style' was a mode of expression common to the age on both sides of the Atlantic. The perception of politics as little more than intrigue and deception characterized the decades from the Restoration to the accession of William III. Indeed, one could easily argue that Locke's work both drew from and contributed to these characterizations. It drew from the Rye House Plot, with which Locke's connection now seems undeniable and which precipitated his flight to Holland in 1683; from Sidney's execution in 1686 in connection with the same plot; and from the attempt to indict Shaftesbury for treason in 1681 and his eventual death in exile.[10] To a great extent, Locke's fears were not paranoiac, but very real, and the roots of this outlook must be seen to lie in a psychological and moral substratum deeper than the actual political turmoil of the time. The paranoid style, which has been broadly described as 'a mode of causal attribution based on particular assumptions about the nature of social reality and the necessity of moral responsibility in human affairs', was the intellectual gift of the Enlightenment, and in no small way a direct bequest of Locke. Those assumptions, reductionist in their attempt to explain social phenomena through the moral nature of men, and to reduce moral philosophy to what would later be called psychology, drew from no work more deeply than from Locke's *Essay*. Locke's hypothesis of a causal connection between human uneasiness and voluntary action – an inference, as Hume noted, 'from character to conduct' – was the crux of the Enlightenment science of man. It also imbued that science with a propensity to mistrust unrestrained power in all hands other than one's own, and ultimately even in one's own.

Wood's recognition of the ubiquity of the paranoid style in politics, then, does not refute the position that the ideological origins of American revolutionary politics drew some support from the sceptical anti-authoritarianism of the British Opposition writers and pamphleteers. It does undercut the neatness and discreteness of these links, and it seriously undercuts the effort to excise the Lockean influence on this ideology. It also prompts us to return to the more interesting question of why such dramatic differences existed between the institutional outcomes of the constitutional upheavals in England and America. On Bailyn's argument, one must understand the triumph of parliamentary sovereignty – epitomizing supremely self-confident politics – in Britain and its defeat in America in terms of majoritarian politics. That is, the opposition writers were only a minority, however influential they may have been individually. Their fears, therefore, produced no systemic or constitutional change. But in America, their pamphlets struck a chord in a revolutionary majority which eventually placed institutional limits on the sovereignty of the legislature. However, this interpretation is not wholly satisfactory. If the paranoid style infected the age rather than particular segments of societies, then numbers are not significant. Once again, in explaining a generalized set of Anglo-American attitudes toward authority, Bailyn's ideological 'template' isolates too little of what might be said to be peculiarly American. Nevertheless, the implications of Bailyn's study of pre-revolutionary ideology for jurisprudence are evident: when ideological issues become the key to understanding social and legal problems of society, then appealing to the old jurisprudence for resolution of the problems simply begs the basic question at issue. Indeed, Burke pinpointed the problem of employing the English criminal law to control colonial opposition in his 1775 speech arguing for a British reconciliation with America. 'It looks to me to be narrow and pedantic', Burke argued, 'to apply the ordinary ideas of criminal justice to this public contest. I do not know a method of drawing up an indictment against a whole people. I cannot insult and ridicule the feelings of millions of my fellow-creatures as Sir Edward Coke insulted one excellent individual (Sir Walter Raleigh) at the bar'.[11]

Although focusing more on political culture than on political ideology, Wood supports the same conclusion. He claims that not only 'different circumstances' from those extant in Britain at the time, but also 'different ideas' ultimately underpinned revolutionary Americans' understanding of law and jurisprudence.[12] Wood's important historical focus on the years between the Revolution and the Founding has added much to our understanding of those 'different circumstances'. On the other hand, he concludes that for all the work done on judicial review, for example, it is still a far from clearly understood aspect of American jurisprudence. And, precisely in the areas of adjudication and jurisprudence, Wood's analysis is no stronger than Bailyn's in adding to an understanding of just which 'different ideas' made American colonial and indeed post-revolutionary attitudes toward law possible, justifiable, or even understandable.[13] However, a look at colonial jurisprudence, and particularly jural argument, helps not only to clarify those 'different ideas' but also to highlight a final limitation in any understanding of colonial legal thought that would rely on either the influence of the British opposition pamphleteers or the 'contagion of liberty' ideology for an explanation of colonial practices.

In terms of legal thought and jural argument, it would seem that American colonials were as busy radicalizing the British opposition writers as the other way round.[14] Contemporary observers such as Burke never bothered to identify or locate the origins of colonial complaints with opposition writers in Britain, despite the citations in their pamphlets. Rather, Burke recognized as central to colonial political argument an unreplicated and 'fierce spirit of liberty' peculiar to colonial conditions, and a commitment to 'popular' government which 'Cato' (Trenchard) at times directly opposed. 'The phantom of a commonwealth must vanish, and never appear again but in disordered brains.'[15] Instead, Burke attempted to explain the American intellectual climate of resistance in terms of the number of lawyers present in the colonies. 'In no country, perhaps in the world,' Burke wrote, 'is the law so general a study'. 'This study,' he concluded, 'renders men acute, inquisitive, dexterous, prompt to attack, ready in defence, full of resources'.[16]

However, the sheer numbers of lawyers in the colonies does little to explain American attitudes toward law when one reflects on the fact that during both revolutionary periods in Britain lawyers counted themselves among the most staunchly conservative, anti-radical defenders of order and tradition. Indeed, only one Leveller, John Wildman, is known to have had any direct connection with !aw at all, other than standing in the defendant's dock.[17] It was not their status as lawyers but their understanding of law which distanced American colonials from Britain. And, in their discussions of law and jurisprudence and particularly in their strongly held conviction of the ability of common men both to know and to judge the law by which they lived, colonials again drew from that deeper substratum of thought – one more philosophical as well as theological in its foundations, and more persistently held over time – than the 'contagion of liberty' and political distrust which has been suggested as the colonials' dominant political 'ideology'. It is the positive and regulative language of judgment, and the belief in the power of ordinary men to know and to judge the laws which guide their conduct, that informs and directs colonial legal thought. And it was to a great extent the epistemological as well as the political thought of Locke which underpinned and directed this thought. For this reason alone, despite the recent dramatic fall in Locke's perceived relevance to American political thought, it is both necessary and worthwhile to turn again, if only briefly, to the character of the colonial reliance upon his thought, and particularly upon its legal and jurisprudential implications.

BRINGING LOCKE BACK IN

The enormous devaluation in the explanatory currency of Locke's thought for historians and theorists of the American Revolution is, of course, in no small part attributable to the influential arguments not only of Bailyn but also of J. G. A. Pocock. However, in Bailyn's case at least, the effort seems never to have been to deny categorically the relevance of Locke's thought, but only to attenuate significantly its dominance in theoretically unsophisticated historical literature. Indeed, Bailyn produces extensive references to Locke from colonial sermons and political tracts, noting that 'Locke is cited often with precision on points of political theory, but at other times he is referred to in the most off hand way'.[18] Certainly it is true that, in practical terms, revolutionary colonists may have been prepared to make rhetorical references to almost any thinker from whom their arguments might obtain a measure of credibility otherwise thought to be lacking in the eyes of their British opponents. Nevertheless, there are many referenced discussions of Locke's work cited by Bailyn in *Ideological Origins* – more than any other European theorist suggested to have relevance to revolutionary thinking other than the authors of *Cato's Letters*, John Trenchard and Thomas Gordon. More importantly, even in the case of Cato, the thinker(s) given greatest emphasis in his analysis, Bailyn is prepared to recognize that 'the skeleton of Trenchard and Gordon's political thought was Lockean – concerned with inalienable rights and contract theory of government'.[19]

Of course, this is not surprising, since the imprint of Locke's thought on eighteenth-century literature, as well as on religion, politics, and law, was as pervasive as it was profound. Indeed, it is not too much to suggest that one can scarcely examine a sermon, a novel, a pamphlet, or a treatise written in eighteenth-century America and remain in any doubt after reading a few lines whether it was written before or after the publication of Locke's *Essay Concerning Human Understanding*.[20] Even those such as John Dunn, who have been perhaps justifiably sceptical about the explicit contribution of the *Two Treatises* to colonial political thinking, are prepared to recognize that on the eve of the Revolution Locke's *Essay* sold and was read in substantial and increasing numbers, and to admit that its reputation was 'vast'.[21] To see the immediacy of the *Essay* to colonial legal concerns requires only a brief excursus into its jurisprudential implications.

LAW AND ADJUDICATION: WHO SHALL JUDGE?

The focus of concern here, both with Locke and his relationship to colonial and early liberal jurisprudence, is with the transmission of a particular conceptual concern about law and its degree of certainty, particularly its moral certainty, and with its ambiguous character as both a limitor and an instrument of social and political control. Locke offered not a structure of government to be copied, but an understanding of the limitations of human reason and its relationship to law; an attitude of uncertainty about unlimited lawmaking power, a sceptical distrust of any and all who made claims to wield it; and a new conception of constitutionalism placing a check with 'the people' outside the bounds of existing government and standing law. In short, Locke replaced an older vision of the possibilities for moral certainty in law and politics with a new theory of knowledge. The political implications drawn from this theory can be seen in the writings and election sermons of New England preachers such as

Jonathan Mayhew, who reverted to arguments from Locke in his *Discourse concerning Unlimited Submission and Non-Resistance to Higher Powers* in order to ground political and legal challenges to Britain.

Historians have readily recognized that in Mayhew's arguments, rather typical 'Whig' claims for the power to resist tyranny are supplemented with new and ominous claims that 'subjects in general' were the 'proper judges [of] when their governors oppress them' and were 'bound' in duty to rebel against such recognized oppression.[22] Indeed, Mayhew's claims for the power of the people to know and to judge the law turned the common law of seditious libel explicitly on its head, by suggesting that whenever subjects

> find themselves thus abused and oppressed, they must be stupid *not* to complain. To say that subjects in general are not proper judges when their governors oppress them and play the tyrant, and when they defend their rights, administer justice impartially, and promote the public welfare, is as great treason as ever man uttered. 'Tis treason, not against one *single* man, but the state – against the whole body politic; 'tis treason against mankind, 'tis treason against common sense; 'tis treason against God.[23]

Of the various writers whom Mayhew later claimed to have influenced his thinking in political matters, only Locke provided the necessary theory of knowledge to support such an argument for the inalienable right of political judgment.[24]

The conception of human knowledge and judgment elucidated in the *Essay* lies at the heart of Locke's civil theory, and it is this view of law that makes the legal and constitutional implications of Locke's political thought so novel. While there is no necessary (logical) relationship between knowledge and politics, Locke created a powerful psychological and religious link between the two in the theory he developed about the relationship between knowledge and power.

In the *Essay* – written, as he insisted, 'not to know all things, but those which concern our conduct' – Locke's theory of moral law was firmly linked to the problem of common men's knowledge. The first step in both Locke's epistemology and his theory of law was to deny the existence of innate ideas and to deny specifically man's innate knowledge of the law of nature. Why he does so is related to man's profound and seemingly unavoidable propensity to err. This propensity is combined in men's mental makeup with a psychological and undeniably religiously grounded yearning to avoid error, with men's desire to be 'right' in their actions, and thus with their felt need to be certain in their judgments – not so much to give their judgments authority, or sheer force, but to give them legitimacy before their own eyes, and finally before God's.

Locke's denial of an innate knowledge of natural law was not a denial of natural law generally or its efficacy, nor a claim that only positive law was 'true' law. 'They equally forsake the truth,' Locke wrote, 'who running into the contrary extreams, either affirm an innate Law, or deny that there is a Law, knowable by the light of nature'.[25] Rather, Locke's denial was based on his recognition that an explicitly known law of nature is not in fact the basis of any system of moral laws in this world. Therefore, men should look askance at those representatives of political or religious power who claim to speak with an authority based on their innate knowledge of God's law.[26] Instead, Locke claimed, 'men have contrary principles', and common men have it within their capability to reason reflectively and to choose among competing moral laws arising from a variety of sources, customary, and civil.[27] In their drive for certainty, men are cautioned to avoid lazy 'enslavement' to the 'Dictates and Dominions of others' whose doctrines 'it is their duty to examine'.[28] They are under no obligation to obey laws whose authority rests on tradition, personal claims to power, or other 'oracles of the nursery'. These laws cannot be coeval with the laws of nature because the men who make them have imperfect knowledge. Therefore, Locke's vision of how men ought to conduct themselves in civil society (that is, the weight which they ought to give to customary and civil law, and the way in which their certainty ought to be attenuated) arises both from his descriptive analysis of the actual uncertainty of man's knowledge of the moral laws, and from an awareness of man's psychological drive for certainty in the laws on which he grounds his conduct.[29] Together, fallibilism and the drive for moral order work to place judgment at the centre of political considerations in a way that can be seen both in Locke's more explicitly political writings and in the writings of those American revolutionaries who employed his arguments to challenge British political and legal authority.

Locke's political argument in the *Second Treatise* is constructed almost entirely in terms of law, and focuses on the problem of adjudication in a manner which has been recognized to depart significantly from previous English writers on either constitutional or jurisprudential thought.[30] Locke thus describes law in the *Second Treatise* along the same lines as in the *Essay*, as rules set to the actions of men – politics arises, or rather the conception of political power arises, with the creation of laws. 'Political power', he writes, 'I take to be a Right of Making Laws, with penalties of Death, and consequently all less Penalties for the Regulating and Preserving of Property, and of employing the force of the Community in the Execution of such Laws and all this only for the Publick Good'.[31] Moving from the state of nature means giving up the individual's natural judicial and executive power to the community. The exercise of political power is then circumscribed and confined by the making and administering of laws within the strictures of the public good. The right of governing and the power to do so (a fundamental, individual natural right and power set alongside self-preservation and the preservation of mankind) are judicial in nature. They are seen as the pronouncing and enforcing of law. However, given men's epistemological difficulties, the exercise of political power is a very uncertain business, and Locke rarely neglects this fact in the *Second Treatise*, just as he had not failed to reinforce in the *Essay* that 'without Understanding, Liberty (if it could be) would signify nothing.'[32] Unfailingly, Locke's references in the *Second Treatise* to the capabilities of a 'rational creature' to derive principles from the law of nature are qualified with the *Essay*'s sceptical evaluation of men's likelihood of actually knowing it.[33] Therefore, as a hedge to error, a check is instituted on the legislative power which is entrusted with the ordinary exercise of the people's sovereign will.

Locke recognized in the *Essay* that men will always sit in judgment over the actions of others. However, the stipulation that none may judge in his own case is a juridical condition that makes absolute or uncheckable rule, whether by an arbitrary monarch or a legislature, untenable for Locke. Civil society is established when men give over their natural powers of judging and executing what they deem uncertainly to be the law of nature 'into the hands of the community', or 'to the publick', yet 'there remains in the People, a supreme power to remove or alter the Legislature, when they find the Legislature acts contrary to the Trust reposed in them'.[34] In this way, Locke creates 'the People' as a legal entity with constituent powers of its own, outside and independent of the legislative power based on the notion of a fiduciary trust. Locke's idea of a trust was legal as well as political, but he was well aware that no routined procedure or court existed to adjudicate breach of trust claims beyond appeal to the people themselves as a body sitting 'in judgment', independent and external to government.

Judicially, of course, what Locke was suggesting was entirely novel: a vantage for judgment about constitutional matters which could not be 'tacked on' to the existing constitutional structure of sovereignty. It eliminated Parliament's de facto judicial function as a 'court' exercising final judgment over its own laws. The maxim 'no one may judge in his own case' prohibits an absolute monarch or an absolute legislative power from uniquely judging whether its legislation pursues or corrupts the public good, which is the 'supreme law'. And Whig lawyers such as Blackstone were quick to note this radical step for what it was – a direct challenge to Parliament's position as the only basis of the rule of law: 'However just this conclusion (the right of the people to exercise checks on Parliament) may be in theory,' Blackstone wrote in 1776, 'we cannot practically adopt it, nor take any legal steps for carrying it into execution, under any dispensation of government at present existing'.[35] For Blackstone, there could be no distinction between the constitution, or frame of government, and its system of laws. On his view, the terms 'constitutional' and 'unconstitutional' were synonymous with 'legal' and 'illegal'. In this, at least, Blackstone simply reflected the traditional notion of constitutionalism prior to the eighteenth century, as a set of principles embodied in the institutions and laws of the nation, and neither external to these institutions nor in existence prior to them. It is not surprising that Locke's revolutionary check would be unacceptable to English Whigs. For them, the entire issue of 'who shall judge' was resolved – Parliament should judge. It could not override the people's will, as Locke's thought implied, because it embodied it. This makes the suggestion that colonials' use of Locke's 'revolution principle' was simply a piece of legitimating rhetoric somewhat illogical.

Locke's jurisprudential break with the traditional line of English constitutionalism is at its core a disagreement over the nature and character of an appropriate civil law. Unlike Locke, Blackstone would later characterize law in a Hobbesian fashion as a rule of civil conduct commanding what is right and prohibiting what is wrong. Further, unlike Locke, Blackstone believed the legitimacy of this law arose because it was prescribed by the 'supreme power' in the state – 'that absolute and despotic power which must in all governments reside somewhere', and was by the English constitution after 1689 vested in Parliament.[36] Therefore, while sympathetic with the colonials' antipathy to the British use of juryless Admiralty courts to prosecute political offenders, Burke clung firmly to the Blackstonian constitutional position that 'we [in Parliament] are, indeed, in all disputes with the colonies, by the necessity of things, the judge.'[37]

However, the purpose of civil law for Locke, as for revolutionary colonists, was not to be the arm of an 'absolute and despotic power' in any form. Freedom is juridical; it is not the absence of all rules, but it 'is to have a standing rule to live by' rather than being arbitrarily ruled by others – socially as well as politically. The purpose of such law is, in Locke's words, to 'enlarge Freedom', to enable man to dispose of his 'Person' and 'Actions' as well as his 'Property' within the framework of the law and to do so by limiting 'the Power and modera[ting] the Dominion of every Part and Member of Society'. Therefore, human freedom, both in and out of society, is a jural status, that is, a relationship between the individual's consent and judgment, and a body of law: 'Where there is no law there is no freedom'.[38] Liberty is also given an epistemological status. It is the capacity to be determined in one's actions by thought and judgment, rather than by force, faith, or unthinking habit.

The only way men can be sure that civil laws do not impose an arbitrary restraint on this freedom is to be governed by 'established and promulgated laws: that both the People may know their Duty, and be safe and secure within the limits of the Law, and the Rulers too kept within their due bounds'.[39] This would seem to counter the first shortcoming of the state of nature, that there be 'established and known' laws.[40] But obviously it is more than a procedural criterion which Locke has in mind here. Locke was not a common lawyer, and given the analysis of tradition and custom in the *Essay*, it is not surprising he explicitly rejects Coke's dictum that the common law was a nearly perfect system.[41] Locke characterized the common law, in contrast, as the 'Phansies and intricate contrivances of men, following contrary and hidden interests put into words.' Substantively, neither appropriate civil laws nor 'indifferent' judgments could be expected from such law, regardless of how established or known. Instead, Locke recognized that men must consent to those 'standing rules' by which they lived. To obtain consent such laws must be publicly known and 'conformable to Reason'. Public law should be stripped of the false authority of tradition and custom.

Therefore, following up the implications of the *Essay*, if properly structured juridically, the state 'hollows out' a certain protected and tolerated moral sphere, as well as judicial space, for each member of the subject population. In the first arena, the individual pursues certain moral knowledge uninhibited; in the second, 'the people' judge when the reach of legislative authority has overreached the bounds of consent. Locke's concern was to examine the foundations (moral, epistemological, psychological) for establishing government and opposing tyranny. He offered American revolutionaries almost no consideration of institutional design. The source of his influence is less the transmission of an explicit political or legal framework than a framework of ideas, and an attitude not about politics alone, but about the certainty of law and the limitations of reason as a guide to conduct. It is an attitude sometimes implicit and at other times explicitly expressed, as in parts of the *Federalist* or in revolutionary debates and tracts.[42] This *mentalité* makes for a new and genuinely liberal conception of law and freedom that was central to legal thought in America both before and after the Revolution. In the decades of the 1760s and 1770s, Americans were engaged in a fierce debate with the supposed authorities and representatives of their legal and political past – a past more and more brought home to them, but in no area more clearly than law, as no longer legitimate when judged 'by their own lights'. The arguments of Locke's *Essay* helped Americans to conceptualize their intellectual and political distance from the English jurisprudence being employed to bring them to heel. It helped colonials to structure their dialogue with Britain, and to legitimate, if only to themselves, their new and openly defiant 'definitions' of 'constitution' and 'sovereignty'. In this way, Locke's thought may be understood as an epistemological framework within which Americans established the logic of their legal and jurisprudential innovations. The dictum of the *Essay* is that men must think and judge for themselves; that no other authority can assure their conduct is rightly guided. 'The floating of other men's opinions in our brains', claimed Locke, 'makes us not one jot the more knowing though they happen to be true'.[43] The further removed traditional maxims and rules are from their source of experience, the less moral 'weight' they should carry. It was an argument colonial Americans made repeatedly as they struggled to bring their own laws into correspondence with American experience.

Jefferson certainly was not alone in recognizing that by framing the question of the limits to the constitutional authority and power of government in terms of the epistemological and moral question 'who shall be judge?', with its implications for both sovereignty and the legitimacy of law, Locke's thought had unleashed the power of public opinion in politics.[44] The claim that 'the people' retain, and should know they retain in the final analysis, the supreme say regarding the rightful exercise of the power delegated to government was the central claim of colonial pamphleteers.[45] Yet, there was at the time nowhere for this claim to manifest itself in a routinized fashion except in the practices of juries. Colonial jurymen had the franchise, but a theory of virtual representation kept their own ideas submerged in the regular political channels, so the turn to juries was not surprising. In this sense, Tocqueville was correct in his observation that the jury system in America functions as 'one form of sovereignty of the people', because they recognized that 'the man who is judge in a criminal trial is the real master of society'.[46] In their discussion of law and jurisprudence and of the ability of men to know and judge the law by which they lived, colonials reflected a more critical understanding of their need to rethink the claims of English jurisprudence than is commonly inferred from references to 'ideology'. The problem of judgment was of central importance in colonial thinking. A central theme of pre-revolutionary discourse, and the very core of the colonials' 'revolution principle' as explicitly and repeatedly reiterated in election sermons, popular pamphlets, and newspapers, was 'the peoples'' capacity – particularly through the institution of the jury – to challenge law. And while the right to trial by jury was embedded in the fabric of the English constitution, as John Adams recognized, the American understanding of it was quite different. In many cases, the defence of trial by jury moved easily into what amounted to ringing affirmations of Locke's theory of limited government and a defence of popular resistance to arbitrary rulers and arbitrary laws.

JURIES AND JUDICIAL INDEPENDENCE IN REVOLUTIONARY AMERICA

The differences between American colonial and British Opposition writers was more than just ones of attitude; there were also differences in the institutional practices through which these ideas filtered. Contrary to the English common law practice giving judges exclusive determination with the court on matters of law, juries held the central place in colonial courts: 'juries rather than judges spoke the last word on law enforcement in nearly all, if not all, of the eighteenth-century American colonies'.[47] Adding to the expansiveness of the jural reach is Alexander Hamilton's claim that in some states all cases were tried by jury.[48] With the exception of equitable actions, which some historians suggest were severely limited in the colonies, judges could neither enter a judgment nor impose a penalty in criminal matters without there first being a jury verdict.[49] The judge's role was simply understood differently. For example, one contemporary source described judges in Rhode Island as holding office "not for the purpose of deciding causes, for the jury decided all questions of law and fact, but merely to preserve order and see that the parties had a fair chance with the jury'.[50] Similar practices were followed in Connecticut and New York.[51]

More importantly, however, the scope of colonial jury determination reached beyond determinations of fact to substantive questions of law. William Nelson has argued that the power of the colonial jury to 'find law' was almost unlimited. He attributes this power to various rules and practices regulating the division of function between judges and juries. For example, Nelson notes that the frequent use of the general issue, which left to juries the ultimate determination of the legal consequences of the facts of the case as well as 'the practice of giving juries conflicting instructions on the law emanating both from counsel and from the several judges of the court', encouraged juries to 'select the rules for determining the legal consequences of facts.' Moreover, 'the infrequency with which jury verdicts were set aside after trial tended to give juries wide power to find law.'[52] Such jural practices existed pointedly in contradiction to both contemporary and earlier, seventeenth-century English common law theory and practice. The practices themselves need explanation, as does the observation that for a considerable period before the Revolution, 'juries were specifically instructed', both by opposing lawyers and leading public figures, that 'they could disregard the judges' opinions of the law and determine the matter for themselves.'[53]

One proposed explanation for the colonials' jury-centred approach to common law – particularly during the years immediately preceding the Revolution – was a deeply ingrained and increasingly 'patriotic' distrust of the independence of the British judiciary.[54] Given the political and legal structure of colonial society, the tension between judges and colonial control as represented by juries is hardly surprising. Colonial judges, it is important to note, even after the Glorious Revolution, held their commissions without the benefit of settled salaries and at the pleasure of the Crown rather than on good behaviour. In practice, this meant the Crown exercised the political power of appointment and dismissal over the colonial judiciary explicitly

denied it in England under the Act of Settlement. Burke was not
alone in recognizing the difficulties this made for securing the
colonies 'a fair and unbiased judicature, as judges, at all levels, from
justices of the peace to chief justices of the supreme courts, were
not only appointed on the nomination of the royal governor, but
were dismissable by the governor's fiat.'[55] Indeed, in America, Adam
Smith's intended praise of the British judiciary in 1763, that 'there
seems to be no country in which the courts are under greater regulation and the authority of the judge more restricted,' was a sword
which cut with a double edge. When colonial assemblies such as that
of Pennsylvania in 1759 sought to remedy this lack of independence
of the judiciary, their efforts were quickly overruled by the Crown
amid torrents of colonial protest.[56] Such judges, as authorized administrative 'arms' of an external and increasingly threatening executive,
were naturally to be suspect as political operatives lacking in 'independent' and neutral judgment.

This jural opposition to an 'arbitrary' executive would seem to
parallel the position of juries in English revolutions. However, the
expanded role of colonial juries was not simply a response to the
'dependent' administration of law by judges acting as placemen of a
government pursuing unpopular policies, as cases such as *Forsey v.
Cunningham* in New York demonstrate. The case, a civil suit for
damages by the victim of an assault (Forsey) against his assailant
(Cunningham), pitted the New York judiciary against the colony's
Crown-appointed Lieutenant Governor, Cadwallader Colden.
Though the case would seem of no particular public significance, it
proved a crucial case for reiterating the colonials' control over jury
trials. Having been fined more than £1500, Cunningham petitioned
New York's Supreme Court to allow an appeal to the Governor in
Council of what he considered an excessive damage award. The
request directly challenged the judicial practice permitting appeals
to jury verdicts only on the grounds of technical errors of writ, not
on grounds of equity. Cunningham was thus knowingly asking that
the Governor be permitted to review a matter of 'fact' and to pass
judgment on the jury's verdict. At this point, Cunningham's own
lawyers recognized the challenge being made to trial by jury, and
refused to continue with the case, leaving Colden to find other legal
representation. As anticipated, the Supreme Court denied Cunningham's petition.

However, acting for an absentee Governor, and anxious to bring
New York's jury system more within the ambit of British practice,

Lieutenant-Governor Colden took the step of accepting Cunningham's plea and ordering the Supreme Court to submit the trial proceeding to the Council. The Court refused, arguing that such an act would overturn 'the ancient and wholesome laws of the land', and would threaten trials by jury in a manner 'repugnant to the Laws of both England and this Colony.'[57] Colden countered with the charge that the Court lacked 'respect for the King's authority' and insisted his interpretation of law was as legitimate as the Courts', and his judicial right to be exercised 'without regard to any man'.[58] The Court's refusal persisted and a lengthy press battle was waged in local newspapers in which Colden's challenge to jury trials was condemned as a 'fondness for showing himself in Law matters, superior to the body of the Law.' A certain 'Sentinel', writing in the pages of the *New York Gazette; and Weekly Post-boy*, ensured that the popular meaning and constitutional significance of this attack on trial by jury was denounced as 'unconstitutional and illegal'.[59] In the end, the Supreme Court's position was publicly heralded by a specially convened grand jury, while Colden was denounced by the New York Assembly and his pleas for support ignored by a generally embarrassed London Board of Trade.[60]

Colonial disagreement with the fundamental understanding of law which underpinned the division between jural and judicial powers in England was persistent and pronounced. The host of devices – including directed and special verdicts, special juries, and the setting aside of verdicts deemed incompatible with judicial instructions – that had been developed in England by Justice Holt, and carried forward after 1756 by Justice Mansfield in order to shrink the jury's space for judgment, were all but ignored in Colonial America. While John Trenchard could suggest in 1722 '[w]e have very good laws' to punish seditious libel, 'and I well approve of them, whilst they are prudently and honestly executed, which I really believe they have for the most part been since the Revolution,' colonial juries disagreed. Despite evidence that colonists 'treated royal authority and parliamentary measures with a merciless contempt and abuse,' Leonard Levy has now noted that with but two exceptions no common-law prosecution for seditious libel succeeded in America in the eighteenth century.[61] Nowhere is this better seen than in the comparative treatments in England and America of seditious libel trials in the early part of the century.

In 1731, the English bookseller and printer Richard Franklin was tried for seditious libel for having printed and published 'A Letter from the Hague', in the *Craftsman*.[62] The fictional 'Letter', which contained both humorous and caustic remarks about English revisions in its current relations with France and Spain, was accused of 'wickedly, maliciously, and seditiously contriving and intending to disturb and disquiet the happy state of the public peace. . . .'[63] Franklin was tried by a special jury composed entirely of lawyers, who were instructed by Chief Justice Raymond to render a special verdict:

> So, gentlemen, if you are sensible, and convinced that that the defendant published the *Craftsman* of the 2d of January last; and that the defamatory expressions in the letter refer to the ministers of Great Britain; then you ought to find the defendant guilty. . . .[64]

Franklin was found guilty, and the conduct of his trial simply enforced the division of jural and judicial responsibility that would remain in force in England until Fox's Libel Act.[65] In colonial America, a very different understanding of this division of responsibility obtained, and the seditious libel trial of John Peter Zenger raised this difference pointedly in 1734, with the Revolution more than forty years away.[66]

In November 1734 John Peter Zenger, the printer of the *New York Weekly Journal*, was arrested and charged with seditious libel against the Royal Governor, William Cosby. The case arose over Cosby's preemptory dismissal of the Chief Justice of the New York Supreme Court, Lewis Morris, when that Justice found against the Royal Governor in a personal equity case. The Governor dismissed Morris and elevated a second judge, James Delancey, in his place. In the pages of the *Weekly Journal*, Zenger complained, among other things, that 'We see men's deeds destroyed, judges arbitrarily displaced, new courts erected without consent of the legislature, by which it seems to me, trials by juries are taken away when the governor pleases. . . .'[67] These remarks became the basis of an indictment for seditious libel.

The Zenger case is one well known and frequently discussed in colonial historiography. Even so, it remains a seminal case in colonial jurisprudence worthy of yet another reconsideration, particularly in terms of its significance in both reflecting and shaping colonial attitudes toward the character of jural power. It is not difficult to see why. Historians have recognized New York's eighteenth-century legal development to be ostensibly more Anglicized and professionally formalistic in character than many of its New England counterparts, and its legal system likewise mirrored more closely than New England's those institutions operating in England.[68] However, the significant lack of sophisticated or, in many cases, even basic English legal knowledge on the part of judges, prosecutors, and juries – recognized as the 'very heart of the English tradition in criminal law' – created the ground for alternative interpretations in the operation of those institutions and in the understanding of law to develop. In a period in which the vast majority of New York as well as other colonial lawyers were trained provincially, and in which the only indigenously printed law books were the laws of the colonial assemblies and some few legal opinions and arguments (together with the texts of some outstanding trials) Zenger's case was of considerable heuristic and pedagogical significance.[69] Reprinted many times, colonials were familiar with its arguments, which are themselves informative both as to the level of technical legal expertise brought against colonial political recidivists and their legal response. Zenger shows both the attempt by crown prosecutors at legal control through more technical and sophisticated common law argument, and the innovative and successful circumvention of this legal formalism accomplished by Zenger's defense lawyers. Equally important, both the prevalence of this case and its popular as well as legal significance are weighted heavily on the jury issue; it would be difficult for the legal practitioner studying Zenger to avoid its distinctly unBritish attitude toward the role and scope of jural power.

The Zenger case itself was enmeshed in the controversial efforts of a series of New York Governors – dating from 1701 – to erect a court of equity in the province. Resistance from both the General Assembly and the popular press had focused on the charge that the 'governor was undermining the right to jury trial by bringing matters of law before a court of equity'.[70] Threats to juries in New York, as elsewhere, were interpreted as a threat to 'constitutional government'. And, the jury issue was already very much alive in 1734, when Zenger published his 'seditious' charges against the governor in issue numbers 13 and 23 of *The New York Weekly Journal*.

Now, Zenger's defence against seditious libel focused not only on claims concerning the freedom of the press but, more importantly, the role of the jury in determining law. Later historians analyzing the case have suggested that the outcome of the Zenger case terrorized 'the partisans of royal prerogative in England and America', who recognized it as a 'dangerous triumph of popular reason and will over the authority of judicial canons and forensic pedantry'.[71]

Their alarm undoubtedly arose from the fact that the English law of libel was squarely and unambiguously against Zenger, yet he was nevertheless acquitted. In the earlier case of Franklin, under that same law, judges of the King's Bench reserved to themselves the power to decide whether words were libellous, permitting the jury to decide only the facts of publication and innuendo. In this way, the jury's verdict was regarded as 'special', that is, restricted to the question of fact, rather than 'general', that is, directed to the question of guilt or innocence. However, when Zenger's case came to trial in 1735 the prosecution and bench were confronting the claim by those accused of seditious speech that only juries of peers were the proper 'judges' of their crimes.[72] The legal citations put forward for Zenger were (and would have had to have been) altogether unconvincing legally. Indeed, they were not intended to persuade the justices in the case at all. Defence rhetoric appealed instead to the 'twelve plain jurymen', and was intended to match their experience of government with their conception of law. It was plainly not a conception of law shared by the judges, so that when Zenger's lawyers, James Alexander and William Smith, went so far as to offer written and oral exceptions to the legality of the judges' commissions, as based on Royal 'pleasure' rather than 'good behaviour', they were summarily disbarred.[73] Undaunted, Zenger's new lawyer, Andrew Hamilton (assisted informally by Alexander), 'appealed to popular notions of government and society'; he 'cited first principles' such as 'the constitution' rather than relying on the technicalities of the common law of libel. In particular, Hamilton directly attacked the existing form of the libel law in two ways. First, by asserting that truthful statements could never be libellous, whether or not they aroused public censure, he challenged the ruling judicial dictum that 'a libel is not to be justified, for it is nevertheless a libel that it is true'.[74] Second, he suggested that the jury not only could determine the law in the case, but that it might challenge the legitimacy of the laws altogether: 'What strange doctrine is it to press everything for law here which is so in England?'[75] The argument for truth as a defence in libel had been suggested publicly in *Cato's Letters*.[76] However, it was Hamilton in *Zenger* who first produced such an argument in court. And, while 'truth' was not accepted into English common law until 1843, it became a recognized element of American jurisprudence from *Zenger* forward. Furthermore, while Hamilton might have drawn the argument on truth from *Cato*, the essential element of Zenger's defence – the appeal to the jury to decide for themselves rather than to be bound by the court's instructions – was never proposed by either Trenchard or Gordon.

Later critics of Hamilton, who represented the English legal perspective, not surprisingly focused on the technical flaws in the defence argument and its appeal to the reason of common men. '[T]his lawyer seems to be above having his points of law decided by the authorities of law', argued one critic, 'and [he] has something in reserve which . . . he calls *the reason of the thing*, but is truly and properly a sketch of his own politics.'[77] From the colonial legal perspective, however, this criticism was quite beside the point. The departure of Zenger's lawyer from proper legal form was not 'careless' or 'lack learn'd'. It was an attempt by a skilled defence counsel to compel the court to focus on the substantive rather than the procedural aspects of the case.[78] While the existing law might have been against Zenger, the law itself no longer matched public opinion, as expressed by the jury's verdict of 'not guilty', despite the court's attempt to direct that they render judgment only on the fact of publication. Responding to the jury's verdict, one observer noted: 'If it is not law it is better than law, it ought to be law, and will always be law wherever justice prevails'.[79] In England, the Zenger case was treated as a legal anomaly without force of precedent. In America, the substance of Hamilton's arguments both for truth as a defence against libel and for the sweeping power of juries to determine law – that is, to challenge offensive law – became staple elements of the colonial legal challenge.[80]

Neither the origin of the Zenger case nor its final outcome can be understood well or solely in terms of opposition politics or simply a distrust of the British judiciary's independent judgments. Zenger's acquittal was not a slap in the face to British rule, although it was a swipe at unchecked royalist control over the appointment and tenure of New York justices.[81] It seems clear, however, that the Morrisites would have objected equally to the arbitrary actions taken, had the Governor been an indigenous rather than royal appointee. At a deeper level, the case was a challenge to the authority of any judge to determine unchallenged what the law governing colonials would be.

In contrast to British legal practices, in the early colonial cases defence attorneys were presenting and juries considering challenges to law, not simply to its administration. They expressed a colonial belief that the 'Jury had a right to do as they please[d]' with respect to law.[82] John Adams argued that even when juries decided contrary

to court direction, their verdicts determined the law, *because* it was
not only the juror's right but also his duty to 'find the Verdict
according to his own best Understanding, Judgment and Conscience,
tho in Direct opposition to the direction of the Court'.[83]

This challenge, then existed well before the Revolution. As we
shall see below, it also extended well after the Revolution, to the
point of constitutional resolution at the Founding. Indeed, even
after 1789, opinions about who was to exercise final judgment about
determinations of law remained divergent.

LEGAL UNCERTAINTY AND JURAL SPACE IN COLONIAL LAW

In part, the tension between juries and judges concerning matters of
law, particularly in cases where the relationship between law and
politics was close, lies in the uncertainty and diversity of the colonial
legal experience. The American court system, which virtually collapsed all English common law jurisdictions, often rendered the
wholesale incorporation of English law inapplicable and pointless.
As Peter van Schaak, reviser of New York's eighteenth-century laws,
wrote in 1786, 'the simplicity of our Courts' renders 'the complex
subtleties' of English common law practice as unsuitable as 'the
appendages of an old dowager's toilette ornamental to the bloom of
nineteen.'[84] All the colonies claimed the 'benefits' of general common
law rights, but they accepted only limited categories of British statutes.[85] The sense that what constituted the 'common' law was in
many colonies a product of selective and conscious incorporation of
English law placed side-by-side with an indigenous colonial product
can be seen in the very wording of formal reception clauses penned
at the close of the Revolution when each state was forced to come
to legal terms with political separation. The Massachusetts Constitution of 1780 contained a clause authorizing the continued effectiveness of all laws that had 'been adopted, used, and approved' in the
Commonwealth.[86] In other colonies, such as New York, evidence
suggests that the basic questions of what law obtained in the colony,
how far English precedent should be considered operative, and who
should decide the answers to such questions, were ones of general
public concern. In New York, for example, adjusting the common
law was the task of the legislature; in pre-revolutionary Pennsylvania
– much to the chagrin of colonials such as John Dickinson – it was

a function performed by the courts. In his *Letter From a Farmer in Pennsylvania*, Dickinson noted that 'our courts exercise A Sovereign Authority, in determining what parts of the common and statute law ought to be extended: For it must be admitted, that the difference of circumstances necessarily requires us, in some cases to Reject the determination of both'. However, Dickinson complained of the 'constructive' practices of the courts, which in many instances 'have also extended even acts of Parliament, passed since we had a distinct legislature, which is greatly adding to our confusion. The practice of our courts is no less uncertain than the law'.[87] Uncertainty was further exacerbated by the lack of written case law, and the complete lack of any collected indigenous case reports until very late in the century. In Massachusetts, for example, American court reports in series did not begin until 1789, suggesting that only the sporadic cases recorded in the legal notebooks of lawyers such as John Adams were available to guide legal practice. Incorporation of particular English common law precedents, forms, and principles would then be seen as at best selective, variable, and, most crucially, a matter of explicit choice and 'the will of each colony'.[88]

This is not to suggest that colonial adjudication was a simple model of 'frontier justice'. Indeed, it was quite technical – but, importantly, there would be scope for choice. Here was something that no English jurist or even English judge in a comparable position might experience. What was to be the basis of this choice? Although the number of lawyers in the colonies was large and continually growing, the ordinary citizen called for jury duty could not have had much of an understanding of the intricacies of common law. However, while to critics of colonial jurisprudence this seemed an argument to limit their function, to colonials themselves technical ignorance and a concomitant reliance on an oral legal tradition of local precedent and the 'simple voice of nature and reason' were believed to enhance and 'simplify' their task.[89] In contrast to the 'torturous jungle' of common law which the Levellers, Hobbes, and Locke encountered in the English court system of the seventeenth century, and which they felt left men uncertain about the security of their property and rights, common law thinking in early colonial American courts took a quite different turn. Again, John Adams noted, 'The general Rules of Law and common Regulations of Society . . . [were] well enough known to the ordinary Juror.'[90]

Jurors knew the law, at least in part, because they made those 'general Rules and common Regulations' within their own communities. William Nelson has inferred from his extensive examination of the colonial court system that jurors came to the courts with similar preconceptions about that law, 'at least to be applied to disputes that frequently came before them'.[91] And, the same peculiar and selective admixture of English law and provincial custom which provided juries with the opportunity to exercise discretion placed judges on an unsure footing. As Wood notes, the mingling of both English law and provincial practice provided 'two Fountains of their Law'.[92] In most cases, there was no indigenous record – in part a result of relying on jury determinations in which the raison d'être of judgment remained unstated. Judges, therefore, had likewise to rely on local memory, reason, and equity 'for the clarifying of their law and for justifying the deviations in their jurisprudence.'[93] In such a situation, recourse to obscure references or unfamiliar English law could only appear to obfuscate the legal issue and to further expand rather than restrict judicial discretion. Litigants claimed 'that the issues of cause' depended 'not so much on the right of the Client as on the breath of the Judge, and what was looked upon as a good plea in one circuit was disallowed in another'.[94] Such a complaint is not anti-British; rather it reflects an uneasiness over the uncertainty of law and the discretion for judicial interpretation it permits. This feeling was probably exacerbated by the fact that nearly every eighteenth-century court sat with more than one judge on the bench, and the common practice was for them to deliver their individual and potentially conflicting charges seriatim to the jury. Furthermore, most of these judges were neither transplants from the ranks of the professional English bar, nor lawyers, nor even formally trained in the law. Rather they were local men, often controversial appointees, such as Thomas Hutchinson, who wrote of his experience as Chief Justice of the Massachusetts Superior Court from 1760 to 1790: 'I never presumed to call myself a Lawyer. The most I could pretend to was when I heard the Law laid down on both sides to judge which was right'.[95] Not surprisingly, the 'rightness' of Hutchinson's judgments were almost universally challenged and despised by colonial revolutionaries.

Because of what have been characterized as the very 'perplexities' of colonial law, judges such as Hutchinson were left free, indeed were forced in many cases, to select and innovate in order to adjust continually to local circumstance. Therefore, one confronts a jurisprudential situation in which selective and innovative legal interpretations and judgments on the part of jurors were viewed as legitimate because such activity was 'founded on the nature and fitness of things'. On the part of judges, however, such legal innovation and selection were viewed as an unacceptable exercise of discretion. At issue was the existence or content of the standards by which judges' decisions could be legitimized as neutral as well as 'right'.

While both the systemic lack of judicial independence and the uncertainty of the corpus of colonial law were certainly heightened by opposition to British policies in the revolutionary era, neither is sufficient to explain the scope and character of the judicial space colonials accorded to juries. The tension between judges and juries must be found in a deeper underlying moral and intellectual milieu of colonial society, which needs to be understood independently of those antipathies engendered by the Revolution. The degree to which conformity to local moral, religious, and political standards was enforced in colonial society has been well documented.[96] Juries served importantly to reflect and enforce, as well as to create, those standards. They did something more, however. They enhanced the belief that the people themselves knew what the law was for their own community. It was a belief that Jefferson would later articulate, that 'the great principles of right and wrong are legible to every reader: to pursue them requires not the aid of many counsellors'.[97] There was no need to judge American citizens by English rules, as 'the people knew very well what violated decency and good order'.[98]

Certainly not all, or even most, of the hostility expressed toward the judiciary by such thinkers as Adams and Jefferson sprang from their antipathy toward Britain. Their political and legal defence of an expanded role for the jury reflected a more basic and positive epistemological and moral vision of men's capabilities as knowers and judges of law and of their own and the public interest.

The role and activity of juries in the American revolutionary conflict suggests that the American Revolution was not only about widening participation in the making of law – sovereignty – but also about widening the space for reflective judgment about laws once made. This second effort was decidedly not the same as widening the 'discretion' of judges. Indeed, while judges might attempt to 'guide' a jury in legal matters, it was not at all clear that an unwilling jury could be coerced, or even circumvented, if, for example, it refused to return a special verdict. John Adams argued that jurors could not, on principle, be expected 'under any legal or moral or divine Obligation to find a Special Verdict where they themselves [were] in no doubt of the Law'.[99] Again, the Zenger case suggests that in practice they could not be coerced. Widening the space for reflective judgment about law instead involved an expansion of the numbers of individuals routinely exercising judgment about the legitimacy of government action, accompanied by an enlargement of the scope for questions about the very constitution of 'legitimacy'. The effort to expand the space for judgment about law through juries involved a recognition that after answering the questions, 'Who shall make the law?', and 'How shall the law be made?', not all the questions of significance to liberty had been asked or answered.

DENOUEMENT ON JUDGES AND JURAL POWERS IN POST-REVOLUTIONARY AMERICA

In the eyes of many Americans such as John Adams, the American Revolution had been completed before the actual fighting with Britain commenced. On this view the 'real Revolution' – by which they meant a 'radical change in the principles, opinions, sentiments, and affections of the people' – had taken place not on colonial battlefields but 'in the minds of the people, and this was effected, from 1760 to 1775, in the course of fifteen years before a drop of blood was shed at Lexington'.[100] However, to others the cessation of fighting and with it the British admission of American independence marked nothing more than the first act in an ongoing drama. In the words of Benjamin Rush, 'the American war is over, but this is far from being the case with the American revolution'.[101] Perhaps nowhere was the evidence of America's continuing revolution more apparent than in the area of legal and jural reform.

The power and scope of jury ability to determine law and the tenure and appointment of judges – central and hotly contested legal issues of the revolutionary period – remained unsettled in its aftermath. In the aftermath of the Revolution and throughout the Founding period, juries functioned alongside courts – and sometimes in opposition to them – as instruments in the consolidation of post-revolutionary law and jurisprudence. The Georgia state constitution of 1777 forbade judges from interfering with the jury's power to determine the law, as did New Jersey, by statute, in 1784.[102] In many quarters confidence and enthusiasm for juries continued throughout the Founding period and well into the first third of the nineteenth century. General praise for trial by jury as a 'cornerstone of liberty' poured forth both from those who participated in framing the Constitution and who affirmed the final document, such as John Dickinson, and those who participated but would not sign, such as Elbridge Gerry.

More important, the powers of juries remained a principal locus for the resolution of a wide range of legal issues within communities. In North Carolina, juries were employed both to 'lay out roads' and to ascertain 'any damages done to private property' in the process.[103] In Georgia, grand juries were empowered to issue public presentments chastizing the state legislature for the promulgation of constitutionally 'suspect' laws.[104] Similarly, in Massachusetts, juries maintained a wide range of lawfinding powers in civil as well as criminal matters. The opening of grand juries continued to serve as occasions in which discourses on the nature of the 'social compact' and of government, as well as the nature of criminal law, were reiterated.[105] Indeed, recent studies have suggested that popular resistance was registered in states such as Pennsylvania to any efforts on the part of an emerging American bar to reform or to significantly 'Anglicize' the law in ways which would reduce the jury's power to determine law. Such resistance continued well into the nineteenth century. Instead, 'popular' law reformers insisted upon 'a code of laws free of Latin phrases and technical terms', and written in 'a language they believe consistent with the plain and simple nature of a Republican form of government' and easily 'legible' to citizens and jurors alike.[106] Republicans writing under pseudonyms such as 'Camden' and 'Zenas' continued to defend the jury's right to disregard any court's recommendations with regard to law. 'Suppose a difference in sentiment' exists 'between the judges and the jury with regard to law . . . what is to be done?' 'The jury must do their whole duty', Camden claimed, and determine the law as well as the fact though in contradiction to court direction. For, as Zenas noted, to ask a juror 'to judge against his own judgment [of law]; in other words to sacrifice his honor and conscience – who would willingly be a juror upon these degrading terms?'[107] In Massachusetts, radical republicans opposed bills as late as 1806 which declared the incompetency of juries in questions of law with arguments reminiscent of their revolutionary claims for jural equality:

The doctrine now attempted to be promulgated, to render the jury incompetent to law, is to depreciate the character of every other man in society but practitioners of it. It is similar to the declaration, that the people are their own 'worst enemies' – that they are ignorant as to every particular on which is founded either the political or legal principles of the constitution and of the laws. Should this once become the prevailing sentiment, in a few years no man would be considered of any weight in society but those connected in the judiciary department. This doctrine would pervade the legislative branch and none of them would be eligible to make laws but those in the practice of them.[108]

Nevertheless, after the constitutional separation from Great Britain, the political relationship of the people to their representatives changed, and the legal implications of recognizing popular sovereignty as the standard of law began to emerge. These changes were inevitable to a changing and expanding self-rule. However, they challenged the ability of both judges and juries in America to know either law or custom by simply 'opening' their eyes. The result was merely to add to the general legal uncertainty extant during the Revolution within the states, most dramatically in the area of civil case law. Reflecting this legal uncertainty, one historian notes that between 1790 and 1820, 'courts in nearly every state for which evidence exists began to grant motions for new trials in civil cases where juries returned verdicts contrary to law, instructions or evidence'.[109] It appears that for an increasing number of newly independent Americans, the demands of achieving some degree of legal uniformity in the aftermath of the Revolution, not only within the newly legitimated 'states' but especially within the nation at large, required a curtailment of the jury's significant lawfinding powers. In particular, legal historians have suggested that jural powers were curtailed for largely economic reasons, because 'the certainty and predictability of substantive rules that a commercial economy required would be to little avail if juries remained free to reject those rules or to apply them inconsistently'.[110] Yet, such practices met with opposition from those who considered any diminution in the scope of jury determinations of law to be a political challenge rather than an economic issue.

For proponents of popular or local control, the question of who knew the law, even in civil cases, remained politically significant. Arguments about the locus, causes, and solutions of uncertainty in the law repeated nearly verbatim those arguments of pre-revolutionary colonials over three decades earlier:

We say that the error lies not with the jury, but within the complex system of English laws adopted as authorities. On this comprehensive system, founded on cases no way analogous either to our constitution or customs, the judges themselves get confounded, and the lawyers sport with their client with a parade of wonderful learning and investigation. It is laughable to hear men talk seriously about the certainty of that which has become proverbial for uncertainty. – 'The glorious uncertainty of the law,' is an observation as familiar as the expenses of it. – Not that it is uncertain as it relates to the verdict of the jury, but its uncertainty consists in the explanation of those who profess exclusively to be its expounders. After we have heard a cause attended with all the variety of opinions given on the subject, the mind of the audience is generally more satisfied by the decision of the jury than from all the comments on the law, however elaborately delivered. The fact is, the jury hear the variety of opinion, and are able on mature deliberation, to judge accurately on the precise point of controversy.[111]

Their proposed solutions were likewise the same – reduce, simplify, or eliminate the vestiges of 'foreign' common law. 'Shall we be directed by reason, equity and a few simple and plain laws promptly executed, or shall we be ruled by volumes of statutes and cases decided by the ignorance and intolerance of former times?'[112] However, while the jurisprudential outlook and the solutions were the same, both the times and the jurisprudential problems had clearly changed. Nowhere could this be more clearly seen than in the constitutional impact of continued jural claims to find law in criminal prosecutions.

A period of significant internal political turmoil leading up to the turn of the century – including Shay's Rebellion in Massachusetts (1786–7) and the Whiskey Rebellion of the 1790s, as well as domestic unrest occasioned by international entanglements – served as the basis for the most significant test of both the reach and scope of post-revolutionary juries to challenge law, and the applicability of English common law jurisprudence to American criminal law. The 'test case' was the prosecution of James Thompson Callendar for seditious libel under the much resisted Alien and Sedition Acts of 1798.[113]

In what appeared to many as a startling retreat from the legal principles of the Revolution, supporters of the acts argued that they were justified under common laws 'received' from Britain, and that the common law was a constitutional part of the law of the Federal

Government.[114] Opponents of the acts, including Madison and Jefferson, immediately responded that such arguments were antithetical to the entire legal thrust of the Revolution. As Madison reminded the acts' supporters,

> The assertion by Great Britain of a power to make laws for the other members of the empire *in all cases whatsoever*, ended in the discovery that she had a right to make laws for them *in no cases whatsoever*. Such being the ground for our Revolution, no support nor colour can be drawn from it, for the doctrine that the common law is binding on these states as one society. The doctrine, on the contrary, is evidently repugnant to the fundamental principle of the Revolution.[115]

Furthermore, it was claimed that any effort to impose upon American law a national, common law jurisdiction was explicitly at odds with the Constitution and with the character of American legal thought.[116] The question was posed: Who would finally judge the constitutionality of such laws?

In the case of James Callendar, prosecuted for seditious libel under the Sedition Act, the argument was directly made that the jury was the final judge of any law's constitutionality. The argument addressed to the jury by Callendar's lawyer William Wirt came to be known as the Richmond Syllogism: 'Since, then, the jury have a right to consider the law, and since the constitution is law, the conclusion is certainly syllogistic, that the jury have a right to consider the Constitution'.[117] Supreme Court justice Samuel Chase, presiding over the case on circuit, agreed that 'if the Federal legislature should, at any time, pass a law contrary to the Constitution of the United States, such law would be void'.[118] However, he called the Richmond Syllogism a 'non sequitur' in law, and refused to permit the jury to consider the argument. Only the judiciary, Chase claimed, was 'competent' to determine whether 'any Law made by Congress, or any State Legislatures is contrary to or in violation of the federal Constitution'.[119] Although Callendar was convicted, his was the only conviction and the last trial under the Sedition Act, which lapsed shortly thereafter along with any remaining claims for a Federal common law of crimes. More important, an attempt was made to impeach Chase based in large part on the outraged reaction of Republicans to his arguments against the jury's right to determine the law. However, the Callendar trial marked the only effort in American jurisprudence to argue that a jury might determine the

Constitution. The peril of instability from such a practice seemed obvious to almost everyone, not the least to John Marshall, who was present at the trial.[120]

Nevertheless the public response to Chase's argument that final 'judgment' with regard to the constitutionality of law should rest with a court suggested the need for stronger and more publicly persuasive arguments in order to legitimate this understanding of American jurisprudence. At least one recent historian has argued that the definitive transferral of the power to determine law occurred not as the result of Mansfieldian 'legal niceties' but because of the public recognition that they had become 'anachronistic':

> They were barriers to the rule of law, in the sense of uniform and predictable rules of conduct within a jurisdiction; they were barriers to the expression of the general will, as voiced through legislative assemblies; and they were barriers to the onward flow of history, for a new world of competitive, acquisitive individualism was beginning to replace the old world of communitarian consensualism which the jury system symbolized and embodied.[121]

Nevertheless, the legal perception of a need for a sphere within politics of common consideration and reflective judgment about law – a vision which jury trials had served to enhance during the revolutionary period – remained strong in several of the political perspectives that helped to shape the nation's new Constitution and its Supreme Court. Both Adams and Jefferson, for example, continued to believe, although to differing extents, that they had found in the jury an institutional locus for answering the question of central importance to legitimate and constitutional government – 'Who shall judge?' However, in the post-revolutionary period, jury activity within the colonies, together with the various positions of key constitutional thinkers such as Adams, Jefferson, Hamilton and Wilson, suggest that the broadened space for judgment demanded in the Revolution could be filled with conflicting theoretical and ideological views on the nature of law and the proper locus of its final determination. In the movement from considerations of juries, to a Council of Revision, and finally to a Supreme Court, the focus of concern remained the need to avoid implicating representatives of either legislative or executive authority in the judgment of public laws in which they might be conceived to have an 'interest'. The effort was to maintain a locus for 'independent' dialogue and debate with expressions of legislative will. It could not be argued that the

Supreme Court was either the logical or necessary historical and theoretical choice for locating this jural power. However, it would seem it was in fact created to fill this need, and created in large measure with both the strengths and weaknesses of earlier jury claims to challenge the law clearly in mind.

PART II
From Judicial Space to Judicial Review
Four Perspectives on the Power of Judgment in American Politics

4 Locating the 'Voice of the People'

> What do we mean by the Revolution? The War? That was no part
> of the Revolution, it was only an effect and consequence of it.
> The Revolution was in the minds of the people. . . .
>
> (John Adams, 1815)

To examine John Adams' jurisprudence provides a convenient entrée
to one strand of legal thought which occupied colonials both during
and immediately after the Revolution. His legal thinking contains
many of the apparent disparities and inconsistencies in argument
that one might expect from any lawyer struggling to legitimate a
radical departure from English jurisprudence – a revolution in the
law – while remaining within the constraints of the language and
existing institutions of the old jurisprudence. Thus while Adams was
author of most, and inspirer of all, of the remarkably innovative
Massachusetts Constitution – the model for several other state constitutions as well as the Federal one – his political ideas have been
equally characterized as out of touch with, even irrelevant to, those
of the Federalists who established our constitutional form. In his
perceptions of political attitudes toward Britain, Adams seemed to
have his finger on the very pulse of colonial radicalism in 1776, when
he recognized that the 'revolution' in the American mind toward
British rule was complete, and 'that the question was not whether,
by a declaration of independence we should make ourselves what
we are not, but whether we should declare a fact which already
exists; that as to the people or Parliament of England', Americans
had always been independent.[1] Yet, in the aftermath of the Revolution, while admitting that the people might institute any government they wished, Adams nevertheless felt compelled to admit his
nostalgic hope that 'they would be wiser, and preserve the English
Constitution in its spirit and substance, as far as the circumstances
of this country required or would admit'.[2]

Adams' more explicit discussions of jurisprudence and legal
thought likewise appear somewhat conflicted. Adams was the foremost proponent of the separation of powers and of an 'independent'
judiciary. He appointed John Marshall as Chief Justice to the

Supreme Court.[3] Yet he never considered, much less proposed, the Court exercise of judicial review which has been so often closely associated with these institutional structures and with Marshall himself. Rather, Adams' notion of the division of powers suggested to his revolutionary contemporaries an archaic picture of mixed government. His 'independent' judiciary, like its English counterpart, was not completely separated from the executive and was no more, as Adams himself admitted, than a 'salutary check' on the other branches.[4] Like Montesquieu, whose views on adjudication he had closely studied, Adams saw very little space within the political sphere for a permanent judiciary to exercise an independent review of legislative action.[5] As we shall see, Adams' own views on the nature of law and the character of jural determinations implicitly precluded such a mechanism at the national level.

However, in his *Thoughts on Government* (1776), Adams did place the power of legislative review with an elected, 'distinct Assembly, which for the sake of perspicuity we will call a Council,' and which would serve as a mediator between the two extreme branches of the legislature 'that which represents the people and that which is vested with executive power'. On Adams' account, such a council could be elected from among the members of the Assembly or even from the constituents at large, could consist of any number of members, 'and should have a free and independent exercise of judgment, and consequently a negative voice in the legislature'. Therefore, while British writers continued to appeal to an 'independent' judiciary to 'balance' the executive in the administration of law, Adams moved well ahead of his British contemporaries in the recognition that such a judicial power 'could not mediate, or hold the balance between the two contending powers, because the legislative would undermine it'.[6] Instead, Adams expected the adjudicatory check on the executive to come from 'the people' in the shape of the jury which would introduce to 'the executive branch . . . a mixture of popular power' and popular judgment and would guard the citizenry in 'the execution of the laws'.[7] It is Adams' views on the powers of juries, then, that help to reconcile, or at least explain, the mixture of archaic reference points and genuine innovation so obvious in his legal and political thought.

THE POWER OF JURIES AND THE 'REASON' OF LAW

John Adams was perhaps the preeminent pre-Revolutionary proponent of the rights and powers of juries. He was a leading legal authority on the subject in colonial Massachusetts.[8] In examining the British constitution, Adams characterized jury trials as one of two 'essential and fundamental' elements, the other being popular election. 'These two popular powers', he wrote, 'are the heart and lungs, the mainspring and centre wheel, and without them the body must die, the watch must run down, the government become arbitrary'.[9]

As has already been suggested, Adams conceived of an even broader role for juries in America. He noted in his diary that 'the common people should have as compleat a Controul, as decisive a Negative, in every Judgement of a Court of Judicature'.[10] Adams equated juries with 'the Voice of the People', and he was vociferous in his opposition to what he considered the British effort to 'render Juries as a mere ostentation and Pagentry and the Court[s] absolute Judges of Law and fact'.[11] Yet, Adams recognized that part of the impetus behind British efforts to suppress the colonials' expansive interpretation and use of jural power generally had been a response to the openly instrumental use to which juries were put in resisting British efforts to impose politically unpopular policies such as the stamp tax or the writs of assistance.

One major legal and political difference between the earlier periods of revolutionary upheaval in England and the Revolution in America was the degree to which the colonials gained and held control over the law – administratively and substantively – via the jury. The colonials' influence in jury selection and the broader scope of colonial jury determination of law were a key to this control. For example, three of the major forms of jury in the American colonies – the grand jury, the criminal traverse jury, and the civil traverse jury – were put in service by the revolutionaries. These juries refused to indict or convict colonial activists for seditious libel, as English juries had also done earlier. However, Americans went beyond English experience, even employing in some cases civil juries instrumentally to impede British control.[12] By employing the existing law of liability, under which officials were held personally liable for harm caused in the performance of official duties, revolutionaries converted efforts to enforce parliamentary legislation into damage suits brought by injured merchants against officials for illegal trespass or confiscation.[13] In such cases, juries almost invariably found for the plaintiff.

However, it would seem that Adams was not the jury's foremost legal proponent for reasons simply of political opposition or political distrust of British aims. Adams expressed at least private reservations about such blatant political manipulation or packing of juries on the part of the colonials, noting in his diary that 'to depend upon the perversion of Law and the Corruption or partiality of Juries would insensibly disgrace the Jurisprudence of the Country and corrupt the Morals of the People'.[14] That Adams neither publicly condoned nor depended upon the potential patriotic bias of revolutionary juries, but rather in some cases battled against it, is evidenced by some of the very cases he chose to represent in the Revolutionary period. He represented loyalists in their civil damage suits against riotous patriots (*King v. Stewart*). He won acquittals for Boston Massacre defendants William Wemms and Thomas Preston in the face of obviously hostile juries and at what he calculated as considerable cost to his reputation and private practice.[15] However, he did so not by making appeals for aid to a royally appointed judiciary on the defensive – as did his other similarly situated colleagues – but by arguing the law directly to potentially hostile jurors. As lawyer for the defence in the *Wemms* case, Adams argued the law – not just the facts – to the jury, and he urged them to rely on the authorities he cited and to 'correctly determine the law itself'.[16] The law he argued to the jury comprised his own interpretive references to Hale, Fortescue, and Blackstone. And, in language reminiscent of Lilburne, Adams told the jury that, having been informed of legal arguments, they were capable of determining its application themselves.[17] Adams' denial that juries were under any legal, moral, or divine 'Obligation to find a Special Verdict where they themselves were in no doubt of the Law', was more than instrumental rhetoric employed to foster the colonial cause.[18] Therefore, it would seem one must look elsewhere for the foundation of Adams' contention that juries had a right to determine the law, not just the facts, according to their 'own best Understanding, Judgment and Conscience, tho in Direct opposition to the Direction of the Court'.

Unlike other Revolutionary proponents of expanded popular jural power, such as Thomas Jefferson, or more anarchic post-Revolutionary proponents such as Lysander Spooner, Adams never rejected the common law outright, but he transformed its applicability to colonials in at least two important respects.[19] First, he recognized that in fact there were questions of the British common law applicable to colonial life in which legal complexity 'would confound a common Jury', and ensuring a 'decision by them would be no better than a decision by Lott'.[20] However, in such cases Adams was confident that juries would recognize this complexity, as well as the judges' potentially greater experience at legal knowledge, and would 'consider a Special Verdict', or ask the 'advice of the Court in the Matter of Law'.[21] Nevertheless, contrary to the jural restrictions guiding English common practice, Adams was clear that he believed such a decision of self-limitation was the jury's to make, and he was quick to add that it by no means followed that juries must accept a judge's determination of the law if it contradicted their own opinion or judgment of law. 'The English Law', as Adams chose to interpret it, 'obliges no Man to decide a Cause upon Oath against his own Judgement, nor does it oblige any Man to take any Opinion upon Trust, or pin his faith on the sleve of any mere Man'.[22]

Second, Adams chose to draw these conclusions about jural refusal to follow the court direction in matters of law by extrapolating on a series of quotations from Blackstone and common law cases. However, characteristically Adams' conclusions in no way followed from, nor even squared with, the existing legal precedent. For example, Adams quoted Blackstone and Hale that juries should use special verdicts 'where [they] doubt the matter of Law, and therefore chuse to leave it to the determination of the Court, though they have an unquestioned Right of determining upon all the circumstances, and finding a general Verdict, if they think proper so to hazard a Breach of their Oaths'. From this position, Adams based the jury's right to challenge the Court's rendering of law where the members of the jury 'are in doubt of it'.[23] This was clearly not Blackstone's intent.

More important, the suggestion that the status of judges' knowledge in relation to the common law was no more privileged than that of any 'mere man' is a statement without support in either the decisions or jurisprudential writings of Coke, Hale, or even Blackstone. Such a statement is no more than a paraphrase of Locke's sceptical rejection of the substance of common law and his condemnation of the authority of common law judges. For both Locke and Adams, an appropriate civil law was one that conformed to the strictures of reason, rather than tradition or history. 'Law is human Reason', Adams wrote. 'The political and civil Laws of Nations should be only particular Cases, in which Reason is applied.'[24] This meant that both in his courtroom arguments to local

juries and in his more widely circulated legal arguments addressed
to the jury of public opinion, such as the 'Novanglus' letters, Adams
resorted as extensively to civilian, comparative law and Enlightenment sources as he did to common law references.[25] Adams' principal
purpose in 'Novanglus' was to challenge the epistemological claim
implicit in common law jurisprudence as put forward by Daniel
Leonard that 'the bulk of the people are generally but little versed
in matters of state', and they lack the knowledge necessary to judge
government. Adams' effort in response is to establish legal credibility
for 'what are called revolution-principles – the principles of nature
and eternal reason' which are nothing more than 'the power of the
people to judge when the ministers of their authority have out-
stripped their power'.[26] Therefore, while Adams was not prepared
to reject categorically the substance of the common law, it is clear
that his vision of it, and the adjudicatory roles of judges and of 'the
people' as jurors within it, was something more than a transatlantic
projection of English jurisprudence of his day. Nor was Adams
arguing, as some have suggested, for America's legal exceptionalism
or uniqueness.[27] He was, rather, transforming the basis of English
jurisprudence as he transplanted it.

ADAMS AND THE WILKITE CONTROVERSY

The extent to which Adams was consciously attempting to expand
radically the powers of colonial juries in determining the law can be
seen perhaps more clearly by comparing the logic of his argument
for the jury's refusal to take direction from the court in matters of
law in *Longman v. Mein* and *Wright and Gill v. Mein* – a pair of
ordinary civil suits for the recovery of debt – with jural arguments
being made almost simultaneously by Wilkite radicals in England.[28]

In *Gill v. Mein*, Adams urged the jury to make its own determination of law despite the judge's directed findings. After the jury
had followed Adams' advice, he then countered an appeal by the
defence for judicial rejection of the jury verdict, supporting his coun-
ter-argument by marshalling quotations from such common law
luminaries as Coke, Barrington, and Blackstone.[29] Even Mansfield,
a judge almost universally despised in the colonies, is stretched far
beyond his own meaning to render support: '[i]f you [the jury] will
take upon you to determine the Law, you may do it, but you must

be very sure that you determine, according to Law, for it touches your consciences, and you Act at your Peril'.[30]

The 'peril' referred to here of course stems not only from God and the terrors of perjury (including damnation), but also alludes to the power of attaint which earlier judges held over juries in order to secure conformity to the court's rendering of law. In such instances, a judge's proximity to the common law was claimed to be superior to that of 'mere men' of the jury, and his judgment of law legally superseded theirs. In the eyes of the contemporary commentators cited by Adams, particularly Mansfield, the judge's privileged position did not change after the power of attaint lapsed into disuse, even though some recognized that now 'the contest between Judges and Juries was of a very different Nature'. Adams chose to ignore this, however, emphasizing instead the clause 'you may do it'. In so doing, Adams deliberately misconstrued Mansfield's clear intent.

Mansfield's position on the exclusion of jurors from determinations of law was being publicly assailed by Wilkite radicals in England at the time, as the controversy taking place there over the prosecution of seditious libel reached its boiling point.[31] Adams was unquestionably aware of the Wilkite cases, and *Rex v. Williams* in particular. In fact, his quotation of Mansfield on juries in *Rex v. Baldwin* was taken almost verbatim from the famous 'Junius' letter to Lord Mansfield reprinted in the *Boston Gazette* around the time *Longman v. Mein* went to trial.[32] However, the differences in legal approach and in the claims made for the reach and scope of jural powers between Adams and the Wilkite defence lawyers are considerable.

In the Wilkite trials, the jury issue was first joined in *Rex v. Williams* (1764). In defending Williams, the printer of the collected edition of John Wilkes' *North Briton*, against a charge of seditious libel, the leading defence lawyer, Serjeant Glynn, argued to the jury that in matters of libel they were the proper judges of the law as well as the fact.[33] Glynn was immediately contradicted by the Chief Justice, Mansfield, and Williams was found guilty. There is little doubt that Glynn's aim in the *Rex v. Williams* case was by English standards a 'radical attempt' to enhance the power of juries and to challenge the constrictive 'reforms' of Holt and Mansfield which threatened to make juries silent complicitors in political trials.[34] However, the declared target of the Wilkites' effort to enhance the scope of jural determination in seditious libel trials was based on their inherent distrust of the political motives of the judiciary. The effort, as one Wilkite historian explains, was only to limit judicial discretion:

'In sum, they opposed judicial discretion for they maintained that all problematic matters were the proper concern of the jury'.[35] Wilkite fears of judicial discretion stemmed from the questionable independence of judges from the Crown and from Crown administration. Quite simply, the Wilkites were sceptical of the effects of George III's claims to ensure judicial independence by giving the judges tenure for life. As John Brewer has noted, Wilkites simply 'pointed to the salary paid to the Speaker, who was a judge, and to the sums obtained by three others who were Commissioners of the Great Seal'.[36]

Therefore, it is important to note that Wilkite reservations were not about whether the judges knew the law, nor about the law itself – the Wilkites conducted no campaign to change or repeal the actual libel law in the name of 'free speech'. They were protesting judges' arbitrary or wilful interpretation of the law, and particularly that of Justice Mansfield. Ironically, their 'radical' claims for jural powers were tied to a legally conservative and, in certain respects, counter-reformist view of law and adjudication. Again, as Brewer notes, the Wilkites' view of the law 'was in the best strict common law tradition. Forms had to be adhered to punctiliously and exactly: a misspelling of the tiniest legal nicety rendered a trial null and void.'[37] While politically radical, the Wilkites remained legally conservative. They grounded their legal and jurisprudential positions in the common law, strictly construed, believing it the surest guarantee of a subject's rights. Evidence suggests that their commitment to close construction was as practical as it was principled. On several occasions both Wilkes and his supporters successfully avoided prosecution or conviction through appeals to technical errors in writs.[38] They rejected legal appeals to natural law, applications of 'reasonable construction' and even equity in law, as potential expanders of judicial discretion and creators of legal uncertainty. A number opposed all forms of mercy for the same reason, favouring instead a legal process of weighted and fixed pains and penalties reminiscent of Beccaria's legal thought.

The only group permitted any scope for judgment on the Wilkite view was the jury. Jury judgments, however, were not intended to challenge the substance of the law; neither were juries expected to be neutral. Both prosecutors and defence attorneys sought to manipulate, intimidate, and otherwise cajole jurors.[39] As in the revolutionary struggles of the previous century, juries were participants in a political struggle, and the legitimacy of their judgments had little to do with their knowledge of the law. 'You need not say any more, for I am determined to acquit him', shouted one juror in a Wilkite seditious libel trial as the judge delivered his charge to the jury.[40]

Reminiscent of earlier Leveller demands for reform, the Wilkites themselves with few exceptions confined their arguments concerning the scope of the jury's power to find law simply to applications of the law of seditious libel, reinforcing the earlier conclusion that the issue at stake was less a legal than a political battle in which the jury was one, albeit important, participant.[41] Indeed, one senses that a political tension existed between any more general argument concerning the jury's determination of law and the Wilkites' intense attachment to the more technical details of common law pleading which traditionally fortified the judges' superior legal position. As in the case of earlier Whig radicals, the Wilkites were concerned with exercising jury control over judicial arbitrariness in what were essentially political trials. Their radicalism carried with it no fundamental argument for restructuring the power or position of the courts, and Wilkite radicalism left no permanent imprint on the face of British law or jurisprudence.

While making reference to the ongoing 'free press' and jural controversies in England, Adams' position and rationale concerning jury judgments in *Wright and Gill v. Mein, Longman v. Mein,* and generally, are quite different. One need not be surprised that the practical support each expressed for the other's cause did not reflect agreement at deeper, jurisprudential levels. An obvious difference lay in the manner in which colonial lawyers such as Adams persisted in supporting their legal arguments by reference to the 'general principles' of Englishmen's common law rights, rather than through resort to the technical 'niceties' of that law as did the Wilkites. This comparative difference formed the basis of an explicit criticism of colonial legal practice by English lawyers. Indeed, as one anonymous barrister complained, in citing Magna Carta the colonials 'do not quote the Text, as Mr Wilkes quoted his *Nullus liber homo* etc, nor do they so much as give any References, to the clause they rely upon: instead of which, a Proposition is framed . . . and then, that Proposition is rested upon with the same Confidence, as if it really contained the literal text of Magna Carta.'[42] However, a second, and more significant difference lay in the scope of Adams' representative claims for jural power. The position which Adams takes on the boundaries of the jury's space for judgment, both as a practising lawyer and as a legal and political theorist, is considerably broader than any power suggested by Wilkite radicals. In Adams' view, the

jury's capabilities to know law reached beyond the politically sensitive criminal law to the more mundane civil level. *Wright and Gill*
and *Longman* were civil suits, and, despite the undercurrents of the
free press issue, there is little to suggest they were 'political trials',
or that any potential or actual tensions between the judiciary and
local opinion existed in these cases. The petitioners represented by
Adams were (Tory) London suppliers; the defendant, Mein, a Tory
colonial.[43] These cases were instead examples of the 'one thousand
instances to one' in which, Adams argued, juries could determine
the law for themselves, independent of the court's direction or, as
Longman's case shows, in contradiction to it.[44]

More important, these cases suggest that Adams' conception of
the character and substance of jural determination is broader than
the Wilkites', insofar as he argued directly in cases such as *Sewell v.
Hancock* for the jury's right to prevent the execution of statutes
considered unconstitutional.[45] In such cases, however, Adams did
not ask the court, as James Otis, for example, did, to exercise routine
common law practice and either to reinterpret or repudiate the
statutes in question.[46] Instead, Adams linked the constitutional challenge to a second right – the right to trial by jury – which he correctly
claimed was abrogated by permitting such cases to be tried in (non-
jury) Admiralty courts rather than in common law courts (by jury).
The jury could then be relied upon to exercise its substantive judgment about the law by rendering a not-guilty verdict.[47] Adams did
not broach the issue of judicial distrust in any of these cases. Nor
did he suggest an enhanced role for the judiciary as such to challenge
unconstitutional laws; he neither needed nor wanted it.

LAW, JUDGMENT, AND THE MORAL SENSE

It is an interesting feature of the *Longman* case that after first
directing the verdict for the defendant, the Court then agreed with
Adams and permitted the jury verdict which defied its instructions
and went against the defendant to stand.[48] The editors of Adams'
legal papers have noted this feature, choosing not to speculate concerning the reasons for what they perceive to be, by English standards, irregular judicial behaviour. The question arises, whether
Adams proposed, and judges permitted, lawyers to argue law to
juries or conceded law-determining power to juries because of conditions of legal uncertainty – conditions in which the judges them-

selves did not know the law?[49] Certainly more recent historical studies of the Massachusetts colonial judiciary suggest that, at all levels in the courts of the period, relatively few judges had either practised law or formally studied it. As one historian notes, 'the key to becoming a judge was not that one was a lawyer, for nearly all Massachusetts judges were not, but that one was a man of substance who commanded the respect of the community'.[50]

This fact, however, only partially aids in clarifying Adams' characterization of judges as 'mere men' in relation to law. Adams is clear that he intends by this to characterize their epistemological as well as moral and political status in relation to law. The characterization should be understood, however, more as a statement of fact than of disparagement. On Adams' view, juries did not assume their power of judgment in matters of law by default, because of judicial ignorance. His position was much more positive. As Adams saw it, 'the general Rules and common Regulations of Society, under which ordinary transactions arrange themselves, are well enough known to ordinary Jurors. The great Principles of the Constitution, are intimately known, they are sensibly felt by every Briton – it is scarcely extravagant to say, they are drawn in and imbibed with Nurses' Milk and first air.'[51] Such a statement conveys something of the character and source of constitutional as well as public law for Adams, as well as something of the way in which men know the law. It is the character and 'reasonableness' of law that makes this knowledge possible. On this criteria, English common law held 'pride of place' neither in Adams' own constitutional thinking nor in the minds of his Massachusetts neighbours from Lenox, Ashfield, or the Berkshires.[52] What then is the character of this 'law of reason'?

Adams has been called a legal rationalist, but there is little in the mass of his writing, public or private, to justify such a characterization.[53] Adams writes in *Novanglus* of a 'principle of nature and eternal reason', the 'law of nature and nations'.[54] However, the bulk of his references to natural law were not to a transcendent moral law which, when made accessible to men through reason, directed virtuous behaviour. His references were to a law of man's nature, of instinct, known through the study of history and through personal experience.[55] He accepted a conception of natural law in the transcendent, rationalist sense as a precondition for a universal moral discourse: 'if there is not such a law [of right reason common to God and men] . . . [then] there is an end of all human reasoning on the moral government of the universe'. As an ideal, positive law ought to be 'pure unbiased reason' unmoved by 'fluctuations of the passions' and 'flights of enthusiasm'.[56] Realities however, suggested to Adams that 'passions and appetites are part of human nature as well as reason and moral sense'. In Adams' thought, however, this disparity was not the result of any inherent limitation or problem in men's knowledge. He did not place the epistemological source of moral, social, and political rules in a transcendent, higher law which would render men's power of judgment highly fallible. Rather, he argued in the *Dissertation on Canon and Feudal Law* that the foundations of law and government were not to be sought 'outside' man but 'in the frame of human nature, in the constitution of the intellectual and moral world'.[57] For Adams, the difficulty was not in knowing the laws of human nature – he exhorted men not to find them but to study them by reading the history of the ancients. The difficulty was not in discovering them, but in obeying and applying them. The difficulty was not the people's power of judgment, but in their power of 'self' control. It is just this recognition that if the vestiges of 'feudal and cannon' law were removed from colonial jurisprudence, then knowledge would present no barrier to the potential for right action that makes Adams in the end appear so bitter in his appraisal of men.[58]

Adams' vision of the laws of human nature meshes with an epistemology in which knowledge is conceived of as inherently practical, and indeed only available in 'compassable' subjects: 'Aim at an exact knowledge of the Nature, Ends and Means of Government.'[59] In law, as in politics, the increase and certainty of knowledge would come not from Lockean moral reflection – Adams considered 'Locke upon Education' as 'manifestly useless, at this Time and in this Place' – but from a ruthlessly formative public, civil education. He argued that, 'in short, the theory of education, and the science of government may be reduced to the same simple principle, and all be comprehended in the knowledge of the means of actively conducting, controlling and regulating the emulation and ambition of the citizens'.[60]

Adams embraced the powers not only of civil education but also the common moral sense as the necessary and sufficient conditions for making, knowing, and judging positive law. He argued that 'if the people are capable of understanding, seeing the difference between true and false, right and wrong, virtue and vice, to what better principle can the friends of mankind apply, than the sense of this difference?'[61] There were, however, inherent limits to both education and moral sense, as Adams understood them, which ultimately entailed corresponding limits in his jurisprudential and adjudicatory theory.

JURIES AND THE EXPANSION OF DEMOCRATIC REPUBLICS

With the proper education and experience – the refiners of the moral sense – men are as equipped to judge the law as they are to make and to live by it, according to Adams. Yet he makes a clear distinction between the power to make law and the power to judge it. While Adams' commitment to democratic principles need not be questioned, his notions of jural rights and powers are not directly derived from that commitment. Adams never claimed that juries ought to have the right to determine or even to challenge the law because they had made it. That is, juries were also for Adams what Tocqueville perceived them to be in post-Jeffersonian America, an expression of popular sovereignty, but the sovereignty of the people's judgment, not their will alone. Both the power to make and the power to judge law are political and judicial derivatives of a larger moral and epistemological position on men's potential to know what is right.[62] In addition, the criteria for 'who shall judge' (that is, jury membership) was necessarily somewhat more restrictive than for citizenship in the voting public. By suggesting that the jury was the 'voice of the people' in regard to law, Adams was insistent that he did not mean by the word 'people' either 'the vile populace and rabble of the country' or a 'cabal or small number of factious persons', but the more 'judicious part' of the populace.[63] The obvious assumption was that jury selection practices would control for this at the local level, and here the question of 'who shall judge' would act to identify knowledge and civil virtue in the form of local reputation.

Adams' views on education, moral sense, and the acquisition of knowledge help to place in context his position on the relationship of judges and juries, and the power of juries to know and thus determine the law. More importantly, these views enable us to understand in a new way the inherent inadequacies of Adams' jurisprudential views as an adjudicatory vision adaptable to the post-revolutionary and constitutional context. Adams' political and constitutional thought has been characterized as out of touch or at odds with that of those who established the country's final constitutional form. Various and conflicting explanations have been offered. For example, some historians have suggested that his estrangement developed as his own political thought changed, and as assessments of the moral condition of the American people and their society grew more pessimistic.[64] Others argue that Adams' 'social and psychological universals failed to describe Americans accurately' and that he exaggerated Americans' uniqueness.[65] Conversely, it is argued that Adams did not understand the uniqueness of the 'American politics', that he thought politically in the 'old fashioned terms' of mixed government and Roman republics, while at the same time his fellow Americans refused to accept those truths he did offer about their ideology and values.[66] However, the implications of Adams' position on the jury suggest that these various interpretations of him are inadequate.

Adams' distance from the other founders came not so much from his vision of politics or political institutions as from his underlying vision of law and judgment. 'The Excellency of a Tryal by Jury', Adams wrote in 1774, 'is that they are the Party's Peers, his equals – Men of like Passions, feelings, Imaginations and Understanding with him'.[67] In his diary Adams' views of the jury were not surprisingly expressed more personally, as the 'Judgment of my Peers, my equals, my Neighbors, men who knew me, and to whom I am known'.[68] The key to the jury's preferred position regarding the law was their proximity to each other and to local moral, civil and political norms, which as individuals they may or may not have made, but which as residents they knew. Throughout his life John Adams thought legally, jurisprudentially, and even politically in 'local' terms. Late in life, in a letter to Jefferson, he recalled 'with rapture the happy times of Revolutionary struggle with England – the golden days when Virginia and Massachusetts lived and acted together like a band of brothers'.[69] His reference to close, familial ties is important. It suggests why he tended to think of wider politics in terms of competing orders of men, each order with its own inherent interests. It also suggests why he praised hereditary institutions as 'an Asylum against Discord, Sedition and Civil War', which he thought expanded republics necessarily entailed.[70] In contrast, Adams made no attempt to disguise his frustration at the absence of communal ties or common understanding among members of the First Continental Congress of 1774. 'Tedious, indeed, is our Business'. 'Slow as Snails, I have not been used to such Ways,' Adams wrote to his wife. 'Fifty gentlemen meeting together, all

Strangers, are not acquainted with Each other's Languages, Ideas, Views, Designs. They are therefore jealous of each other – fearful, timid, skittish'.[71] 'America' for Adams, was 'a great unwieldly body'. The lack of a national linguistic and political affinity was, for Adams, not less severe than that which had separated England from her colonies. This disillusionment at politics among strangers reached its peak by the eve of the Constitutional Convention: 'How is it possible,' he wrote, 'that whole nations should be made to comprehend the principles and rules of government, until they shall learn to understand one another's meaning by words'.

The problem for Adams, however, was much deeper than its linguistic manifestation. It was not that Adams' view of human nature had changed. It had not. From his earliest reflections on his own 'litigious Braintree' and his 'encroaching, grasping, restless' neighbours, to his final remarks on living in an 'enemy's country', Adams' assessment of the flaws of men was always brutally frank, sometimes carping.[72] Nor did he exempt himself from such scrutiny. However, such explications of character, whether or not they reflect the 'true John Adams', underestimate his confidence in the epistemology of local law and particularly local judgment, and therefore ignore an important basis for his disenchantment as the scale of politics and judgment changed. The Revolution, in which men had lived and acted like a band of brothers, had only temporarily masked the great diversity of opinion inherent in colonial politics with a layer of apparent uniformity of opinion about the shortcomings of the British constitution and Parliamentary sovereignty. This diversity suggests the degree to which the real issue for Adams was the need to serve local causes and to solve local problems with local solutions, such as the jury.

In this sense, Adams' political and jurisprudential views were neither necessarily or even essentially antiquated, as some historians have suggested. Adams' reliance on the history of ancient republics and on Montesquieu was purely instrumental: they were the reinforcement, not the origin, of his attachment to locality. Adams expressed hope in 1776 that the people of Massachusetts would call themselves a 'commonwealth', and in 1780 they did. For Adams, a 'commonwealth' was one people, united by affective ties of blood and common heritage.[73] Unlike the anti-Federalists, Adams could at least conceive of politics on a national scale, but it would have to reproduce these affective ties through established 'orders of men'. Although it was rejected both normatively and descriptively by his fellow countrymen, Adams' version of a 'mixed and balanced' separation of powers suggested one method by which politics on such a scale might operate.

What Adams offered was a theory of community, of 'commonwealth'. What he clearly did not have, however, was a theory of the state, and here his position on juries had its most obvious political and jurisprudential impact. He could not conceive of judgment on a national scale.[74] As in a Newtonian universe, separation of powers made for the orderly, mechanical resolution in law of a plurality of interests of competing power-holders. But, in such a structure there was no single, locatable, or final point of judgment about law at the national level to fill the role held by juries at the local level. Adams conceived of a national judiciary as 'independent' in exactly the same unsatisfactory sense as it had been in Britain. It was to be distinct, though not entirely separate, from the executive, and its space for judgment no more or less. If he believed that '[l]awful, orderly government should not yield to transient whims of the majority or selfish passions of the minority', then at the national level he had no legal way to stop government if it did.[75]

Adams never confronted and therefore never resolved a corollary and central problem of pre-Revolutionary jurisprudence, that of protecting the judiciary from either Executive or Legislative encroachment. Rather, Adams believed that he had successfully circumvented this issue with his position on the scope and power of jury judgment. Such powers, however, were premised by an epistemology of law utterly and irrevocably dependent upon local government and on the jurors' first-hand sense of the law. Such immediate knowledge and consensus disappeared in national government, and did so at exactly the same time as the demand for a reconsideration of the locus and instrument of 'judicial space' was emerging.

John Adams' frustration with the problems of judgment and of government on an expanded scale is evident in the aftermath of the Revolution. After arguing for more than a decade that 'the people' were the proper locus of 'control' over an arbitrary government, he then argued that the most urgent task within the constitutions of the newly independent America was to check the power of the multitude.[76]

Although absent from the constitutional convention, Adams hoped that his *Defence* might 'lay before the public a specimen of that kind of reading and reasoning which produced the American constitutions' – such as the Massachusetts Constitution of 1780 – and that such reasoning could be generalized to meet the demands of a 'wholly national' government.[77] However, without reformulation on the question of final judgment, Adams' constitutional schemes left final legal determination with the same, though perhaps expanded, version of those 'turbulent majorities' who, Madison complained, ruled the state legislatures and produced 'fluctuating and indigested' laws.[78]

Adams' designs disregarded the issue central to law and politics as it emerged after the Revolution: who shall judge whether an act produced legitimately by a 'turbulent majority' conformed to the constitution? The debate over this question, which could only intensify at the national level, was not subject to a simple institutional or even legal answer. It was rather, as we shall see, a philosophical as well as a practical political question to be argued and rethought many times over. Adams himself grappled with the problem in his 'quasi-mixed' conception of government without ever truly understanding it, as his attitude toward the prospects for self-rule grew more pessimistic.[79]

5 Law in the Context of Continuous Revolution

> The great honor of science and the arts, that their natural effect is, by illuminating public opinion, to erect it into a Censor, before which the most exalted tremble for their future as well as present fame.
>
> (Jefferson to Adams, 1816)

In sharp contrast to Adams' fears of American declension, Thomas Jefferson's political and legal thought is buttressed by psychological optimism and inner certitude. Altogether missing from Jefferson's thought is any note of the tragic, or of the doubt, anguish, or uncertainty which come from the consciousness of the chasm separating ideals from harsh reality.[1] 'It is part of the American character', he wrote, 'to consider nothing as desperate; to surmount every difficulty by resolution and contrivance.'[2] Altogether absent is any uncertainty or fear of some future judgment. Such doubts did not of course escape John Adams, just as they had not escaped John Locke. 'What is there in life', Adams wrote to Jefferson, 'to attach us to it but the hope of a future and better? It is a cracker, a rocket, a firework at best'.[3] Jefferson was less interested in the rewards of an afterlife about which we could know nothing with certainty. He had faith in the rewards and ultimate recognition of ideals in this one: 'men's destiny was somehow to be realized and judged on this earth and right here in America'.[4] Jefferson's 'faith', which was basic to his social philosophy, extended politically to a confidence in the majority to choose wise leadership, and in each individual to judge for himself what served his needs. This faith was not shaken even by the 'turbulent majorities' feared by Adams and Madison:

> The commotions which have taken place in America, as far as are yet known to me, offer nothing threatening. They are proof that people have liberty enough, and yet I could not wish them less than they have. If the happiness of the people can be secured at the expense of a little tempest now and then, or even a little blood, it will be a precious purchase. Let common sense and common honesty have fair play, and they will soon set things to rights. . . .[5]

There is little question that these differences in attitude, particularly between Adams and Jefferson, are reflective of other more fundamental disagreements over religion, philosophy, and politics which Jefferson readily recognized.[6] But we are interested in these fundamental differences insofar as they pertain to their positions on the character of human judgment and the role of the courts and juries in the new political order.

JEFFERSON AND THE RECONSIDERATION OF JURAL JUDGMENT

Despite great differences in attitude toward the nature and basis of moral and political judgment, Jefferson and Adams did share powerfully stated commitments to trial by jury. In Jefferson's words, 'trial by jury' is 'the only anchor ever yet imagined by men by which a government can be held to the principles of its constitution'.[7] In keeping with general colonial discourse, Jefferson described the jury as an 'inestimable institution', which 'curbed judges and represented the people in the judicial branch.'[8] Jefferson even went so far as to claim that if called upon to decide 'whether the people had best be omitted in the legislative or the judiciary, department,' he 'would say it is better to leave them out of the legislative', as 'the execution of laws is more important than the making of them'.[9] For this reason, he criticized the proposed Federal constitution for its lack of an explicit guarantee of trial by jury in civil cases and proposed revisions of the Virginia constitution to include jury trials in all courts.[10] He suggested to the Abbé Arnoux that while juries were most competent to judge the 'facts' of a case, they were equally responsible to 'exercise control over the judges'. Moreover, should jurors believe such judges to be 'under any bias whatever in any cause', they should 'take on themselves to judge the law as well as the fact' of the case. As a caveat, however, Jefferson added that jurors should never exercise this lawfinding power unless 'they suspect partiality in the judges'.[11]

In his belief that the principal legal role of juries was to 'curb' a distrusted judiciary rather than to inform or assist them in law, Jefferson appears to return to a legal position not unlike the earlier Leveller and later British opposition writers and pamphleteers. Indeed, in suggesting books on the subject of juries to the Abbé Arnoux, Jefferson explicitly recommended Walwyn's *Juries Justified*,

Henry Care's *Security of Englishmen's Lives*, Hawles' *Englishman's Right*, and John Jones' gloss on Hawles, *Juror's Judges of Law and Fact*.[12] Therefore, despite the considerable advance beyond issues of judicial distrust being made in colonial arguments as to the power of juries to find law and to challenge unconstitutional laws, Jefferson's message to Arnoux remains, if anything, more legally conservative than the very pamphlets he is citing. 'The people are not qualified to Judge questions of *law*,' Jefferson writes, 'but they are very capable of judging questions of fact'.[13] The suggestion that the people were 'incapable' of knowing and judging law was an admission usually to be found only in Tory recriminations of colonial action, and an admission that even earlier British radicals had avoided making. Nor was Jefferson's comment simply a post-revolutionary afterthought. At the very height of the Revolution – and despite Jefferson's own explicit efforts to secure the inclusion of trial by jury in all cases within the Virginia constitution of 1776 – he was just as explicit that juries should be confined to finding 'facts' and proposed no role for them in the consideration of law.[14]

That Jefferson saw the importance of the jury less in purely legal terms than in political and educational ones may partly explain his more conservative stance on the character of the jury's legal scope. He characterized the jury as the 'school by which [the] people learn the exercise of civic duties as well as rights'.[15] The principal purpose of education generally was a jural one: 'to qualify [individuals] as judges of the actions and designs of men'.[16] Jefferson's theoretical work (and practical proposals) emphasized education as a prerequisite for government. It is interesting to compare Jefferson's position on education with that of Benjamin Franklin, who stressed the importance of inculcating powers of persuasion and organization, which he considered important for politics. Jefferson's educational agenda, in contrast, was to inculcate the republican 'standards' by which men might judge the performance of government. 'Man is an imitative animal', Jefferson wrote. 'This quality is the germ of all education in him'.[17]

Jefferson proposed public education for the poor, who would not naturally develop a republican creed. As he wrote to Judge John Tyler (Governor of Virginia) in 1810, 'I have indeed two great measures at heart without which no republic can maintain itself in strength'. The first was to institute a form of general education, so as to 'enable every man to judge for himself what will secure or endanger his freedom.' The second measure was 'to divide every county . . . that all the children of each will be within reach of a central school'. However, it is important to note that Jefferson's preeminent educational concern was to shape the political will of the citizens, rather than to enhance their 'independent' or 'critical' faculties of judgment. As he wrote to Madison in 1826, this formative, even 'creedal', vision also lay behind the founding of the University of Virginia: 'It is in our seminary that that vestal flame is to be kept alive. . . . If we are true and vigilant in our trust, within a dozen or twenty years a majority of our own legislature will be from one school, and many disciples will have carried its doctrines home to their several states, and will have levened the whole mass'.[18] It was not an education to encourage persuasion, discussion, or polemic, particularly in matters of law. Indeed, Jefferson proposed that appointments to the Chair of Law and Civil Polity at the University be strictly regulated along political lines, 'to guard against the dissemination of [Federalist] principles among our youth, and the diffusion of that poison, by a previous prescription of the texts to be followed in their discourses'.[19]

Therefore, while Jefferson agreed with John Adams about the fundamental importance of juries, Jefferson's position on the actual function of juries and their limited scope of lawfinding powers suggests a position far more reflective of 'British' jurisprudence and certainly more legally conservative than perhaps any of his fellow Founders. Indeed, Jefferson's position on juries poses an apparent paradox. For a thinker whose political views might be characterized as radically republican – even democratic – Jefferson's jural position remains firmly in the mould of that common law jurisprudence which colonials thought antithetical to republican thought. However, in a new and still emerging American politics, Jefferson saw the actual function of juries quite differently; just as he held quite radically different views from Adams and most other colonials on the character of law, moral judgment, the sources of men's epistemological certainty, and the character of men's jural equality. It is these differences which underpin Jefferson's basic disagreement, as he saw it, with Adams, over the 'direction' to give to a national government: Jefferson 'to strengthen the most popular branches and extend their permanence'; Adams 'to strengthen the more permanent branches and to extend their permanence'.[20]

LAWS FROM THE NATURE OF MEN

Adams held a position on judgment based on men's jural equality before God. Judgment in this life – which inextricably bound together questions of knowledge to questions of religion, morals, and politics – presupposed, and was preconditioned by, beliefs about the next. In politics as well as religion, men must judge for themselves, or at most entrust judgment to those who know them and share a common language of interests. To so judge required that politics centre on local levels or, if it must be expanded geographically – as Adams reluctantly recognized by 1821 – comprise strata of homogeneous orders.

For Jefferson, in contrast to both Adams and Locke, the essence of men's jural equality rested less on a belief in a soul or in men's jural status before God than it rested on the similarity of men's bodies.[21] While Jefferson did not explicitly employ a metaphor to characterize the political activity of men and government, implicit within his writings is an organic premise: the physical constitution of man is the basis of the constitution of his social and political character. Unlike Adams, who presented a 'science of government', Jefferson directed himself to a 'science of man', from which he *derived* both his ethical and political thought. The pursuit of man's happiness, which for Jefferson is to be equated more with 'needs' than with 'interests', is the 'natural' purpose of government, and it is possible only if the constitution of government parallels the constitution of man.[22] Laws employed to any other end, particularly to an opposing end, are then both in legal and physiological terms 'unconstitutional' and 'corrupting'.[23] For Jefferson, as for Locke and Adams, government had a moral foundation and served moral purposes. The differences among the three rest on the questions of how and to what extent men can be said to know the foundation and the purposes with certainty.

While Jefferson did not develop a systematic theory of human nature and human knowledge, his views on these subjects were certainly consistently held. These views provided the cornerstone of his jurisprudential and political thought. It is interesting to note the extent to which Jefferson's own epistemology represents a more materialist and accordingly less sceptical gloss of statements contained in Locke's *Essay*.[24] For Jefferson as for Locke, the constitution of man is built upon his senses, and 'the business of life is with matter':

When once we quit the basis of sensation, all is in the wind. To talk of immaterial existences is to talk of nothings. . . . Rejecting all organs of information therefore but my senses, I rid myself of the Pyrrhonisms with which an indulgence in speculations hyper-physical and antiphysical so uselessly occupy and disquiet the mind. A single sense may indeed be sometimes deceived [*sic*], but rarely: and never all our senses together, with the faculty of reasoning. They evidence realities; and these are enough for all the purposes of life, without plunging into the fathomless abyss of dreams and phantasms. I am satisfied, and sufficiently occupied with the things which are, without tormenting or troubling myself about those which may indeed be, but of which I have no evidence.[25]

Jefferson's claim that a reliance on knowledge drawn from the senses is 'enough for all purposes of life' is a virtual paraphrase of Locke's own statements from Book II of the *Essay*.[26] However, altogether missing is Locke's accompanying threnody of the potential for error in man's interpretation of his perceptions which accounts for the fact that 'men's Principles, Notions, and Relishes are so different', and are likely to remain that way.[27] Indeed, his more robustly 'materialist' epistemology provided Jefferson with the moral certainty that is missing in Locke.[28] Thinking, or reason itself, is an 'action of matter'.[29] The implication of this position in political terms is that our opinions are not voluntary, 'but rather linked to the physiological character of the body'.[30]

Jefferson employed differences in physical 'organization and experience' not only to explain his political disagreements with Adams, but also more generally to characterize larger political groupings such as Whigs and Tories. 'The terms of whig and tory belong to natural as well as civil history. They denote the temper and constitution of mind of different individuals.'[31] Jefferson went further to characterize the 'nature' of political factions in these terms, suggesting that the 'sickly, weakly timid man, fears the people, and is a Tory by nature. The healthy, strong and bold, cherishes them and is formed a Whig by nature.' He left little question that the terms 'Whig' might be replaced with 'Republican', and the term 'Tory' with 'Federalist'.[32]

Jefferson's own 'habit of mind' has been described by Bailyn as a 'relaxed', 'generous receptivity to pre-formed patterns', 'a reluctance to doubt, to question, to examine, within broad limits, what was given'.[33] Such a characterization would seem at odds with Jefferson's total rejection of Blackstone and the entire corpus of common law. However, the apparent contradiction dwindles when one recognizes that the sources of Jefferson's jurisprudential thought lay more in France rather than in England.

In general, Jefferson indiscriminately blended his own physiological and epistemological positions not only with those of the Scottish philosophers of common sense such as Reid and Stewart, but more importantly the French physiological-psychologists and Idéologues, particularly Helvetius, Condorcet, de Tracy, and Cabanis.[34] He apparently cared little to scrutinize the differences among them. It is clear, however, that Jefferson's materialist-sensationalist rendering of Locke, his unremitting belief in the irresistible progress of science and its salutary effects on social life, his profoundly non-Calvinist vision of the absence of evil in men and the world, are the intellectual product of his years in France and his close association with de Tracy and Condorcet. Such views comprise Jefferson's original contribution to American political thought, since they were views espoused, on the whole, by no other Founder. They also underpin his contribution to American jurisprudence and constitutional thought, and this can be seen nowhere to greater effect than in Jefferson's views on the power and function of juries.

Above all, in matters of jurisprudence, Jefferson shared with Condorcet (as well as Turgot, Tracy, and Beccaria) an enthusiasm for the educational role served by juries. What he did not share was Condorcet's rendering of physiological psychology into political priorities: the belief that the purpose of politics was to pursue truth; the extreme concern with the 'rationality' of legislation which led to the imposition of a 'calculus of consent', and an application of the theory of probabilities to juridical questions.[35] Rather, Jefferson preferred to emphasize the improved possibilities for social cohesion which he believed would follow from a recognition that political differences were 'natural'; 'as no two faces, no two minds, probably no two creeds' were alike. For Jefferson, the overriding implication is that men's moral responsibility for their political creeds is reduced; '[d]ifferences of opinion, like the differences of face, are a *law of our nature*', and should be viewed with the same tolerance.[36] For Adams' in contrast, reduction of responsibility lay with the admission of ignorance and uncertainty which men could adjust with a measure of self-control.[37]

Given Jefferson's connection between a healthy body and a

'healthy' political orientation, it is not surprising that, unlike Adams, he showed little or no interest in examining political regimes of the past, or in exploring the political theories of his contemporaries. Jefferson himself wrote no extended political treatise.[38] What genuinely interested him was not the study of politics, but the study of man's nature. It is exactly in this light that he and fellow scientist (physician) Benjamin Rush eagerly perceived an expanded potential for the colonial Revolution: 'All the doors and windows of the temple of nature have been thrown open, by the convulsions of the late American Revolution'.[39] The *Notes on the State of Virginia*, written in 1782, midway between the Revolution in which Jefferson participated and the Founding in which he did not, comprises Jefferson's most developed and complete consideration, theoretical and practical, of the interrelationship of nature, politics, and law. The *Notes* contains lengthy descriptions of Virginia's topography, geology, and ecology, as well as its environs, laws, constitution, and commerce. Here the hypothesis of a connection between a 'healthy' body and a 'healthy' political orientation is the basis of a descriptive and prescriptive discussion of the interplay between environment, physiology, and government. Jefferson saw the physical environment of his agrarian Virginia lending itself to the development of robust, healthy individuals essential to a Republican constitution, and noted that 'those who labor the earth are the chosen people of God, if ever He had a chosen people, whose breasts He has made his peculiar deposit for substantial and genuine liberty'.[40]

In line with the mandate of nature, which the Revolution had made it possible to follow, Jefferson reviewed Virginia's government and laws in the *Notes*, suggesting changes which would adapt them more clearly to this natural Republican 'constitution' of its citizens. As he later recalled, he saw no reason why, 'without the negatives of Councils, Governors, and Kings to restrain us from doing right', the entire legal system of Virginia might not be 'reviewed, adapted to our republican form of government, and . . . corrected in all its parts, with a single eye to reason . . .'[41] At issue, however, was the character of this 'reason' as well as the space for reflective judgment about such laws.

REASON AS WILL, AND THE PROBLEM OF REFLECTIVE JUDGMENT

In the *Notes*, Jefferson proposed changes in the Virginia laws of entail and inheritance, which would extend land ownership and an agrarian life-style to greater numbers.[42] He described such laws as 'enforcing a law of nature'.[43] On the proscriptive side, Jefferson proposed a sharp curtailment in immigration to Virginia and the importation of the products (rather than the producers) of even small crafts, such as carpenters, masons, and smiths. Otherwise, Jefferson wrote, 'they will bring with them the principles of the governments they leave, imbibed in their early youth; or if able to throw them off, it will be in exchange for an unbounded licentiousness, passing, as is usual, from one extreme to another. It would be a miracle were they to stop precisely at the point of temperate liberty.' Political opinions, on Jefferson's analysis, are not developed, held, or transmitted through rational argument or exchange of views in which an independent and reflective judgment might temper and revise initial positions. Rather, Jefferson claims, once 'naturally' – and, thus, involuntarily – formed, 'these principles, with their language . . . will transmit to their children. In proportion to their numbers they will share with us the legislation. They will infuse into it their spirit, warp and bias its directions, and render it a heterogeneous, incoherent, distracted mass.'[44]

This statement of the natural 'necessity' of diverse political opinions somehow immune to rational reconsideration are neither casual speculations nor conclusions drawn from Jefferson's own observations and experience. They are social and political implications *deduced* from Jefferson's physiologically informed epistemology and political thought. And it is here that the first of several difficulties in this theory can be highlighted.

Both in reducing men's moral responsibility for the 'creeds' they hold, and in counselling toleration, Jefferson recognized the potential diversity of opinions, but he had no clear sense of how to accommodate it politically. If men's opinions are not voluntarily held and if their creeds are 'naturally' different, individuals would seem to lack the faculty of critical or reflective judgment on their own political and moral opinions. Thus, Jefferson proposes homogeneity coupled with early and formative education as the 'natural' substitute for political debate and reasoned consensus achieved through political persuasion and reflective argument.[45] Jefferson identified politics with the social cohesion underlying it; laws flowed directly from the nature of men, that is, 'from their habits, their feelings, and the resources of their own minds'.[46] Yet, when men of differing natures and habits engage in lawmaking, disagreement is inevitable. How then would differences be resolved? Who would judge in such a natural conflict, and by what criteria would the conflicts be adjudicated? In such a case the answer could only be: 'the majority will.' In Jefferson's epistemology, will, reason, and judgment are seemingly conflated, and identical. Therefore, Jefferson is able to claim – in contrast to the general thrust of both American political thought and practice – that 'the will of the majority, the natural law of every society, is the only sure guardian of the rights of man'.[47]

Politically, Jefferson's materialism undercut the use of reason and reflective judgment, and thus any recourse to 'constitutional' principles in resolving conflicts or challenges produced by laws based on conflicting opinion. In the parallel between the constitution of man and the constitution of government he consciously departed from what he called the supposed 'magic' in the term 'constitution', which was so important to earlier revolutionaries such as John Adams. In contrast, Jefferson contends: 'The term constitution has many other significations in physics and politics; but in jurisprudence, whenever it is applied to any act of the legislature, it invariably means a statute, law or ordinance which is the present case'.[48] The constitution, as such, is not a standard of legal judgment above the ordinary legislature. It is the aggregate sum of the laws made, and thus alterable by the legislature. Jefferson wrote that he felt 'safe . . . in the position that the constitution itself is alterable by the ordinary legislature. Though this opinion seems founded on the first elements of common sense, yet is the contrary maintained by some persons. . . . I answer that *constitutio, constitution, statutum, lex* are convertible terms'.[49]

Jefferson's conflation of reason and will in calling for 'the free right to the exercise of reason' also precluded the use of any transcendent moral principles as a generalized standard of reflective 'judgment'. His naturalistic conception of epistemology emphasizes the reliability of sense knowledge as a sure guide for determining the 'right' – that is, the most generally desired – course of action. He preferred to 'rest his head on a pillow of ignorance' with regard to the question of whether a natural or moral law, in any universal or generalizable sense, existed.[50] However, his positivistic emphasis on the reliability of sense knowledge – on a 'patient pursuit of the facts'

to give 'sure knowledge' 'enough for all the purposes of life' – alone
would preclude acceptance of it.[51]

Unlike Locke, for Jefferson moral certainty was not just psychologically, but epistemologically, achievable directly, through each
individual's moral sense. '[The] moral sense of right and wrong,
which like the sense of tasting and feeling in every man makes a
part of his nature.'[52] The epistemological basis of man's moral principles was thus as radically individualist as the basis of his political
opinion. But, in what was again no more than a paraphrase from
Locke's *Essay*, he argued that 'the great principles of right and wrong
are legible to every reader; to pursue them requires not the aid of
many counselors. . . . Your own reason is the only oracle given you
by heaven, and you are answerable, not for the *rightness*, but the
uprightness of the decision'.[53] However, in sharp contrast to Locke's
intentions, Jefferson recognized that the only measure of individual
moral principles was the individual's confidence in his own 'uprightness'.[54] The individual lacks an 'independent' or external standard
on which to question either his moral principles or by implication
his own political creed. While each person is potentially different in
the social and political opinions he espouses, all are potentially
equally certain of the moral uprightness of their own position, and
in particular of the laws flowing from their nature. In his materialist
epistemology, Jefferson thus paradoxically increases the legitimacy
of public opinion as the basis of law while decreasing men's psychological predisposition to question the certainty of their own views.

LEGAL CERTAINTY AND POLITICAL UTILITY

It is not surprising that in the *Notes on the State of Virginia* Jefferson
could not conceive government as anything other than 'checks and
restraints'.[55] In a political vision in which legal certainty rests with
men's subjective impression of the honesty and integrity with which
they hold their own opinions, a politics of persuasion or discussion
could be expected to make little headway. However, as the *Notes*
show, Jefferson believed that even the homogeneity of the Virginian
people – which in principle should reduce creedal conflict – would
require a governmental structure of checks and restraints:

> The senate is, by its constitution, too homogeneous with the house
> of delegates. Being chosen by the same electors, at the same time,

and out of the same subjects, the choice falls of course on men of the same description. The purpose of establishing different houses of legislation is to introduce the influence of different interests or different principles. . . . We do not, therefore, derive from the separation of our legislature into two houses, those benefits which a proper complication of principles are capable of producing, and those which alone can compensate the evils which may be produced by their dissensions.[56]

However, Jefferson's position on checks and balances differs from that of other proponents, such as Madison and Montesquieu, in that Jefferson saw no 'negative' element of human nature which required limitation. Given a natural, homogeneous political culture, checks and restraints are the order of government, since Jefferson believed that every government – every representative structure – degenerates. This is not, however, because men themselves are intrinsically bad or 'flawed', but rather because political power is corruptive – it made men 'wolves'. Therefore, those who 'rule' by representing the people will eventually succumb to its corruptive effects. 'It can never be too often repeated', Jefferson reminded his fellow countrymen in revolution, 'that the time for fixing every essential right on a legal basis is while our rulers are honest, and ourselves united. From the conclusion of this war we shall be going downhill.'[57]

On the other hand, while what appears to be Jefferson's 'paranoia' about politics was shared by others in the revolutionary period, he was almost alone among his American contemporaries in sharing with the French physiological-psychologists the belief that man's natural condition is never static, but always progressing, and that change should not be resisted by government. 'As new discoveries are made,' he wrote, and 'new truths disclosed . . . manners and opinions change with the change of circumstances' and 'institutions must advance also, and keep pace with the times'. Therefore, Jefferson concluded, 'we might as well require a man to wear still the coat which fitted him when a boy' as to confine him to an earlier 'constitution of government'. No set of political principles is final or guiding except the principle that 'each generation has a right to choose for itself the form of government it believes most promotive of its happiness'.[58] Either way – for reasons of degeneration or progress – constitutional laws must remain mutable.

Nothing in either government or political culture remains static on Jefferson's theory. 'Nothing', he writes, 'is unchangeable but the inherent and inalienable rights of man'.[59] Rights, however, like the laws which protect them, flow from the nature of men. They are 'accidents of substance', that is, expressions of basic human needs.[60] The obvious conclusion is that while the recognition and protection of some rights is always the foundation of government for Jefferson, the actual content of those rights and the structure of government accompanying them are subject to change. Certain rights are at any given point in time inalienable, but no rights are for all time and in all cases immutable.[61] The question arises once more of who shall 'judge', when through corruption the political representatives of the legislature no longer protect the rights of the people, or when the 'needs' of the people have undergone progressive change?

On Jefferson's theory, there can be no stronger foundation of the legitimacy of the majority of 'the people's' unquestioned right to determine all governmental matters than that men possess a direct, infallible knowledge of their most basic needs. 'If every individual which composes their mass participates of [*sic*] the ultimate authority, the government will be safe.'[62] 'The people' do not reflectively judge what is best, they will it. When the 'voice of the people' speaks, it does not bring government 'back' to its original constitution or principles, it continuously alters and adjusts this government to fit the needs of the living majority. Thus Jefferson agreed with Thomas Paine that the Constitution would need to be recast by each succeeding generation, and that the dead – and with them their political and constitutional principles – had no right to bind the living.[63]

In contrast to Locke's own epistemology, Jefferson's theory dramatically secularized the problem of judgment in questions of constitutional principle in a way that commended public opinion as the legitimate basis of law and judgment. The will of the literal majority of aggregate individuals composing 'the people' is, for Jefferson, the natural law to which legislative action is to be compared and adjudged. 'Every man', he argued, 'every body of men on earth, possess the right of self-government. They receive it with their being from the hand of nature. Individuals exercise it by their single will, collections of men by their majority, for the law of the majority is the *natural law* of every society of men'.[64]

In both his earlier position on juries, and his theory of an absolute and effectively sovereign majority will, Jefferson appeared to some merely to echo in a new context two basic presumptions of the very parliamentary sovereignty against which the colonies had revolted. Madison, in particular, objected to Jefferson's suggested identification of the majority will with natural law on the basis of its coercive implication for the minority. It suggested to him that minority needs were not recognized (by public opinion) as rights. 'On what principle', Madison asked, 'is it that the voice of the majority binds the minority? It does not result, I conceive from a law of nature, but from a compact founded on utility'.[65] Jefferson's response suggests the extent to which he differed from Madison not only in his conception of the law of nature, but also in his conception of utility. 'Nature', Jefferson wrote, 'has constituted utility to man as the standard and test of virtue'.[66] Jefferson's theory of law implies a relativistic law from the nature of man, clearly knowable and differing among societies, based on the 'natural' utility of the laws agreed to by the literal majority in each:

> Men living in different countries, under different circumstances, different habits and regimens, may have different utilities; the same act, therefore, may be useful, and consequently virtuous in one country which is injurious and vicious in another differently circumstanced.[67]

Jefferson's proffered substitution of political utility for the legal certainty of existing constitutional laws drew more fundamental objections from Madison.[68] Such a substitution followed logically from Jefferson's materialist position that the dead have no rights (that is, no needs) and from his progressive jurisprudential premise that age works against rather than in favour of statutory legitimacy. However, Madison feared, such deductions bore little relationship to the realities of 'general uncertainty and vicissitudes' which these nearly continual constitutional reassessments would produce. Jefferson's general disregard of any psychological need for continuity or the ordering principle of habit had been noted earlier by those objecting to his proposal to revise *ex nihilo* the legal code of Virginia.[69] For Madison, the 'numbness' of habit was a small and necessary price to pay in order to forgo the 'anarchy' and 'violent struggles' which would ensue with generational revolutions in the laws and the rights they protected.[70]

Jefferson appears never to have denied the legitimacy of Madison's fears about his majoritarian theory. 'An elective despotism was not the government we fought for'.[71] However, he maintained, in print at least, a rather sanguine attitude about such majority-led revolutions. In fairness, it would seem he often meant by that term no more than periodic plebiscitary elections in which old rules of governing were sweepingly rejected in favour of new rules, new forms, and new leadership. It is perhaps in this sense that Jefferson described his own election of 1800: 'as real a revolution in the principles of government as that of 1776 was in its form'.[72] However, it is clear that, at least in theory, Jefferson countenanced a more literal enaction of the term than electoral politics. He wrote, characteristically, to allay Madison's fears concerning the turbulence within the states in 1787: 'a little rebellion now and then is a good thing; and as *necessary in the political world as storms are in the physical'*.[73] To others perhaps less sensitive than Madison, he wrote that 'the tree of liberty must be refreshed from time to time with the blood of patriots and tyrants. It is its natural manure'.[74]

POLITICS IN THE ABSENCE OF JUDICIAL SPACE

Jefferson's political and jurisprudential thought posits revolution, then, as the necessary manner of resolving constitutional debate. As suggested above, democratic politics, on Jefferson's theory, is destined to be characterized by opposing forces, each equally convinced of the 'integrity and uprightness' of their position. However, the institutional implications of this in Jefferson's jursiprudential and political thought need to be more closely examined.

While Jefferson posited that 'no man having a natural right to be *judge* between himself and another, it is his *natural duty* to submit to umpirage of an *impartial third'*, he offered no repository beyond 'the people' in their revolutionary capacity to perform this role routinely.[75] Jefferson identified all 'independent power' with 'absolute power', and nowhere did he follow up the implications of this identification more closely than in the conceptual problem of judicial space.[76] From his earliest revolutionary writings, Jefferson took the position that independent judgment in legal/constitutional matters would be trusted 'nowhere but with the people in mass'.[77] Therefore, it is not surprising that the *Declaration*, as presented by Jefferson, reads like a legal brief: syllogistic in argument, it is a case clearly presented to the 'national jury' of American colonials (and perhaps to all mankind) for their judgment, and not to the English justices or to the Parliament of Great Britain. For Jefferson, 'the people' represented the third corner of the argument – an umpire 'independent' and therefore 'absolute' – between colonial proponents of change and the British Executive.[78] Having determined the 'facts' of

Britain's crimes against the colonies, the only available process of rendering a verdict was an exercise of political will – the majority revolted.

In the aftermath of the Revolution, Jefferson had no institutional alternative to the 'majority will' of 'the people' to function as the 'independent' and absolute voice in constitutional matters. His alternative was thus to institutionalize and routinize a form of majority revolution. Nowhere were the problems in this theory more evident than at the national level. Jefferson's 1801 Inaugural Address spoke of the 'sacred principle', 'that although the will of the majority is in all cases to prevail, that will, to be rightful must be reasonable.' Yet he offered no institutional mechanism by which the 'reasonableness' of this will might be legitimately determined except perhaps in the arena of national majoritarian politics, and such an argument was plainly circular. Jefferson's solution was therefore to divide the branches into 'independent' and absolute spheres of decision-making, each of which retained the right to decide for itself the 'reasonableness' or constitutionality of matter before it. 'My construction of the Constitution', Jefferson wrote, 'is that each department is truly independent of the others, and has an equal right to decide for itself what is the meaning of the Constitution in the cases submitted to its action'. In terms of constitutional jurisprudence, this meant 'that each of the three departments has equally the right to decide for itself what is *its duty under the Constitution*, without any regard to what the others may have decided for themselves under a similar question'.[79]

Such constitutional compartmentalization suggests that Jefferson, like Adams, had little conception of democratic institutions on a national scale. The relativistic character of political utility, as he conceived of it, militated against the application of general principles and rules over such a diverse area and population. Indeed, when Jefferson catalogued his library in 1783, he classified the statutes of Massachusetts, Connecticut, and other states under the heading of 'Foreign laws', along with Bermuda and Barbados.[80] And, the striking absence of the concepts 'public interest' and 'national welfare' which others have noticed in Jefferson's thought may simply reflect the absence of the necessary material substratum.[81] What he offered as a substitute was a vision of the political culture of homogeneous areas which translated most readily into a compact theory of politics, law, and, most importantly, constitutional 'judgment'.

In this way, Jefferson's theory of 'independent' and absolute arenas of decision-making, which collapsed the functions of will and judgment, extended as well to the constituent parts of the constitution – the states. Jefferson's commitment to localism and to 'states' rights' rests as his answer to the problem of 'judgment' about law in an expanded republic. As author of the Kentucky Resolutions, Jefferson argued that each state retained the right 'to judge for itself, as well of infractions [of the compact] as of the mode and measure of redress'.[82] Jefferson's various drafts of the Resolutions suggest the power of each state to declare federal legislation 'ab initio, null, void, and of no force or effect'.[83] Unlike Adams', Jefferson's commitment to localism was not a hedge to the problem of knowledge in collective judgment; it was a direct political and jurisprudential recognition of the 'independence' of collections of men who were *certain* of their own needs and utilities.[84] The desire for local control and local autonomy was one of the Jeffersonians' most basic political tenets, though even here problems of institutional routinization plague Jefferson's own thought. A clearly alarmed Madison queried his friend concerning the Resolutions. 'Have you ever considered thoroughly the distinction between the power of the *State*, & that of the *Legislature*', Madison asked, 'on questions relating to the federal pact?' 'On the supposition that the former is clearly the ultimate *Judge* of infractions', he continued, 'it does not follow that the latter is the legitimate organ, *especially as a convention was the organ by which the pact was made*'. As Madison correctly surmised, unless Jefferson could resolve this theoretical confusion, he could not in practice 'shield the General Assembly against the charge of usurpation in the very act of protesting the usurpations of Congress'.[85] Indeed, Jefferson's frequently analysed rejection of the exercise of judicial review by the Supreme Court under John Marshall is, I would argue, derivative of his jurisprudential theory and not – as is usually supposed – the basis of it. He saw the judiciary as a threat to the Jeffersonian republic (that is, as a 'corps of subtle sappers and miners' at the foundation of republican rule) not because it was the last bastion of defeated Federalist party members in flight – that is, not for simply partisan reasons. Rather, it is clear Jefferson believed that the judiciary alone should not be 'independent' in this sense. Such 'independence' allowed the Court uniquely to occupy and develop the space for judgment about law which should be left to the determination of each individual and aggregately to the literal majority will of 'the people'.

Beyond the compact theory, Jefferson could offer no institutional solution for the complexities of democratic politics on a national scale. He offered no theory of republican politics; he offered a theory of 'republican' physiology of politics and law on which a vision of governmental operation is based. During his presidency, Jefferson carried out in practice even the most controversial implications of this theory. He pardoned individuals convicted under the Sedition Act of 1798, which he determined to be unconstitutional and thus refused to enforce. He denied the unique authority of the Supreme Court to determine matters of constitutionality implied in *Marbury v. Madison*. He purchased Louisiana without either constitutional authorization or congressional approval, considering it an act of political decision-making and 'judgment' 'beyond the Constitution'.[86]

As a product of both an epistemological individualism and a faith in human nature far more radical than that of Locke, Jefferson's constitutional jurisprudence is perhaps unique among the Founding Fathers. It represents, however, a strain of thinking about the power of individual branches of government to determine constitutional questions within their own sphere which remains alive in American constitutional jurisprudence. Similarly, Jefferson's political thought clearly inspired a powerful strain of republicanism which carried well into the nineteenth century, and perhaps into the present. However, in its conflation of the reason and will in our judgments about law, Jefferson's vision accentuated, in theory and practice, two problems that have also remained central to liberal political thought in America – the paradox of majority rule and minority rights, and federalism.[87] In the popular sovereignty of the New American Republic, the people no longer stood – as they had for Locke – as a constituent power *outside* the government.[88] They practised 'self-rule' and considered the executive and legislative branches as 'nothing more than the agents of the people, and as such, have no right to prevent their employers from inspecting their conduct as regards the management of public affairs'.[89] The position of 'the people' as an 'impartial' third corner in judgment is thus compromised. Jefferson's jurisprudence clearly recognized this paradox. And yet, despite Madison's urgent warning that 'wherever the real power of Government lies, there is the danger of oppression,' Jefferson just as clearly chose to dismiss its implications. He believed that since, given the 'constitution' of man, that 'judgment' could not be exercised 'impartially' in democratic politics, then it must be subsumed under it, in the form of majority will. In the Jeffersonian vision, judging for oneself the constitutionality of every law means determining for oneself its 'fitness' to serve our political needs, and as such is basic to democratic self-rule. In his jurisprudence, the space for reflective judgment about law is simply coextensive with the political sphere of clashing needs and demands. For Jefferson, at least, that was the meaning of the 'revolution of 1800'.

DENOUEMENT ON JEFFERSON'S JURISPRUDENCE

Both Adams and Jefferson had prior assessments about the adequacy and necessity of localism as the centre of jurisprudence which proved inadequate for the expanding nation. Adams believed that there was a consensus at the local level as far as the Revolution was concerned – that the basic principles were known and agreed upon. This commitment to local judgment finds a corresponding willingness in his legal writings and courtroom arguments, to invest juries with a large degree of law-determining powers. However, examining the statements of dissenters from the 'town resolves' of Petersham, Massachusetts (1773), suggests that Adams overestimated the degree of consensus even within his own state.[90] Recent historical research, for example, has provided some evidence that even at the point of Revolution 'the growing geographical mobility of pre-revolutionary society was leading to a breakdown of the local publics on which local legal institutions had depended.'[91] In addition, the Massachusetts Constitutional Convention of 1780 reflected the conflict between two conceptions of 'independence' with regard to the judiciary, as can be seen by comparing the 'Address of the (Massachusetts) Convention' with the response of the dissident townships. The first conceived of an 'independent' judiciary as being as free from the influence of the people as from the other governmental branches. The second, suggesting later Anti-Federalist arguments, believed the best way to keep the judiciary 'independent' from government, conceived of as the legislative and executive organs, was to secure its dependence on the people through election.[92]

Jefferson's political sympathies, in contrast to those of Adams, were 'naturally' (that is, philosophically) far more national in character, and the role of juries in determining or challenging law at local levels is correspondingly less significant for Jefferson than his confidence in the people at large to continually adjust the law through more direct political means. In his proposed constitution of 1776, Jefferson had intended to extend the power of trial by jury quite broadly, 'whether of Chancery, Common, Ecclesiastical, or Marine law'. However, in his more mature considerations the corrective legal, to say nothing of the revolutionary function of juries had dissolved for Jefferson into the body of 'the people', and into its only remaining institutional locus – the legislature.[93] However, examinations of the social and intellectual history of Jefferson's Virginia have suggested that the state underwent a profound change in the immediate post-Revolutionary period. These changes amounted to a social 'revolution' of which Jefferson himself seemed unaware, and which he certainly could not have foreseen. Jefferson feared the effects on social and political culture of the seemingly irresistible attractions of a new society of expanding commercialization. However, between 1790 and 1830 Virginians seem instead to have succumbed to a southern romanticism which mimicked his position on the rights of states in compact, but was otherwise 'more conservative, less optimistic, and less antislavery' than the Jeffersonian vision of common life.[94] Such accounts suggest that Jefferson, as much as Adams, died a stranger to the new political society whose emergence he had so profoundly helped to make possible.

6 The Politics of Judicial Space

> We are laboring hard to establish in this country principles more and more national, and free from all foreign ingredients, so that we may be neither Greeks nor Trojans, but truly Americans.
>
> (Hamilton to King, 1796)

From Alexander Hamilton's perspective, no mechanical structure 'checking and balancing' orders of men, such as Adams proposed, could alone save a 'factious' people from destroying itself. Nor could men rely, as Jefferson seemed to suggest, on the improvement of human nature through technological progress and education. Although their individual visions differed, both Adams and Jefferson held out hope that a new 'science' of politics (or man) would vest final judgment about public law with a community or an order of homogeneous and likeminded men.[1]

However, Hamilton offered another understanding of the nature of popular government and the function of judgment within an expanded political sphere. On this view, to conduct 'self-government' in the absence of shared communal values and among men that one does not know well, if at all, requires both a set of rules or laws of sufficient generality to acquire assent and a politically 'independent'– that is, neutral between contending parties – public adjudicator to interpret and apply these rules in particular cases. Courts, in general, thus play an important role in Hamilton's theory of state, which he prefered to characterize as 'limited constitutionalism'.

However, in the drafting of a national constitution, Hamilton also contributed significantly to the conceptualization and creation of a 'supreme' court, with unprecedented and controversial powers of reflective judgment over the will of the majority, in the form of legislative review. To Jefferson, as well as to a number of newly independent 'Americans' who actually participated in drafting the new Constitution, vesting such powers of final judgment in such a court appeared to go back on the 'revolution principles' which legitimated their newly won popular sovereignty. Nevertheless, in a series of arguments culminating in *Federalist* 78, Hamilton sought to justify publicly the need for such judicial power within a scheme of self-government which he argued was consistent within at least one interpretation of the jural principles underlying American revolutionary jurisprudence. It is a governmental theory predicated on the belief that a sphere for reasoned discussion and reflective argument conducted independently of legislative determinations of political will must be sustained within the political sphere. It is a jurisprudential argument for the need to maintain a judicial space within a liberal politics of popular sovereignty.

THE NEW POLITICS AND THE NEW LAW

Hamilton's disagreements with Jefferson were as deeply legal and jurisprudential in nature as they were economic and political. At the theoretical level, they differed profoundly not only in their understandings of the nature of man, but in their understandings of the character and function of law. More important for my considerations here, they differed significantly in their conceptions of the nature of the judicial task, the character of judicial 'independence', and the function and scope of jury determinations. These differences both reflect and condition their positions on the best structure of the 'union' entailed by national government.

Hamilton accused both Adams and Jefferson of a failure to recognize that the introduction of 'factions' or parties in the aftermath of the Revolution substantially diminished the difference between a judiciary dependent upon continuous legislative or executive reappointment and one dependent upon popular election. 'When the deliberative or judicial powers are vested wholly or partly in the collective body of the people,' Hamilton contended, 'you must expect error, confusion and instability.'[2] In Jefferson's jurisprudential thought, a judiciary partially 'restrained' through elective control was consonant with keeping the right to government and the substance of law firmly in contact with the will of the people. Therefore, Hamilton's suggestion that such a development compromised judicial 'independence' suggests only the degree to which the two thinkers differed in their understanding of this term and its relationship to political order. Their understanding of the role for juries in the new republic differed as well.

Hamilton agreed with both Adams and Jefferson that Americans would need in some cases to cling to trial by jury. However, he did not accept that either a jural power diffused among the people or a 'frequent recurrence to fundamental principles' would satisfy the more pressing needs of a newly independent nation for security and stability.[3] The Anti-Federalist attachment to the jury as a means of making judgments about the content and applicability of law, and their concomitant criticism of the national 'consolidation', implicit in the Constitution, mirrored Jefferson's sentiments. At the basis of their positions on both juries and 'union' was a belief that the requirements of stability and order could be met only in a republic in which 'the manners, sentiments and interests of the people' were similar. From Hamilton's perspective, they were correct to see that national government would reduce the importance of the affective ties of local, social, or cultural similarity in ordering self-rule. However, Hamilton's political thought clearly relied for stability on arguments from self-interest rather than affective ties. He relied, in contrast, on the Lockean claim that there were more basic human similarities of 'common' or 'public' interest which a developing economy of manufacture and division of labour might engender, and which government might draw on for support and stability.

Hamilton wrote *Federalist* 83 in part to assuage the more general fears that the framers intended to limit the scope of jury power by omitting an explicit constitutional guarantee to trial by jury in all civil cases:

> The friends and adversaries of the plan of the Convention, if they agree in nothing else, concur at least in the value they set upon trial by jury. Or if there is any difference between them, it consists in this: the former regard it as valuable safeguard to liberty, the latter represent it as the very palladium of free government.[4]

However, the difference between Hamilton and the Constitution's immediate Anti-Federalists 'adversaries' was in their differing perceptions of the necessary limits of the political function and scope of jury power in the new government.[5] The power of juries to check the improper use of law at its despotic extreme did not, from Hamilton's perspective, exhaust the role of a newly independent people in shaping the law. He himself recognized the need for juries in criminal trials – particularly in 'political' trials for seditious libel – to protect liberty by controlling the arbitrary application of otherwise legitimate authority:

> It is vain to say that allowing [Judges] this exclusive right to declare the law, on what the Jury has found, can work no ill; for, by this

privilege they can assume and modify the fact, so as to make the most innocent publication libelous. It is therefore not a security to say, that this exclusive power will but follow the law. It must be with the jury to decide on the intent – they must in certain cases be permitted to judge of the law, and pronounce on the combined matter of law and fact.[6]

At the same time, he argued that with regard to even the criminal law of libel, the court should be 'the constitutional advisers of the jury in matters of law', and that jurors 'may compromit their conscience by lightly, or rashly disregarding their advice.' Yet, Hamilton continued to endorse the standard trailer that jurors might 'still more compromit their consciences by following [judicial advice on law], if exercising their judgments with direction and honesty they have a clear conviction that the charge of the court is wrong.' In response to this tension between judges and juries over the interpretation of the 'true law' in the most politically controversial of public crimes, libel of a public official, Hamilton argued successfully for a fundamental revision of New York law to include 'truth' of the allegedly libellous statement as evidence in defence.[7]

However, at the theoretical level, Hamilton questioned in *Federalist* 83 whether one could recognize 'readily the inseparable connection between the existence of liberty and the trial by jury in civil cases.'[8] He acknowledged that the strongest argument in favour of trial by jury in such cases might be as security against corruption of judges. However, in sharp contrast to the jury's strongest Jeffersonian and Anti-Federalist supporters, he argued that the force of this consideration was diminished by others. 'The sheriff, who is the summoner of ordinary juries, and the clerks of courts, who have the nomination of special juries, are themselves standing officers, and acting individually, may be supposed more accessible to the touch of corruption than the judges, who are a collective body.'[9]

From Hamilton's perspective, judges in the new American republic were no more 'other' or suspect of corruption than any local political official. Hamilton neither understood nor sympathized with the spirit of the New England town meeting, with its belief in and dependence on the controlled virtue of face-to-face relations as the alternative to government. And here, the relationship of Hamilton's social thought and general characterization of human nature to his jurisprudence is readily apparent. The tensions in the new post-revolutionary society were not, if they had ever been, between a virtuous people and a corrupted distant government. 'The people' were now their own rulers – the sphere of 'politics' had enlarged to include them as well as the organs of government – and the requirements of justice entailed as much the need for protection from 'themselves' as from some distant 'power'. In such a polity, the threat to liberty would no longer come from kings, but from demagogues.

REASON, WILL, AND JUDICIAL INDEPENDENCE

Hamilton's characterization of the struggle between reason and will within the nature of uneasy men is well-known and well-documented. His characterization of the basic human drives involving the desire for esteem, for gain, and for power, which in politics and government could be channelled for good or ill, punctuate all his works, reaching a zenith in his speeches at the Constitutional Convention and in his contributions to the *Federalist Papers*.[10] In Hamilton's thought, man is neither inherently evil nor perfectible, but, rather, fallible. Like Locke's uneasy man, Hamilton's man teeters between suggestibility and a zeal to impose his own opinions, and 'unthinking habit'.[11] Man's inherent goodness cannot be relied upon. 'It is not safe to trust the virtue of any people', he writes. 'One great error is that we suppose mankind more honest than they are.'[12] Nor, in contrast to Jefferson's opinion, were Americans justified in believing that their revolution had broken the mould of history, and rendered them 'wiser or better than other men'.[13] What the Revolution had done, in Hamilton's terms, was to bring forward – as all great political convulsions do – 'human nature in its brightest and blackest colors'.[14] And, Hamilton's legal experience suggested that it often came forth in its 'blackest colors' at local levels:

> The spirit of faction . . . ill humors, or temporary prejudices and propensites . . . in small societies frequently contaminate the public deliberations, beget injustice and oppression of a part of the community, and engender schemes which, though they gratify a momentary inclination or desire, terminate in general distress, disatisfaction and disgust.[15]

Some of the first cases Hamilton handled as a lawyer were the defences (in 65 different civil and criminal prosecutions) of those convicted under three major 'anti-Loyalist' statutes passed in the wake of revolutionary victory: the 'Confiscation Act', the 'Citation

Act', and the 'Trespass Act'. The purpose of the statutes as passed by the 'patriot' New York Legislature between 1779 and 1783 was explicitly to 'penalize Loyalists and to nullify their influence in the community after the Revolution'.[16]

The Confiscation Act made 'adherence to the Enemy' a crime equivalent to high treason under English law, but unlike the latter it required no overt action or witnesses. Rather, it ascribed 'adherence' to anyone who had voluntarily moved to or stayed behind enemy lines. Penalties were stiff. Conviction entailed forfeiture to the state of all real and personal property and banishment from New York under penalty of death. Under this act were prosecuted officials such as provincial governors, members of the Provincial Council, justices of the Supreme Court of Judicature, and a number of New York's leading merchants, landowners, and noted citizens.[17] Under the Citation Act, loyalist citizens were prevented all recovery for debts on contracts made before or during the Revolution. The Trespass Act facilitated suits by Patriots against Loyalists for having occupied, injured, or destroyed 'occupied' property.

Hamilton lamented the 'violent spirit of persecution' which prevailed in post-revolutionary New York, and which he believed was systematically depleting the state of its most productive and talented citizens: 'Our state will feel for twenty years at least, the effects of the popular phrensy'.[18] His view of patriotic passion as a pretence in many cases obfuscating mere greed and petty personal motives was echoed by others:

> In some it is a blind spirit of revenge and resentment but in more it is the most sordid interest. One wishes to possess the house of some wretched Tory, another fears him as a rival in his trade or commerce and a fourth wishes to get rid of his debts by shaking his creditor or to reduce the price of living by depopulating the town.[19]

In defending Loyalists prosecuted under the Acts, Hamilton recognized and confronted the same challenge to his loyalty as Adams had earlier in the Boston Massacre cases. Hamilton, however, cast his response in national terms, that is, the need to resist the persecutorial use of law in the interest of 'national character' and the public good.[20] He made similar admonitions as early as 1775 regarding mobs of roving 'New Englanders' who were harassing Tory printers in New York. 'Though I am fully sensible how dangerous and pernicious Rivington's [one such Tory printer] press has been,' Hamilton wrote,

'and how detestable the character of the man is in every respect, yet
I can not help disapproving and condemning this step.'[21]

Hamilton's commentators and legal interpreters have frequently
identified his 'basic reason' for making such arguments as a 'Machiavellian' admonition to avoid 'half-way measures' when punishing
political opponents. However, such an interpretation elides the substantive (and controversial) legal and jurisprudential arguments
Hamilton put forward as defence attorney for the Tories prosecuted
under these acts. Clearly, in both his pamphlets and court briefs,
Hamilton is aware that he is offering advice to framers of law, not
to clever holders of naked power. Hamilton was as concerned with
the contempt for the value and habit of law induced in those who
profited from punitive laws as with the hatred and despair of those
selectively oppressed by them. Both concerns can as easily be understood as claims for the psychological power and value of law itself
in the maintenance of stability. It is the importance of the psychological force of law that he would later make the cornerstone of his
theory of state. 'When the minds of these [citizens] are loosened
from their attachment to ancient establishments and courses, they
seem to grow giddy and are apt more or less to run into anarchy.'[22]

Hamilton had little confidence in the 'reasonableness' of the 'popular will' as manifested in the legislatures. On the contrary, he always
sought to measure or reconcile this will against what he considers a
higher, that is, more general and more politically neutral, standard.
The Treaty of Peace, signed in 1783, and the Proclamation issued
shortly thereafter by the Continental Congress appeared to protect
former Loyalist citizens (and aliens) from such punitive legislation.
However, the New York Legislature had chosen to exercise their
power to 'reinterpret' the Treaty language to permit their applications of these acts. In so doing, a question of the relative legislative
powers between the newly created federal and state levels of government was immediately raised, as the articles of Confederation (XIII)
provided that 'every state shall abide by the determination of the
United States in congress assembled, on all questions which, by
this confederation, are submitted to them. And the articles of this
confederation shall be inviolably observed by every state, and the
union shall be perpetual'.[23]

These cases raised the problem which Hamilton, in *Federalist* 7,
considered the Confederation's greatest weakness – the lack of any
institutional locus of definitive judgment (independent of the legislature) on questions of constitutionality and of conflict of laws

between the state and national levels. Hamilton argued in *Letter from Phocion* that the anti-Loyalist acts contradicted both the constitution of New York and the 'fundamental principle[s] of law' contained in the law of nations and made explicit in the Treaty of Peace.[24] This legal argument was made possible for two reasons: first, the New York state constitution of 1777 recognized the law of nations as part of the common law; and second, that constitution, as an amalgam of common law, old British statutes, and provincial laws, expressly called for the rejection and abrogation of other statutes 'repugnant to the constitution'.[25] In this way, the complex and uncertain character of New York's legal corpus presented both the problem and the occasion for a novel solution, since it was on this basis that Hamilton introduced his first arguments for judicial review in the trespass case of *Rutgers v. Waddington*.[26]

The defendant in the case, Joshua Waddington, had served as the agent in the takeover and operation of a brewhouse and malthouse abandoned by Elizabeth Rutgers when New York was captured by the British in 1776. Two British merchants repaired and occupied the property under military order, paying no rent until 1780 and afterward paying a yearly rent until 1783. Given the exceptional circumstance of occupation in time of war, no justification for the defendant's action was provided under the ordinary common law of the state, and the case could have been removed to Chancery for a decision based on equity. However, Hamilton argued that the defendant confronted no insufficiency of law, since the law of nations was a recognized part of New York's common law and additionally held justifiable the use of abandoned property in war. The problem, then, was a direct conflict between the state's common law and its Trespass Act, between a law which Hamilton considered 'higher' by virtue of its greater universality, and the reach and scope of the power of the state legislature. In addition, the Treaty of Peace agreed to by the Continental Congress implied a general amnesty 'relinquishing any right to reparation for injuries arising from the war.'[27] Therefore, the Trespass Act was likewise in conflict with the powers of Congress to make treaties in the name of the United States.

Contained in Hamilton's draft legal briefs for the *Rutgers* case is the novel argument that the state court had the power to declare an act of the state legislature void, to judge that the legislature had exceeded its authority because its statute conflicted with a law of greater authority – in this case, the law of nations. In conscious recognition of the novelty of the claim, Hamilton opens his fourth draft brief (of six) by straining to bring to the statutory context a common law principle from Viner on Title Law: 'A New case must be determined by the law of Nature and the public good.'[28] Likewise the citation which Hamilton offers in the same brief to legitimize the court's power of review is the dictum of Coke – 'A statute against Law and reason especially if a private statute is void'.[29] Such a reading of Coke's rule of construction goes, of course, far beyond its original legal or political intent or understanding. And in his brief Hamilton anticipates this objection: 'This would render the act nugatory'. His prepared answer is: 'No objection if it did'.[30] His briefs contain the first formulation of the argument that there are laws, based on reason and the nature of men, which are of greater legitimacy and therefore authority than the will of 'local law'. Hamilton's argument in Rutgers reappears in *Federalist* 22 (the precursor to 78) in his discussion of the bias of 'local views and prejudices' and 'local regulations' over 'general laws', and in his reassertion that the 'crowning defect' of the Confederation was the want of an independent judicial power.[31]

Hamilton's *Rutgers* brief challenged existing jurisprudential and political thought. It also, however, was written to win his client's case. Therefore, the brief contains a judicial 'out' (as well as a slap at the legislature) by arguing also for the more accepted practice – indeed the one Coke actually had in mind – of liberally construing the statute so as not to violate the law of nations, by excluding the defendant from its application:

> Statutes to be construed according to the Intention of the Legislature; which intention is to be ascertained by supposing the framers of the law wise and honest and well acquainted with all the merits of the case to be determined upon; and under this supposition asking ourselves[:] What could be the intention of wise, honest and well-informed men in this particular case?[32]

This last alternative was, not surprisingly, the argument accepted by the judge. In delivering his opinion in the *Rutgers* case, Mayor Duane explicitly denied any intention of exercising Hamilton's proposal of judicial review by voiding the statute. In an ironic twist to the revolutionary events that had made the *Rutgers* case possible as well as necessary, Duane paraphrased Blackstone's rule of legislative sovereignty, only this time in support of American legislators:

> The supremacy of the Legislature need not be called in question;

if they think fit positively to enact a law, there is no power which can controul them. When the main object of such a law is clearly expressed, and the intention manifest, the Judges are not at liberty, altho' it appears to them to be unreasonable, to reject it: for this were to set the judicial above the legislative, which would be subversive of all government.[33]

Duane chose instead to follow the common law rule of statutory construction that 'when a law is expressed in general words, and some collateral matter, which happens to arise from the general words is unreasonable, there the Judges are in decency to conclude, that the consequences were not foreseen by the Legislative; and therefore they are at liberty to expound the statute by equity, and only *quoad hoc* to disregard it'. Rutgers is a complex opinion which relied for its perceived legitimacy on appeal to old forms of common law adjudication ill-adapted to the jurisprudential problem at hand. The resulting decision, unavoidably political in its impact if not its reasoning and justification, split its findings half in favour of the plaintiff and defendant and clearly satisfied no one, particularly not the New York legislature.

That Duane's use of old, established forms was of little consequence in fending off the fury of the legislature's reaction is not surprising, since the 'intent' and the 'foreseen consequences' of the act – legally to punish aliens and alien sympathizers as a class – were perfectly obvious to everyone. The issue was not legislative intent, but legislative power and whether any legitimate authority existed which might challenge the majority will. The New York Assembly responded to the decision in *Rutgers v. Waddington* with the following resolution.

Resolved, that the adjudication aforesaid is in its tendency subversive of all law and good order, and leads directly to anarchy and confusion; because, if a Court instilled for the benefit and government of a corporation may take upon them to dispense with an act, in direct violation of a plain and known law of the State, all other Courts either superior or inferior may do the like; and therewith will end all our dear bought rights and privileges, and the Legislatures become useless.[34]

Employing the tactic followed by other state legislatures disgruntled by judicial decisions, a motion was made within the Legislature to replace Duane with a new Mayor 'as will govern by the *known* laws of the land'. While this recommendation failed to pass in New York, judges in other states such as Rhode Island lost appointments based not simply on decisions rendered but simply on courtroom comments made concerning legislative power. In *Trevett v. Weeden*, the constitutionality of a 1786 Rhode Island enforcing act was challenged. This legislative act placed fines on anyone refusing to accept paper money and, for expediency, created special three-man courts to try offenders. Weeden's lawyer, James M. Varnum, challenged the act's establishment of three-man courts as an unconstitutional denial of trial by jury.[35] However, as the Rhode Island charter contained no explicit clause regarding trial by jury, the defence argument echoed the revolutionary appeals to fundamental liberties of Englishmen and to laws of greater authority than that of the legislature.[36] One Superior Court judge hearing the case referred to such arguments as 'mere surplusage', and the case was dismissed for reasons of improper jurisdiction. Nevertheless, several participating judges did recognize in court the strength of Varnum's arguments concerning the conflict between the act and fundamental claims to trial by jury. Following the example of the New York legislature in *Rutgers*, the Rhode Island Legislature excoriated these judges for their attempt to 'abolish the legislative authority', and three members of the court failed to be reappointed.

The dictate that judges must adjudicate by 'known laws' signalled a jurisprudential claim on the part of the legislature of its right and power to judge the content of such laws, a right which fitted easily with claims of legislative supremacy that in the revolutionary era had been made by men who recognized that they stood outside the political nation. The same space for judgment about law carved out of the old adjudicatory process by juries in the Revolution was now effectively being reclaimed by state legislatures, particularly in tandem with other explicitly political bodies such as state Councils of Revision.

The New York Constitution (1777) established a Council of Revision, which included the Governor, Chancellor, and judges of the Supreme Court. A mirror of the British 'King in Council', the Council of Revision existed not as a judicial body, but rather, in part, as a more acceptable substitute for the executive veto which earlier experience had taught colonials to distrust. The proposed purpose of the Council was to 'guard the rights' of the Executive and Judiciary from Legislative encroachment. It was empowered to consider and revise laws it believed inconsistent with the 'spirit of [the] constitution', and to advise the Legislature of laws 'hastily and inadvisedly passed' (Article 3). Its powers were advisory, and its objections could be overriden by a two-thirds majority of each legislative house.[37] Its 'judicial' status was also highly suspect. Indeed, while the judge in the *Rutgers* case denied Hamilton's extended offer to exercise 'judicial review', he equally denied the claim of the plaintiff's lawyers (including the Attorney General of New York) that the earlier failure of New York's Council of Revision to veto the Trespass Act 'should be considered a judicial decision binding on the court. Duane responded by drawing a distinction between the function of a court, and that of a political advisory body composed partly of judges:

> But surely the respect, which we owe to this honorable Council, ought not to carry us such lengths; it is not to be supposed, that their assent or objection to a bill, can have the force of an adjudication: for what in such a case, would be the fate of a law, which prevailed against their sentiments? . . . The institution of this Council is sufficiently useful and salutary, without ascribing to their proceedings, effects so extraordinary; nor is it probable, that the high judicial powers themselves, would in a feat of judgment always be precluded, even by their own opinion given in the Council of Revision.[38]

The concept of a Council of Revision commanded significant support up to and through the Constitutional Convention, particularly among those who identified liberty, stability, and limited government with fending off encroachments to power by one department on another. Such a Council could serve either to dilute the Executive and therefore 'attract the Confidence of the people', or it could serve – as Madison saw it – as a 'defensive authority . . . consistent with republican principles', and as a way of giving the judiciary 'an additional opportunity of defending itself against legislative encroachments'.[39] However, as one of the strongest proponents of the Revolutionary Council, Madison never conceived of it as a judicial body, but as the political alternative to one. He seconded James Wilson's observation at the Constitutional Convention that such a Council would involve participating judges directly in policy-making, not adjudication:

> Laws may be unjust, may be unwise, may be dangerous, may be destructive; and yet not be so unconstitutional as to justify the Judges in refusing to give them effect. Let them have a share in

the Revisionary power, and they will have an opportunity of taking notice of these characters of law, and of counteracting, by the weight of their opinions the improper views of the Legislature.[40]

Others, such as Nathaniel Ghorum of Massachusetts, 'did not see the advantage of employing Judges in this way.' 'As Judges,' Ghorum argued, 'they are not to be presumed to possess any peculiar knowledge of the mere policy of public measures. Nor can it be necessary as a security for their [the judges'] constitutional rights'.[41] For many, the similarity between such a Council and the much resisted Privy Council of the Revolution era evoked the image of a permanently operating 'censor' of laws, which by operating without the benefit of public consideration or discussion failed to appeal to the judgment of that greater 'censor' – the people. Therefore, while the Council of Revision is sometimes identified by contemporary analysts as a precursor to judicial review, it is important to recognize that both its supporters and detractors did not conceive of it in this way. And no one was less willing to view it in this light than Hamilton.

Hamilton consistently opposed the creation of such a Council at either the state or national level. His opposition is particularly interesting because it is consistently cast in jurisprudential terms, that is, in terms of the need for the complete judicial independence of judgment rather than in the language of protecting the judiciary from territorial encroachments. From Hamilton's perspective, involving the judges in such a Council might, as its supporters claimed, serve the psychological function of bolstering the confidence of the people in an otherwise feared and distrusted Executive or Legislative power, but it would do so by compromising or misrepresenting the very elements that engendered that confidence – judicial independence and neutrality.

At both the Constitutional Convention and later in *Federalist* 73, Hamilton offered both legal and political objections to such a Council: first, that, by participating in it, 'the judges, who are to be the interpreters of the law, might receive an improper bias from having given a previous opinion in their revisionary capacities'; and second, that such close association with the Executive would comprise their independence of judgment and threaten to make them administrative functionaries of the Executive. 'Thus,' Hamilton reminded them, 'a dangerous combination might by degrees be cemented between the executive and the judiciary departments'. He concluded that it was 'impossible to keep the judges too distinct from every other avocation

than that of expounding the laws', and that it was peculiarly dangerous to place them in a situation to be either corrupted or influenced
by the Executive.[42]

For Hamilton, the dangers of anything less than the courts' appearance of complete independence of judgment over law were to the
people, the 'public justice', and the 'public security'. The answer to
the question of why Hamilton believed with Montesquieu that 'there
is no liberty if the power of judging be not separated from the
legislative and executive powers' was at once simple and legalistic.[43]
Otherwise, the fundamental principle of jurisprudence would be
broken: a man may not be judge in his own case. The simultaneous
expansion of the space for both political will and judgment when
'the people' were constitutionally brought into the nation by the
theory of popular sovereignty, and the conflations of what he *believed*
were the separable functions of legislation and adjudication, were
from Hamilton's perspective the central problematic of the revolutionary aftermath. James Madison agreed with Hamilton, at least
in the diagnosis of the problem:

> No man is allowed to be judge in his own cause, because his
> interest would certainly bias his judgment, and, not improbably,
> corrupt his integrity. With equal, nay with greater reason, a body
> of men are unfit to be both judges and parties at the same time;
> yet what are many of the most important acts of legislation but so
> many judicial determinations, not indeed concerning the rights
> of single persons, but concerning the rights of large bodies of
> citizens?[44]

Madison's solution was different, however, and it is useful to compare briefly his position on judicial independence with that of Hamilton, as it clearly reflects the differences in their political as well as
jurisprudential thought.

Madison assumed that such a violation of the fundamental principle of jurisprudence was an inherent and inevitable part of 'democracy' understood as popular sovereignty with its attendant 'factions',
'spectacles of turbulence', and contention. In the absence of a Council of Revision, Madison believed the jurisprudential conflict within
democracy might be tempered (and such judgments as men would
make about the limits of their own rights and the rights of others
rendered more politically neutral) through the structural adjustments
and diffusion of faction produced by an expanded union and representation.[45] These adjustments of size and representation would

not preclude violation of the principle that no one judge in his own case, but it would at least preclude the anarchy of everyone judging. At the same time, Madison hoped, it would make it less likely that the legislature would wantonly violate private rights, since it would be 'refined and enlarged through the medium of a chosen body of citizens whose wisdom may best discern the true interest of the country and whose patriotism and love of justice will be least likely to sacrifice it to temporary or partial considerations.'

From Hamilton's perspective, diffusion of factions over a large territory alone was no answer to the problem of neutral and independent judgment about law, if for no other reason than that it seemed wishfully to deny the realities of the behaviour of popular assemblies upon which both he and Madison were in firm agreement. Alternatively, and as a response to the same problem, Madison introduced at the First Congress a series of amendments which, after consideration by the Senate and ratification of the states in 1791, emerged as the first ten amendments to the Constitution, or the Bill of Rights. It is clear that for Madison the amendments served a number of functions, each of which has been the subject of extensive examination. The most obvious reason, and certainly the one most supported by his own statements, was that they would 'satisfy the minds' of the Constitution's opponents, and bring stability to the new government by thwarting the Anti-Federalists' efforts to call a second convention.[46]

From the Anti-Federalist perspective, the substance of a bill of rights should serve as an epistemological replacement for the certainty of political and legal judgment based on local standards and community norms which they considered secondary only (if not identical) to the natural law, and which they rightly believed national government would supersede. In this sense, the bill of rights should provide a perpetual set of 'certain', if generally worded, standards by which continually to judge government and, if necessary, resist it. They frequently offered as their model the Virginia Bill of Rights (1776), which declared that 'all man have certain inherent rights, of which, when they enter into a state of society, they cannot by any compact divest their posterity; namely the enjoyment of life and liberty, with the means of acquiring and possessing property, and pursuing and obtaining happiness and safety.' However, within the Virginia bill, the explicit content as well as the conditions of the breach of these 'natural rights' are left to the people to 'judge', through 'a frequent recurrence of [unspecified] fundamental principles'.[47] The certainty of such a bill of rights, from the Anti-Federalists' perspective, lay in the fact that *they* were left to judge, as they had been at local levels, the content as well as the application of the limits of government.

This understanding of a bill of rights struck at the very stability Madison hoped to produce by restricting, not enlarging, the space for exercise of popular judgment about law with a strictly enumerated bill of rights.[48] Madison's Bill of Rights, by and large the one finally ratified, offered no statements of broad principle or ambiguous appeals to preserve unspecified 'natural rights'. It offered the traditional civil rights that a now alien political and legal system had offered its subjects as a defence against abuse of the royal prerogative. Several Anti-Federalists rejected Madison's narrow proposals as no 'more than a pinch of snuff; they went to secure rights never in danger'.[49] But for Madison it was precisely their traditional, well-worn status which he thought would make them so readily knowable and understandable as to be a double-edged political limit: legislatures would *know* the limits of their powers; the people would likewise know these limits and the area over which they could judge the law would in this way be restricted.[50] By firmly linking men's knowledge of the limits to their will and their efficacy in respecting those limits, the power of the judiciary remained for Madison a peripheral issue which he never fully explored. From Madison's perspective, with or without a Council of Revision, the jurisprudential problem thrown up by popular sovereignty would have to be resolved (as Jefferson believed) by political struggles within a pervasively 'political' sphere. Hamilton, in contrast, believed that it was precisely the insignificance of judicial power within America's newly established popular sovereignty, that is, the collapse into the legislature of both the power to make law and to judge its reconcilability to any standard it chose, that made for jurisprudential and political insecurity: 'it is one thing to be subordinate to the laws, and another to be dependent on the legislative body.'[51]

JUDICIAL SPACE AND JUDICIAL REVIEW

Hamilton believed the claim that instability was inherent in the nature of popular government 'very disputable'. However, he also believed that popular sovereignty introduced instability because it theoretically legitimated will in place of reason and reflective judg-

ment as the standard of law. In his understanding and arguments for
the role of a judicial power independent from executive and legislative functions and powers, and yet equally 'representative of the
people', Hamilton sought to reorient the psychology of self-rule
from the people's distrust of government as 'other' to a self-critical
appraisal of their ability to know with certainty what was right for
the 'public good': 'Why has government been instituted at all?
Because the passion of men will not conform to the dictates of reason
and justice, without constraint'.[52]

From a jurisprudential perspective, Hamilton's suggestion that the
people in practice 'seldom judge or determine right' repeats Locke's
assessment, not only of their uneasy natures, but also of the limits
of men in particular instances either to know or apply with certainty
the general laws which should guide their conduct, or – as either
individuals or members of insular localities – to correctly assess the
'public good', the 'general interest'.[53] One of Hamilton's central
assumptions about human nature involved the fallibility of human
reason, and it is fallibility that moves the issue of judgment to centre
stage in his political thought. In his earliest essays, such as 'The
Farmer Refuted' (1775), he argued that men were 'endowed with
rational faculties, by the help of which to discern and pursue such
things, as were consistent with [their] duty and [their] interest'.[54] In
the 'Camillus' essays (1795) he reiterated Locke's claim for the power
of 'natural reason, unwarped by particular dogmas', to discern the
natural law.[55] However, Hamilton never claimed at any point in his
work that men did in fact know the natural law. A belief in natural
law as the basis of man's natural rights rested ultimately for Hamilton, as it had for Locke, in faith, not knowledge. It is the axiom –
accepted without proof – at the foundation of government. In this
sense it is transcendent of political reality, and recognizable only in
the breach: 'to grasp at a more extensive power than [a people] are
willing to entrust, is to violate that law of nature, which gives every
man a right to his personal liberty'.

Therefore, the 'science of policy', of administering government,
had to be based on knowledge more certain than our knowledge of
natural law – the knowledge of human psychology. It is Hamilton's
continuous refrain that to govern themselves men must look self-
critically at themselves as individuals and in groups. Such an examination was not intended to leave them, like Adams, appalled by what
they saw. It was, rather, intended to urge them to question whether
they alone knew, with the certainty that popular sovereignty claimed,

that their laws were right, that is, consonant with any standard higher than the victory of narrow, factional interests. For Hamilton, the Constitution (or any constitution) served as 'that supreme law of every society – its own happiness', around which public opinion is morally as well as politically obligated to conform.[56] Its political legitimacy derived from consent; its moral legitimacy derived from the unique independence of its judiciary – that is, from the expanded space within the public realm for the assertion of minority challenges to the exercise of public authority and for the regularized adjudication of such challenges by some standard independent of the immediate desires or decisions of legislative will. Its certainly derived neither from its simplicity nor clarity as such a standard. Rather, the Constitution was certain because its content, as well as the content of any other law, could be given final 'meaning' in any given case by only one interpreter: 'A constitution is, in fact, and must be regarded by the judges as, a fundamental law. It therefore belongs to [judges] to ascertain its meaning as well as the meaning of any particular act proceeding from the legislative body'.[57]

Hamilton's belief that a court should judge whether a particular law was consonant with the 'public good' suggests the sharpest formal departure of any framer from a popular sovereignty directed by majority will. His claim that the legitimacy of law is to be found not only in its source but in its consonance with reason paralleled a claim taken directly from Locke – that the 'voice of the people' was the superior power within the state but it was not the 'voice of God'.[58]

JUDGMENT AND THE CENTRE OF LIBERALISM

Hamilton's jurisprudence suggests yet another solution, within the structure of a national state, to the central jurisprudential and political problems of epistemological uncertainty and revolutionary judgment first introduced into liberal political thought by Locke. Hamilton's jurisprudence begins with an affirmation of the existence of rational standards of justice independent of the will of man, but with a sceptical attitude about man's ability within the political sphere to exercise the reflective judgment necessary to apply such standards impartially. Hamilton developed the implications of this moral fallibility in his considerations of politics and judgment. The essence of the political legitimacy of law is consent; the essence of the moral and jurisprudential legitimacy of law is that there is some standard independent of the desires or decisions of the maker by which it can be judged. Both the psychological security and political stability within liberal constitutional self-rule rests on 'the people's' belief that it is possible to have both. Hamilton's jurisprudential theory replaced Locke's 'extraordinary' (and extra-constitutional) appeal of the people 'to heaven' for God's judgment based on such natural laws with an 'institutionalized' procedure by which the people would appeal to a Supreme Court for a judgment based on a constitutional law. Such a Court would not, like a Council of Revision, stand as a continuously operating censor, reviewing every expression of legislative will. Rather, the power of appeal remained, as it had for Locke, in the hands of the people.

Having effectively broken the mould of British common law theories of jurisprudence in the creation of a Constitutional court, Founders such as Hamilton showed a reluctance, and an apparent disingenuousness, by refusing to recognize it openly. It is in large part Hamilton's refusal in *Federalist* 78, as well as the studied ambiguousness of the new Court's character and function, which has kept Court historians, constitutional lawyers, jurisprudential theorists, and Supreme Court justices engaged in the interpretive controversies which have ceaselessly occupied them to the present. Running throughout Hamilton's jurisprudence is the implicit recognition that despite the Court's structural independence from the other 'political branches', and its proffered independence ('disinterestedness') from potential political factions, it was a 'political' institution operating within rather than 'outside' the political sphere. Transforming political questions into legal questions did not change their political character or impact, but it fundamentally changed the character of the Court adjudicating them.

The purpose of establishing an independent point of judgment outside the legislative sphere of interests was to counter demagogic appeals by bringing 'disinterested' reason and reflective judgment to bear on public law and public understanding. Such a point of judgment entails that the 'political' sphere is recognized to be larger than the legislative organ, and that the Court functions within this larger sphere rather than, as was the case with the English court system (and bar) of the period, in a private law sphere of its own.[59] Despite Hamilton's protestations within the *Federalist* of the comparative weakness of the new Court, others who either supported or opposed it recognized both its novel, political character and the potentially expansive latitude inherent in the new space it was to occupy within the polity. Speaking in support, Charles Pinkney of South Carolina characterized the new Court as 'the keystone of the arch, the means of connecting and binding the whole together, of preserving uniformity in all judicial proceedings in the Union'. 'In republics,' he claimed, 'much more (in time of peace) would always depend upon the energy and integrity of the judicial than any other part of the government – that to insure these, extensive authorities were necessary'.[60] However, speaking in opposition, Robert Yates' assessment of the Court's new position was perhaps even more astute:

> The real effect of this system of government, will . . . be brought home to the feelings of the people, through the medium of the judicial power. It is, moreover, of great importance to examine with care the nature and extent of the judicial power, because those who are to be vested with it, are to be placed in a situation altogether unprecedented in a free country. They are to be rendered totally independent, both of the people and the legislature, both with respect to their offices and their salaries. No errors they may commit can be corrected by any power above them, if any such power there be, nor can they be removed from office for making ever so many erroneous adjudications. . . . [T]hey are empowered, to explain the constitution according to the reasoning spirit of it, without being confined to the words or letter. . . . They will give the sense of every article of the constitution, that may from time to time come before them. And in their decisions they will not confine themselves to any fixed or established rules, but will determine, according to what appears to them, the reason and spirit of the constitution. The opinions of the supreme court, whatever they may be, will have the force of law; because there is no power provided in the constitution, that can correct their errors, or controul their adjudications. From this court there is no appeal.[61]

Strictly speaking, Yates' assessment that no appeal existed to the Court's judgments was erroneous in two respects. 'The people' did retain an ultimate voice in constitutional law through the power of constitutional amendment. More important, Hamilton argued explicitly that the Court 'represented' the people and, as such, it ultimately relied as much as any political institution on the support of public opinion and consensus for adherence to its final judgments.[62] However, Hamilton felt the need to go further and to attempt to placate fear of the Court's employment of 'arbitrary' discretion within this new space by suggesting an analogy between the Supreme Court adjudication and British common law forms of adjudication with which it had very little in common.[63] Indeed, Hamilton argued it was not 'artificial reason' but the 'rules of *common sense*' which formed the basis of legal and constitutional interpretation.[64] Recognized as a law *sui generis*, the Constitution was intended to meet the exigencies of a new legal and political structure and therefore to apply to questions without precedents and to be interpreted by recourse to principles consonant with a 'knowledge of national circumstances and reason of state which [are] essential to right judgment'. The issue remained to be settled of how far the 'unprecedented' reach of such judicial considerations might extend.

The question ultimately arises of the content or meaning by which Hamilton intended the Court to inform its adjudication of the Constitution, in the absence of precedents and knowledge of the natural law. Hamilton's public denials of the novelty and the problems inherent in the judicial task had both intended and unintended consequences: it served, as he perhaps hoped, to obfuscate the issue and deflect the more immediate objections to the Constitution; it also served, through his inapt and instrumental comparisons of constitutional with common law adjudications, to cloud a central premise of his own jurisprudential and constitutional theory – that the legitimacy of the judge's task arose from men's acceptance of their own fallibility, rather than from the justice's inherent epistemological superiority or knowledge of the law. Hamilton's jurisprudence attempted to create a middle ground between the anarchy of unrestrained individual liberty and judgment, and the despotism of an unrestrainable sovereign power – a space for judgment – within a liberal polity whose driving forces would be the urgencies of individual or factional interest and whose unifying impulse would necessarily come from a government pursuing policies of an integrated, common, or public interest. However, in attempting to reduce the uncertainty created by the preponderance of either of these antipodal forces, Hamilton's theory of the state radically limited the inhabitants of this judicial space to a single Supreme Court. More important, Hamilton made no effort to undercut any added legitimacy the Court and Constitution might obtain from gratuitous comparisons with 'higher beings' and natural law, even though he never claimed such status for either.

The result for post-revolutionary jurisprudence was to encourage a strand of argument about any judicial role in the new republic which emphasized politically benign characterizations of its 'oracular' or 'mechanical' function. Ironically, the exigencies of legitimating an image of judges 'declaring' or 'finding' such law relies on a claim for their privileged, epistemological superiority which stands sharply at odds with the entire course of American thinking about law and so, quite naturally, has proved impossible to sustain. Politically, such a view of judgment, resting on 'declaratory' rather than discursive reasoning, has encouraged the charge that in the judicial (as well as the other branches of government) the people were left out of the Constitution which 'provided a public space only for the representatives of the people and not for the people themselves'.

As Hannah Arendt has argued, 'the Revolution, while it had given freedom to the people, had failed to provide a space where this freedom could be exercised. Only the representatives of the people, not the people themselves, had an opportunity to engage in these activities of "expressing, discussing, and deciding" which in a positive sense are the activities of judgment'.[65] Such a position, however, is drawn from examining only one strand of thinking about the role and locus of judgment in American post-revolutionary politics. Alternative views which sought to bring the people into the judicial power were present even among the strongest advocates of judicial review, most notably James Wilson. Wilson's more epistemologically 'democratic' revisions of the Hamiltonian argument for judicial space are all the more worth considering in large part because he modelled his understanding of the Court's judicial role on the jurisprudential principles and practices the colonial jury.

COMMON SENSE JUDGMENT AND THE DEMOCRACY OF MAJORITY RULE

> A judge is a blessing, or he is a curse of society.
>
> (James Wilson, 1790)

James Wilson has been called an 'unequivocal advocate' of majority rule and certainly his common sense epistemology underpins an argument for the widest possible implementation of popular sovereignty in the form of constitutional government, direct and actual representation, widespread suffrage, and majority rule by 'the people'.[66] This democratic impulse expressed itself not only politically but also legally, in Wilson's rejection of Blackstonian common law jurisprudence, with its claims for a parliamentary sovereignty 'superior' to the people ruled by it, and for the epistemological 'superiority' of common law judges. Yet it is indisputably true that prior to, during, and after the Constitutional Convention, Wilson joined Hamilton as the preeminent spokesmen for a degree of wide-ranging judicial power at the national level that opponents considered intrinsically anti-democratic. Unlike Hamilton, however, Wilson chose to challenge this 'anti-democratic' characterization and to offer a theory of constitutional jurisprudence which could reconcile the apparent incongruity between popular sovereignty and the Court's function in liberal self-government.

JUDGMENT AND DEMOCRATIC SELF-RULE

From the introductory advertisement to his first article (written in 1768 but not published until 1774) to his final lectures on American law, Wilson relied on the critical force of a common sense epistemology of law. In essence, Wilson set his 'common sense' epistemology – which he drew significantly from a study of the Scottish Common Sense thought of Thomas Reid – against the political 'nihilism' which he argued must follow from Hume's radical epistemological scepticism. Such 'absolute scepticism' on Wilson's account placed 'absolute will' in the form of parliamentary sovereignty at the centre of British politics and law. In contrast, Wilson developed his own version of Reid's significantly less sceptical claims that 'to judge of first principles, requires no more than a sound mind free from prejudice, and a distinct conception of the question', in order to secure a politically more confident rendering of Locke's 'revolution principle' that the people (in this case American colonists) might judge for themselves which laws they were obliged to obey.[67] In terms of jurisprudence, Wilson considered Blackstonian common law 'despotic' not simply because it rested on too 'sceptical' a foundation of knowledge without confidence in the 'power' of reason of the people, but because this 'scepticism' was used by Blackstone to support the view that there can be no law without a 'superior'.[68]

Against a Blackstonian argument for 'superiority' as the ground of obedience, Wilson pitted the democratic common sense principle of validity by consent and common opinion. 'All men are, by nature, equal and free', Wilson claimed, and thus 'no one has a right to any authority over another without his consent: all lawful government is founded on the consent of those who are subject to it'.[69] By tying obligation to consent, and consent to direct rather than virtual representation, Wilson claims that the American people cannot be considered legally bound by the authority of a Parliament to whose laws they have not consented. Their continued allegience is no more than a 'duty founded on principles of gratitude'. Wilson's argument, however, moves well beyond the issue of inadequate representation in Parliament. Americans, he claims, have a right to judge for themselves which British laws they will obey because they are capable of knowing which laws (within their own colonies) custom – an 'intrinsick evidence of consent' by common 'experience as well as opinion' – has determined to be applicable to their circumstances and therefore worthy of incorporation.[70]

Wilson's arguments epitomized the colonials' revolutionary challenge to Blackstone's defence of a parliamentary claim to theoretical and historical supremacy by offering evidence of the process by which the assemblies and legislatures of the American colonies had selectively incorporated only those common law and statutory enactments of England which, in the words of one such legislature (Maryland), were not judged 'inconsistent with the condition of the colony'.[71] Even rules of common law having the force of 'experience and opinion' in England were, Wilson noted, purposely withdrawn by conscious 'discontinuance and disuse' within the colonies.[72] Such modified legislative independence, established firmly as custom on the principle that the American colonists knew and could judge for themselves which laws were appropriate for their own conditions, provided the basis for Wilson's 1775 resolution before the Pennsylvania convention that they publicly and officially judge British laws such as the acts 'altering the charter and the constitution of the colony of Massachusetts Bay' and those 'shutting the port of Boston, and for quartering soldiers on the inhabitants of the colonies' to be unconstitutional.

Wilson argued that it was not necessary to prove by elaborate or demonstrative reasoning that such acts were unconstitutional. Their unconstitutionality rested upon 'plain and indubitable truths' accessible to the reasoning of ordinary men: 'We do not send members to the British parliament: we have parliaments (it is immaterial what name they go by) of our own'.[73] Wilson also followed Reid in recognizing the problem of error and the evidence of experience that 'men may to the end of life be ignorant of self-evident truths. They may, to the end of life, entertain gross absurdities'. But such errors were due to partiality, interest, affection, fashion, or even social isolation. Common judgment might thus be perverted by education, by authority, and by party zeal.[74] However, Wilson believed even more firmly than Reid that the 'active' powers of reason and judging could be improved in ordinary men through early 'instruction' and the experience and development of rational 'reflection'.[75]

Wilson's belief in the potential for, as well as the political importance of, developing the individual's powers of reflective judgment explains his unique claim among the Founders that 'the sole or the primary' purpose of government was not the protection of private property but rather 'the cultivation and improvement of the human mind'.[76] Wilson's position on the centrality of reflective judgment in republican politics shaped and supported his positions on both democratic lawmaking and the role of juries in post-revolutionary America at both the state and national level. It provides, as well, the key to understanding Wilson's unrivalled advocacy of the institution which, on an understanding different from his own, has come to be identified as paradigmatically anti-democratic: the Supreme Court with judicial review.

In contrast to the view of majority rule which underlay parliamentary sovereignty, Wilson contended that absolute sovereignty always resides in the people even after government has been formed, thus making the American Constitution 'materially different' and 'better' than the British.[77] Because sovereignty resides in the people, Wilson claimed that it 'should be exercised by them in person if that could be done with convenience'. Representation is thus second best to direct participation in self-rule and, as he informed the Constitutional Convention, 'representative' legislatures 'ought to be the most exact transcript of the whole Society', since 'representation is made necessary only because it is impossible for the majority of the people to act collectively'.[78] The common sense principle that a 'universally held opinion' has a status of law suggests a legitimating forum larger than the majority of the members of the legislature: majority rule is but a 'practical principle'.[79]

As early as 1779, Wilson challenged the 'democratic' theory contained in the Pennsylvania Constitution of 1776, which established the principle of majority rule within a unicameral legislature and justified all governmental measures by reference to this majority's will. Throughout the next three years, Wilson engaged in a fierce public debate – frequently carried forward in the local newspapers – with the radicals of western Pennsylvania over whether a bicameral legislature was necessary to democratic rule. However, Wilson's support for bicameralism – which garnered him the reputation of an anti-democrat – was couched neither in the Madisonian terms of encouraging necessary counterfactions nor in the more 'elitist' language of John Adams' 'mixed government' and the need for incorporating aristocratic or intellectual groups within the legislature. Instead, Wilson sided with his opponents from the west in insisting that representatives to both houses be popularly elected: 'May merit and unbiassed voice of the people be the only title to distinction ever known in Pennsylvania'.[80] The principal purpose of Wilson's two houses was to reduce error in reproducing the common sense of the people by encouraging public discussion. It was not simply to permit each house to 'check' or 'restrain' but to 'inform' the other.[81] Hasty and impetuous action, unreflective of the reason as well as the feeling involved in the common sense judgment of the public could be reduced if the two houses of representatives were made to discuss publicly and 'to justify their conduct in the judgment of their constituents upon whom they are equally dependent'. One political implication of Wilson's democratic epistemology was that ordinary men not only were capable of knowing the law but they had a strong political need to know it, if only to deflect the 'fury of legislative tempests' he fully recognized as consequent to democratic rule: 'Kings are not the only tyrants'.[82]

JURIES AND DEMOCRATIC SELF-RULE

In Wilson's theory of politics and jurisprudence, one way in which common men come to know, to shape, and thus to admire the law is through their participation on juries. Indeed, the jury is Wilson's model of political participation and democratic epistemology in action. When Wilson asks who can and should know the law, the answer is that 'the science of law should, in some measure, and in some degree, be the study of every free citizen, and of every free man'. This knowledge enables men to be just and 'independent'. Such knowledge is possible, not only because of the make-up of man but the make-up of the law: 'The knowledge of those rational principles on which the law is founded, ought, especially in a free country, to be diffused over the whole community'.[83] Juries, by diffusing the common understanding of the law, serve this function:

The rights and duties of jurors, in the United States, are great and extensive. No punishment can be inflicted without the intervention of one – in much the greater number of cases, without the intervention of more than one jury. . . . Is it not, then, of immense consequence to both, that jurors should possess the spirit of discernment, to discriminate between the innocent and the guilty? The spirit of just discernment requires knowledge of, at least, the general principles of the law, as well as knowledge of the minute particulars concerning the facts.[84]

Wilson's views on the powers of American juries were considerably more expansive – and he thought better – than those of his English counterparts. Importantly, he saw no clear separation of powers between judges and juries over the determination of law and facts. The province of factual determination was clearly the jury's to decide. However, in matters of law, Wilson's confidence in the reasoning powers of ordinary men militated against the English common law position that the judge alone had knowledge of the law. After all, Wilson noted, 'in many respectable courts within the United States, the judges are not, and for a long time, cannot be gentlemen of professional acquirements'.[85] In other words, on practical grounds alone there may be cause to argue that juries know the law as well as judges. However, Wilson's argument for the expansive powers of juries rested on those deeper theoretical commitments that he shared with other American revolutionaries. For example, in matters of criminal law – and here issues of treason and sedition are his constant referent – juries are the final authority in 'judging' the law, regardless of the qualifications of the judge. Wilson notes, 'it is true that, in matters of law, jurors are entitled to the assistance of the judges; but it is also true, that, after they receive it, they have a right of judging for themselves'. In those instances, where the fundamental principles of the country must be known and applied, the jury becomes the key democratic institution – 'the selected body who act for the country'. Such a jury, judging in criminal trials in which the commonly held political principles of the country have been challenged, Wilson calls 'a jury of the country'.[86]

In contrast to any desire to distrust or 'check' judges, which support the Jeffersonian and Anti-Federalist claims for jury powers, Wilson's role for juries is underpinned by a more positive presumption of the need for jural cooperation. He speaks of juries and judges cooperating in a dialogue of 'mutual assistance' as well as 'mutual checking'.[87] Their aim throughout is cooperation in avoiding error in law to which judges as well as juries are susceptible. After all, writes Wilson, 'a man must have an uncommon confidence in his own talents, who, in forming his judgments and opinions, feels not a sensible and strong satisfaction in the concurrence of the judgments and opinions of others'.[88]

JUDICIAL REVIEW AND 'JURIES OF THE COUNTRY'

Wilson's most direct challenge to Blackstone's jurisprudence was to the legal knowledge the common people could be presumed to have. Blackstone had claimed not only that the powers of Parliament are 'transcendent and absolute' but also that in Parliament the House of Lords served a judicial as well as legislative function, uttering final judgments on the validity of its own laws. Blackstone argued that the law of Parliament was 'to be sought by all, unknown by many, and known by few'.[89] Judges accordingly were assumed to possess a knowledge of the law superior to that of juries, and, by the same token, Parliament held legal authority superior to that of the people. Wilson challenged the first claim in his discussion of juries. He challenged the second in his proposals at the Constitutional Convention (and after) for a national Supreme Court with powers of judicial review.

In response to Blackstone's claims for the supreme judicial function of Parliament, Wilson argued there was 'nothing in the formation of the House of Lords; nor in the education, habits, character, or professions of the members who compose it; nor in the mode of their appointment, or the right, by which they succeed to their places, that suggests any intelligible fitness, in the nature of this regulation'.[90] Wilson contended that the same argument militated against leaving the power to determine law finally, without a mechanism of review, in state or national legislatures. Sovereignty lay in the people, and Wilson wanted to dispel the notion that the legislative power alone was the 'people's representative'.[91] Not surprisingly, Wilson's initial vision of the judicial institution to which the people may attach themselves was shaped by his understanding of the character and function of juries.

The experience of the lack of a national judiciary in the Confederation period culminated for Wilson in his participation in the formation of a national 'jury' at the Trenton Trial (1782) in order to weigh the legal claims of two competing states. This 'jural' solution, recognized by Hamilton in *Federalist* 7, raised the call for some comparable body to exercise judgment and to resolve competing legal challenges under the new national Constitution.[92] Wilson reiterated the need for a national 'jury' on the law at the Constitutional Convention when he first supported (together with Madison) a Council of Revision. By permitting participation by members of a national judiciary in this 'Revisionary power', Wilson argued for the power of 'opinion' to counteract or correct 'improper' views of the Legislature. When the Convention rejected the Council, Wilson proposed a separately conceived power of judicial review of both state laws and acts of the national legislature.[93] Wilson's proposal for a power of judicial review was supported at the Convention by Madison and by the voices of a significant number of delegates who held otherwise widely divergent views.[94] However, Wilson alone offered a theoretical understanding of this new court's role that remained coherent with a theory of democratic 'participation' in reflective judgment.

The function of judicial review in Wilson's account was neither to 'disparage the legislative authority', nor to 'confer upon the judicial department a power superior, in its general nature.' It was to avoid the errors that may arise in legislation, perhaps not in the immediate perception of basic political principles, but in the legislative reasoning that constitutes their development. Judicial review, like Wilson's common sense reinstitution of Locke's 'revolution principle', was not intended to be a principle of 'discord, rancour, or war' but rather 'melioration'. The balance achieved between the court, the legislature, and the people in the achievement of justice would require 'much discussion and inquiry' if the errors of judgment produced by bias and partiality, by 'jealousies and attachments', were to be exposed 'in order to be avoided'. Wilson was confident, however, that, when considered properly, such balancing of feeling and reason in the common sense politics of ordinary men would be viewed in a favourable light by the legislature itself.[95] To support the power of judicial review in the *Lectures on Law*, Wilson quoted Elias Boudinot's statement from the House debates on the judiciary. And, in fact, Boudinot's sentiments summarize nicely the revisionary power Wilson projected for judicial review:

It has been objected that, by adopting the bill before us, we expose the measure to be considered and defeated in the judiciary of the United States, who may adjudge it to be contrary to the constitution, and therefore void, and not lend their aid to carry it into execution. This gives me no uneasiness. I am so far from controverting this right in the judiciary, that it is my boast and my confidence. It leads me to greater decision on all subjects of a constitutional nature, when I reflect, that, if from inattention, want of precision, or any other defect, I should do wrong there is a power in the government, which can constitutionally prevent the operation of the wrong measure from affecting my constituents. I am legislating for the nation, and for thousands yet unborn; and it is the glory of the constitution, that there is a remedy for the failures even of the legislature itself.[96]

In Wilson's vision, the Supreme Court with judicial review functioned on the model and the principles of the jury of the country, as 'the selected body who act for the country'. The reasoned and discursive 'common sense' judgment of the people was vested in it, yet Wilson never treated this power as analogous to sovereignty. Sovereignty, even over the Constitution itself, remained with the people, who were at liberty to correct those ultimately unpersuasive judgments of the court through constitutional amendment – the 'revolution principle' – when such judgments did not stand the test of 'universal opinion'. Wilson's own experience on the Court suggests the efficacy of this power. His most extensive opinion delivered, while on the Court was *Chisholm v. Georgia* (1793), suggesting that innovation cannot be made in the philosophy of men's common life 'without using new words and phrases, or giving a different meaning to those that are received.' Wilson proceeded to offer his own understanding of the terms 'state' and 'Sovereign' which closely follow the democratic theory he had developed over the entire course of his career. A 'state' is 'a complete body of free persons united together for their common benefit, to enjoy what is peacefully their own, and to do justice to others. It is an artificial person'. Accordingly, Wilson concluded that the citizens of Georgia had a constitutional right to sue the state in which they live and to have their claims adjudicated.[97] The response to the decision followed true to Wilson's confidence in the ability of the people, but it could hardly have been the result Wilson expected. Proponents of 'state sovereignty' reacted immediately against what they believed to be a 'perversion' of common language and opinion. They accused Wilson of political 'partiality' in the cause of the national Federalists against their 'state's rights' opponents. Within a year Congress passed a resolution employing the 'revolution principle' to amend the constitution in order to secure a meaning of the 'sovereignty' of states that would prevent individual citizens from pressing a legal suit against them. The eleventh amendment, effectively barring such suits, was ratified in 1798, the year of Wilson's death.

7 Government by Discussion: Continuing Debate over Judicial Space

American speculative thought about the general nature of law is marked by a concentration almost to the point of obsession on the judicial process, that is in what the courts do and should do, how judges reason and should reason about particular cases.

(H. L. A. Hart, 1983)

RETHINKING THE JURISPRUDENCE OF JOHN MARSHALL

In the task of searching for ways to 'interpret' the American Constitution and to understand (so as to delimit) the function of the Supreme Court, constitutional and jurisprudential theorists have almost invariably begun with Marshall's principal opinions. He remains 'The Source', even as widespread uncertainty and disagreement persist about the actual character of his contribution to understanding the court's function or indeed about any particular opinion he may have written. Nevertheless, from the perspective of jurisprudential innovation, the differing perspectives on the role of courts and juries in maintaining a space for reflective judgment within the sphere of popular politics that we have already examined *preceded* Marshall's major opinions (such as *Marbury*). Indeed, importantly, there is every reason to believe that Marshall's jurisprudence drew from, rather than added to, at least two of these perspectives, those of Hamilton and Wilson.

To begin with, the persistent belief that nationalism and party allegiance might 'explain' both Marshall's opinions on the court and the underlying motivation for his 'imposition' of judicial review on an unwary public through his 'unprecedented' claims for the powers of the judicial branch, just does not stand up to close scrutiny.[1] Nor is the argument that Marshall's decisions and claims for the scope

137

of court power were without 'political' motivation and drawn from the certain and unambiguous text of the Constitution itself any more robust.[2]

More promising – though, as it turns out, no more adequate – is a recent argument of a new legal historian. Taking off from the inadequacy of these previous understandings, William Nelson has recently offered an alternative thesis about the roots of Marshall's constitutionalism which has the advantage of bringing greater coherence to a number of Marshall's apparently conflicting opinions.[3] Marshall's opinions were not straightforwardly or consistently 'pronationalist'. Against *McCulloch v. Maryland*, William Nelson has claimed, one may set *United States v. Hudson and Goodwin*, or *Wilson v. Black Bird Creek Marsh Co*.[4] While *McCulloch* upheld the power of the federal government to establish a national bank, *Hudson and Goodwin* opposed the efforts of some leading Federalists to establish a national, common law of crimes and to give federal courts the power to try common-law, as opposed to statutory, crimes. In addition, the decision in *Black Bird Creek* denied that the federal government's power superseded that of the states in the regulation of inter-state commerce in the absence of congressional legislation to that effect. Nor, Nelson argues, is the Constitution a sufficiently 'unambiguous' document to support the argument that Marshall's interpretations were, or could have been, in every case 'textually determined'.[5]

At least one proposed alternative to these discarded views is the claim that Marshall's jurisprudence is rooted in an effort to apply eighteenth-century 'governmental techniques' to the judicial resolution of 'nineteenth-century problems'.[6] On this view, Marshall's key opinions sought to apply an eighteenth-century practice of 'government by consensus' drawn from his experience of local rather than national government and modelled more on the 'judicial' powers and practices of juries than on those of courts. In particular, Nelson argues, the Chief Justice drew on that peculiar power of American colonial juries to determine law at local levels as evidence of a degree of 'widely shared' and 'enduring consensus' that could serve as his guide in matters of constitutional jurisprudence by clearly separating matters of 'law' from ones of politics:

> Marshall proposed that the courts have final authority to determine legal questions in a legal manner, that is, that nineteenth-century courts, like eighteenth-century courts, resolve by appealing to

widely shared values those questions susceptible of such resolution. On the other hand, Marshall deferred political questions – those which shared values could not answer – to the majority's will as expressed through the politically oriented legislative branches.[7]

Unfortunately, there would seem to be at least two problems with this interpretation of the basis of Marshall's jurisprudence which undermine its explanatory effectivness. While it is certainly right to suggest that the lawfinding powers of juries at local levels (both before and during the revolutionary era) evinced a considerable degree of local consensus about certain legal and political values, it was precisely this localized 'consensus' that the framers recognized was challenged by the creation of national government. More important, such local consensus (and along with it the reliance on juries' powers to find law) was, on Nelson's own account, 'disintegrating' by the last decade of the eighteenth century – well before Marshall might have chosen to appeal to it.[8] Those Hamiltonian contributions to the *Federalist Papers* which espoused the need for such a national court with powers of review, entailed arguments intended to persuade, cajole, and to build a national consensus, rather than to rely on any existing one at local levels. Indeed, perhaps no one was more aware of the collapse of the older paradigm of 'consensual' politics at both local and national levels than Alexander Hamilton, and during the Virginia ratification debates Marshall chose to share and defend Hamilton's position on the necessarily peripheral role for juries in non-revolutionary and national politics.[9]

Therefore, it is not an adversion to a localistic 'governmental technique' of consensual politics that characterizes Marshall's constitutional jurisprudence. Rather, his opinions more readily demonstrate an effort to *build* a national consensus on disputed constitutional questions through the jurisprudential application of another governmental technique which one might call 'politics by discussion'.[10] Only by understanding his effort in this way can we recognize the ready parallels between Marshall's jurisprudence and that of both Alexander Hamilton and James Wilson.

On the one hand, Marshall shared Hamilton's legalistic conception of constitutional structure as a hierarchy of laws which placed judgment and judicial authority firmly at the centre of liberal politics. The principal focus of Marshall's two most important decisions regarding the scope and reach of judicial power – *Marbury v. Madison* and *Cohens v. Virginia* – turns on the consideration of who

exercises final judgment in a political system which places final political authority with the people. Marshall's decision in *Cohens*, in
particular, represents a direct denial of Jefferson's claim that each
state, through its own judiciary, might 'independently' determine the
constitutionality of its own laws:

> [I]f upon a just construction of that instrument [the Constitution],
> it shall appear that the State has submitted to be sued, then it has
> parted with this sovereign right of judging in every case on the
> justice of its own pretensions, and has entrusted that power to a
> tribunal in whose impartiality it confides.[11]

The *Cohens* opinion has been called 'strikingly reflective of nearly
all the basic attitudes and techniques with which [Marshall's] contribution as Chief Justice has come to be indentified'.[12] If so, what can
readily be seen in this, as in at least four of Marshall's other principal
opinions, is his agreement with Wilson's appeal for a democratic,
ordinary language of law. Indeed, Marshall's jurisprudence has been
characterized as 'the perfect model and logical extension of the
need to speak a contemporary language that all Americans could
understand and heed'.[13] Although there are two passing references
in *Cohens* to Bacon's *Abridgements* and Coke's *Commentary on
Littleton*, the opinion bears no resemblance to a common law judgment. In fact, there is no reference to either natural law, fundamental
law, or to English common law cases. The only case reference in the
seventy-three-page opinion is to *Marbury*. In support of the decision,
Marshall cites only the *Federalist*, the Judiciary Act, the Constitutional Convention, and a panoply of appeals to reasonableness,
arguments from the 'nature of government' and the 'nature of the
Constitution', from the 'general spirit of the instrument' (of judicial
power). The opinion is thus jurisprudentially grounded on the appeal
to the 'self-evident principles' he insisted all Americans should be
able to recognize if they would but reason impartially. Yet, Marshall
never takes any simple, or automatic, 'consensus' for granted, offering instead what is a lengthy and highly repetitive attempt to persuade 'the people' that in claims against a state, 'it is necessary for
the purposes of justice, to provide a tribunal as superior to influence
as possible, in which that claim might be decided'.[14] Political stability
requires some sort of final authority within the political order. That
is, there must be a way of settling constitutional questions – even if
only provisionally – a way of ending debate, at least for now, and
enacting decisions that arc made at the close of that debate. It is

precisely because consensus may be lacking, or any effort to impose the majority will threatens error, that the Court becomes the locus on Marshall's account for an appeal to reflective judgment and discussion. The rejection of 'parliamentary sovereignty' had secured the principle that legislatures would not retain the sovereign power of making such decisions through the exercise of will. The problem then remains of how to reconcile fallibilism with the need for practical decisions, including decisions with enormous political and legal consequences. A 'space' for judgment had been opened in American politics by the recognition that these two conditions must be satisfied, and Marshall, along with Wilson and Hamilton, intended that the Court would move in to fill it. However, insofar as sovereignty remains with the people and the power to amend, it would not occupy that space alone.

There must be some final constitutional authority, and yet the legal and jurisprudential history of the new American republic determined that the legitimacy of this authority could not depend on claims of 'superior' legal or moral knowledge. Marshall generally recognized that the jurisprudence that sustains the Court represented a political and legal break with common law methods, and in cases such as *Fletcher v. Peck* and *Dartmouth College v. Woodward* it also represented a sharp break with common law substance.[15] 'The difference between the instruments in the examples taken from Vattel, or from the books of common law; and the Constitution of a nation is, I think, too apparent to escape the observation of any reflecting man.'[16] In this, Marshall reflected James Wilson's vision of judicial review as an institution carrying forward the jurisprudential claims of the Revolution's challenge to hierarchic common law theories of epistemology and politics. However, in other instances, Marshall just as clearly chose to rely on Hamilton's defensive and disingenuous disclaimers of *Federalist* 78 that the Court was in reality like its English 'predecessors' – an 'oracle' of reason, declaring and finding law, but refusing to enter the 'thicket' of politics. In doing so, Marshall effectively dislodged judicial review from its origins in the jural debates of the American Revolution. He set 'the people' and the Court once again at opposite poles of jurisprudential discourse, defied the challenge of popular sentiment to Court 'reason', and established the framework for the competing roles of the Court and the Congress which yet persist in America today.

JUDICIAL RETRENCHMENT AND JUDICIAL SPACE

Excluding anarchy or despotism has still left plenty of room in the spectrum of political ideologies for fundamental political disagreement, no less than a civil war, in American history. In this sense, Louis Hartz was wrong in his assessment of the political implications of early American commitments to liberalism.[17] More to the point, our lack of a 'feudal past' precluded the easy inheritance in America of an entrenched social and political deference that might have accepted without challenge or debate the participation of our judicial institutions in the unprecedented geographic and economic expansion that reshaped American society in the nineteenth century.

Instead, throughout that period, the Supreme Court, as the institution created to adjudicate conflict in the public sphere, but also courts and judges generally, remained the subjects of intense public criticism and debate. In this sense, judicial review was not born, nor has it 'flourished', in Louis Hartz's words, on the corpse of philosophy in America – as the most recent debates over the relevance of theories of pragmatism, conventionalism, or philosophic nihilism to questions of the Court's function continue to demonstrate. (Even the denial of the relevance of philosophy to this question has sparked philosophic debate.[18]) As a result, the character of the Supreme Court's 'independence' within the political sphere remained persistently difficult to identify and maintain. The popular urge both to make and to reflectively judge the law is a phenomenon which political and legal historians have commonly noted as indicative of the Jacksonian era:

> [I]n the several states the power of the judges became more and more restricted in the era that accompanied the rise of Andrew Jackson and the reorganized Democratic Party . . . with the emphasis shifting more and more to the jury. In many jurisdictions judges were prevented from commenting on the evidence. In some, juries were made the judges, of law and fact.[19]

However, this attachment to juries was not simply or exclusively a Jacksonian phenomenon. Rather, the arguments for expanded jury determination of law made throughout the ninteenth century mirrored to a remarkable extent those peculiarly American arguments for 'the people's' capability to know the law and to judge its constitutionality which had been put forward during and immediately after the revolutionary period. While, as earlier, distrust of the judiciary functioned as one element to enhance this reliance on 'the people's' jural capabilities, equally at work was a more purposive, Jeffersonian appeal, which emphasized the jury's role in expressing the will of the community, and the community's function as the only legitimate source and judge of 'right' laws.[20] As one delegate to the 1853 Massachusetts convention to revise and amend the state constitution requested:

> [W]henever the rights which we reserve to the people are invaded by any law, I ask, that in that case, a jury coming from the people may be allowed to come in and give their judgment, and rescue the people, in the name of their declared rights, from an unconstitutional law, or from an unconstitutional interpretation of that law.[21]

Against the tide of renewed debate over which institution – the jury or the judiciary – was best suited to routinely occupy the space for public judgment which eighteenth-century American constitutional thought had created, the novel aspects of Marshall's jurisprudence which de-emphasized both the applicability of common law techniques of adjudication, and, particularly, precedent as an intrinsic or necessary legitimizer of judicial decisions in constitutional matters, met with sharp popular resistance. In some cases, judges such as Massachusetts Chief Justice Lemuel Shaw, whose adjudicatory techniques most closely followed those of Marshall, confronted efforts at constitutional amendment designed to overturn their more controversial judgments.[22] For a judiciary thus placed on the defensive, one alternative became the jurisprudential retrenchment of James Kent and Joseph Story.

One judicial historian has aptly characterized the difference in adjudicatory techniques which distanced Kent and Story from Shaw:

> Where Kent and Story might rest a decision on a technical distinction, Shaw grounded it on rough common sense. Where Kent and Story might string together sets of authorities, Shaw completely ignored them. And where Kent and Story might pursue legal principle to its consistent, logical conclusion, Shaw emphasized its ambivalences and suggested that it could lead to contradictory results in diverse instances.[23]

However, the differences in the juristic theories and practices of these judges cannot be understood, as is sometimes suggested, as simply the differences between a 'frontier theory' of law and a more mature nineteenth century jurisprudence. The mid-nineteenth-century judicial system over which Shaw presided in Massachusetts was simply no legal frontier. Rather, their approaches comprise differing responses to the problem of acquiring contested occupancy of a newly created judicial space. Kent's lament that judges were without a known and certain law of their own was a sizeable hint that the best technique for defusing the politically controversial position of the judiciary was to deny its inherently political character and to invite comparisons with English common law courts. Both Kent and Story wrote America's first extended legal treatises on the Constitution and American law. In contrast to Marshall, both incorporated masses of historical references and authorities, as well as English precedents, in an effort to establish the universality (and therefore justness) of certain propositions and legal principles by 'demonstrating the ubiquity of their presence'.[24] Story's *Commentaries* – dedicated to John Marshall – are notable for their attempt to reproduce for American jurisprudence the English common lawyer's understanding of the detached and independent function of the Court in relation to the political sphere, while at the same time savaging Jeffersonian political and constitutional thought. Almost in passing, Story denies the right of juries to determine the law.[25]

The inapt model of English common law jurisprudence embraced by American legal thinkers and judges in the middle of the nineteenth century has carried with it both practical and theoretical implications. In practice, the judiciary acquired occupancy of the space for judgment in American constitutional government through an 'oracular' claim for legitimacy that mimicked the English judiciary's claim to sit 'outside' the sphere of politics. Although the debate persisted until 1895, in *Sparf and Hansen v. United States* the Supreme Court effectively repudiated the right of a jury to determine for itself the law in a federal criminal case.[26] However, the denial of judicial space legitimized judicial function in the popular mind at the expense of eventually incurring popular 'disenchantment' and intransigence when the 'myth' wore thin in the early twentieth century. The urge to create a 'science' of law for America, and in so doing to 'neutralize' the political impact of Supreme Court adjudication, produced the drive for system, doctrinal deductiveness and predictability, and above all certainty, which underlay the 'mechanical jurisprudence' of the late nineteenth century. The myth that America too might have its version of the English 'oracular' vision of adjudication was inevitably dispelled. However, the identity of

British and American judicial function, of a unity of concerns within Anglo-American legal thought has remained a constant theme within the corpus of twentieth-century American constitutional jurisprudence. More recently, it has led one Court analyst to suggest that American constitutional law is the construct of 'the artificial reason' which only lawyers and judges may be expected to know, and, therefore, that 'rights will be best and most reasonably respected if reasoning about them goes forward within its special discipline.'[27] However, such attempts to neatly separate questions of constitutional law from politics and to consign their interpretation to the 'artificial reasoning' of the common law model run counter to the fundamental epistemological and legal claims of American jural thought since the early eighteenth century. Indeed, the position of the Court in occupying a judicial space within American politics is inescapably 'political' despite all efforts by justices to assume an 'impersonal' or 'neutral' standpoint on any particular decision. Efforts either to restrict or mask this phenomenon by resorting to 'professional' over 'public' legal reasoning threaten to place this institution under great strain.

It is perhaps appropriate that a discussion which has gone so far to separate the conceptual and theoretical understandings of the role and function of courts underpinning English and American jurisprudence should end on a note of practical disclaimer. This work is not concerned with questions of how the Supreme Court operates, or ought to operate, in practice. It has nothing to say about how badly or well courts and judges function within that space which is inherent in the complex institution of the American judiciary and Supreme Court and missing from what are often considered their English institutional counterparts. It has not attempted to provide a justification for the existence of a Supreme Court with powers of judicial review, but rather to enhance our understanding of how and why this particular institution evolved in the United States, and by underscoring a neglected but important aspect of the standard treatments, to throw some new light on the dilemmas of that court within the American system.

In practice, a smoothly functioning parliamentary sovereignty *may* operate so as to virtually represent, to pursue the common welfare, and to protect the 'fundamental liberties' of the British people. In contrast, the Supreme Court may reach far beyond the bounds of acceptability by public opinion in its practice of constitutional adjudication. However, the differences with which this study is concerned are ones of theory, not practice. In practice, Parliament can, and does, resolve through discussion and political choice many conflicts of public welfare and private liberty similar to those that Americans rely on the Supreme Court to resolve through judicial review. Yet, the differences in our constitutional and jurisprudential thought, and the implications of these theories in practice are quite stark. British legal and jurisprudential thought is informed by the choice of a unified and sovereign control over law which rests with Parliament. Therefore, British jurisprudence immediately catapults the judiciary out of any central position in constitutional thinking in a manner foreign to American legal traditions. British courts do not receive their powers from a constitution whose legal authority and public legitimacy are independent of the expression of parliamentary will.

It is precisely the denial of this principle of judgment which makes a conception of jurisprudence in what H. L. A. Hart has called 'the narrow English style', 'lying outside the scope of political philosophy or theory', appropriate for a description of English court practice but totally inappropriate for that in America.[28] Given such a perspective, it is easily understandable that Hart would assess the perception of judges as 'legislators', or as anything less than the 'objective, impartial, erudite, and experienced declarer[s] or law', as an Englishman's 'nightmare'.[29] However, contrary to Hart's perceptions, English nightmares are not our own. The preeminent American nightmare, vivified by its revolutionary experience, is that a frenzied or tyrannical majority will reach out to supress the 'rights and fundamental liberties' of citizens, and the Court will do nothing to resist this intrusion through the constitutional mechanisms available to it. In contrast, until recently the British have accepted with equanimity the fact that their court system is neither practically nor theoretically precluded from the possibility of serving as the administrative functionary carrying out statutory removals of the 'right to silence', or imposing restrictions on the exercise of a free press or the right to publish when the government considers it to be 'damaging' or 'prejudicial' not simply to 'national security' but to Britain's international relations or interests generally.[30] A British constitutional writer has succinctly, if starkly, summarized the difference in judicial perspective which the denial of judicial space makes possible:

> The courts are free to act, however, only within a sphere of small diameter, for the possibility of interpretation is limited by the legislation passed. If legislation results in oppression the judges

are powerless to prevent it. In England the judges are the censors of the administration, but they are bound by Acts of Parliament. But 'Parliament' means a partisan majority. A victory at the polls, obtained, perhaps, by mass bribery or deliberate falsehood or national hysteria, theoretically enables a party majority to warp the law so as to interfere with the most cherished of 'fundamental liberties.'[31]

Yet, the practical manipulation of judicial space by the Supreme Court can create its own bad dreams, as Alexander Bickel laboured so brilliantly to point out. No solution has yet been arrived at to resolve with any finality the problems which judicial space creates for American jurisprudence, and debates cast in the common law mould, over judicial 'discretion' and 'interpretation', are most unlikely to offer satisfactory, much less definitive, solutions at the constitutional level. 'Interpreting' the Constitution has not consisted in finding a 'privileged' meaning which inheres unchallenged in the document, or in 'the people' at large. Such an epistemological claim for certainty (and privilege) on the part of judges is exactly what was lost in the eighteenth-century move from a private sphere of 'judge-made' common law to the public space of American constitutional and public law. In this sense, American constitutional law is not, and cannot be, a seamless web. The appeals in even Marshall's most controversial decisions, such as *Marbury*, *McCulloch*, and *Cohens*, to 'general principles', 'the nature of government', and the 'nature of a constitution', were efforts of moral and political persuasion, not attempts to legitimize Court decisions through claims of epistemological certainty.

To recognize this makes judicial review, in theory, a 'limited' agreement to allow an independent judiciary to adjudicate political disputes which are brought to it, even as they continue to be discussed in the political sphere. It serves as an instrument for confirming or rejecting problematic laws – laws which for one reason or another threaten to fail the test of rational consent. It offers liberal, political self-rule an opportunity for stability, but not the moral or psychological certainty that our political decisions are indisputably 'right'. It is basic to liberal citizenship that in certain questions neither 'truth' nor numbers can be determinative, but only reasons and arguments. It is the ability to live with uncertainty, or at the very least, to trade the certainty of sovereign will for an independent space of reflection, reasoned argument, and judgment within the political sphere which has allowed for a politics of continuous discussion and a stable, if impermanent, resolution of political conflict in American law.

Notes

PREFACE

1. *The Creation of the American Republic, 1776–1787* (New York: W. W. Norton, 1969, p. 292. Wood himself suggested an understandable degree of puzzlement over the phenomenon of judicial review, which he saw as an outgrowth more of colonial legal thought about the morality of law than about law's fundamentality (p. 457, fn. 43). However, he should be in no way implicated in the solution to this puzzle offered here.

2. John Murrin and A. G. Roeber have noted that unlike other colonial leaders, the Governor of an historically projury Rhode Island, Stephen Hopkins, raised the jury issue only in an unofficial pamphlet, and Virginia avoided the subject of juries in its resolutions against the Stamp Acts. 'Trial by Jury: The Virginia Paradox', in Jon Kukla (ed.), *The Bill of Rights: A Lively Heritage* (Richmond: Virginia State Library and Archive, 1987), p. 110. However, Richard Bland's 1766 pamphlet, 'An Inquiry into the Rights of the British Colonies' made clear that Virginians were worried about the British expansion of the use against offending colonials of trials before juryless Courts of Admiralty as depriving them of 'legal Trials in the Court of the common Law' – trials which would have been before juries. Murrin has also examined the spectrum of jural commitments in seventeenth-century New England – from the extremes of a 'projury' Rhode Island and instances of 'jury madness' which in some cases included an expansion of the role of civil juries which 'far exceeded anything imagined for them in England', to the more antijury New Haven and the severely weakened jury performance of Connecticut. His argument establishes the heterogeneous character of colonial jury experience and suggests the need for a degree of caution in generalizing about such practices. See 'Trial by Jury in Seventeenth-Century New England', in D. Hall, J. M. Murrin, and T. Tate (eds), *Saints and Revolutionaries: Essays on Early American History* (New York: W. W. Norton, 1984), p. 201. For another recent look at the differing historical development and decline from prominence of Connecticut's civil juries in the early eighteenth-century, see Bruce Mann, *Neighbours and Strangers: Law and Community in Early Connecticut* (Chapel Hill: Univ. of North Carolina Press, 1987).

3. Clinton Rossiter (ed.), *The Federalist Papers* (New York: Mentor, 1961), no. 83, p. 499.

1 POLITICAL THOUGHT AND HISTORICAL PROBLEMATICS

1. H. L. A. Hart, *Essays in Jurisprudence and Philosophy* (Oxford, 1983), p. 123. Hart recognizes the centrality of this question as the 'one salient feature of American jurisprudence' and contrasts it sharply with English jurisprudential thought. To suggest some of the reasons why these differences in legal perspective exist is a central aim of this study. Looking back, such analysis is perhaps helpful in understanding why efforts both at codification and at developing constitutional common law have been rejected in America. See, for example, Madison's polite refusal of Jeremy Bentham's offer to draw up a complete codification of American law, including a digest of all statutes and the 'reduction of unwritten to text law'. Gaillard Hunt, ed., *The Writings of James Madison* (New York, 1900–10), vol. VIII, p. 400. Despite recent arguments for its creation, America has no single, recognizable technique or body of 'constitutional' common law. See Guido Calbresi, *A Common Law for the Age of Statutes* (Cambridge, Mass., 1982).
2. The list of participants currently engaged in this debate is lengthy, but for a sampling of authors and arguments, see Marshall Cohen, ed., *Ronald Dworkin and Contemporary Jurisprudence* (Totowa, N. J., 1983); H. A. L. Hart, *Essays in Jurisprudence and Philosophy*; 'A Symposium: Law and Literature', *Texas Law Review*, vol. 60, 1982.
3. John Dunn, 'Consent in the Political Theory of John Locke', in Dunn, *Political Obligation in its Historical Context* (Cambridge, 1980), p. 29.
4. Dunn, *Political Obligation*, ch. 3. Dunn's work on Locke is only one very fine example of this more deeply contextual approach. See also Quentin Skinner, 'History and Ideology in the American Revolution', *Historical Journal*, vol. 8, 1965, pp. 151–78; or, more generally, Q. Skinner, *The Foundations of Modern Political Thought*, 2 vols. (Cambridge, 1978).
5. J. G. A. Pocock, *Politics, Language and Time* (New York, 1971), p. 107; Nathan O. Hatch, *The Sacred Cause of Liberty* (New Haven, 1977); Steven M. Dworetz, 'The Radical Side of American Constitutionalism: Locke and the New England Clergy, Revisited', a paper presented at the New England Political Science Association Annual Convention, Trinity College in Hartford, Connecticut, 5 April 1986, p. 4. I owe this insight, as well as its Latin translation, to Dworetz.
6. Stephen T. Holmes, *Benjamin Constant and the Making of Modern Liberalism* (New Haven, 1984), p. 65.
7. Hannah Arendt, *On Revolution* (Harmondsworth, 1963), p. 238.
8. Hannah Arendt, 'Truth and Politics', in *Between Past and Future* (Harmondsworth, 1954), p. 235.
9. See Samuel H. Beer, *Federalism and the National Idea* (Cambridge, Mass., forthcoming).
10. See Thomas C. Grey, 'Origins of the Unwritten Constitution: Fundamental Law in American Revolutionary Thought', *Stanford Law Review*, vol. 30, 1978, p. 849, fn. 23.
11. Other studies have suggested the degree to which this central concern

of liberal epistemology and moral theory has produced diverse results for politics in different institutional contexts. See Henry G. Van Leeuwen, *The Problem of Certainty in English Thought, 1630–90* (The Hague, 1963). For an excellent discussion of the concerns with certainty in revolutionary France, see Cheryl B. Welch, *Liberty and Utility: The French Ideologues and the Transformation of Liberalism* (New York, 1984).

2 HISTORICAL TRANSFORMATIONS AND LEGAL LEGACIES

1. J. P. Reid, 'In an Inherited Way: English Constitutional Rights, the Stamp Act Debate, and the Coming of the American Revolution', *Southern California Law Review* vol. 49, 1976, p. 1109. The importance of Reid's contribution – as well as that of several other new legal historians referred to in the discussion below – to a renewed examination of American revolutionary constitutionalism has been recently studied to great effect by Jack P. Greene. See 'From the Perspective of Law: Context and Legitimacy in the Origins of the American Revolution', *Southern Quarterly*, vol 85, Winter 1986, pp. 56–77. The discussion below is indebted to Greene's careful presentation. An illuminating examination of the contribution of both old and new law school historians is also found in Stanley Katz, 'The Problem of Colonial Legal History', in J. P. Greene and J. R. Pole, eds, *Colonial British America: Essays in the New History of the Early Modern Era* (Baltimore, 1984), pp. 457–90.
2. J. P. Reid, 'In an Inherited Way', p. 1109.
3. J. P. Reid, *In a Defiant Stance: The Conditions of Law in Massachusetts Bay, the Irish Comparison, and the Coming of the American Revolution* (University Park, Pa., 1977), p. 2.
4. J. P. Reid, 'The Ordeal by Law of Thomas Hutchinson', *New York University Law Review*, vol. 49, 1974, p. 602. Here Reid is building on some suggestive findings by a second new legal historian, William Nelson, in *The Americanization of the Common Law: The Impact of Legal Change on Massachusetts Society, 1760–1830* (Cambridge, Mass. 1975).
5. J. P. Reid, 'In a Defensive Rage: The Uses of the Mob, the Justification in Law, and the Coming of the American Revolution', *New York University Law Review*, vol. 49, 1974, p. 1087; Greene, 'From the Perspective of Law', p. 65.
6. Jack P. Greene, *Peripheries and Center: Constitutional Development in the Extended Politics of the British Empire and the United States, 1607–1788* (Athens, Ga., 1986), p. 25.
7. Lewis Morris, *Some Observations upon the Charge Given by the Honourable James De Lancey, Esq. . . .* (New York, 1734), cited in Green, *Peripheries and Center*, p. 26.
8. William Nelson, 'The Legal Restraint on Power in Pre-Revolutionary America: Massachusetts as a Case Study, 1760–1775', *American Journal of Legal History*, vol. 18, 1974, pp. 7, 10, 14, 23–4, 26, 28. Nelson

developed this thesis with regard to the power of juries at greater length in his *Americanization of the Common Law*, pp. 3, 8, 21, 23, 28–30, 165–71.

9. J. P. Reid, *In Defiance of the Law: The Standing Army Controversy, the Two Constitutions, and the Coming of the American Revolution* (Chapel Hill, 1981) pp. 3, 48, 121; Thomas C. Grey, 'Origins of the Unwritten Constitution: Fundamental Law in American Revolutionary Thought', *Stanford Law Review*, vol. 30, 1978, 863–7, 892.

10. Reid, *In Defiance of the Law*, pp. 3, 48, 121; Grey, 'Origins of the Unwritten Constitution', pp. 863–7, 892; Greene, 'From the Perspective of Law', p. 64. A major theme of Reid's work has been 'that American constitutional ideas were British constitutional ideas, and that there were few differences in legal thought between the two parts of the empire.' At the same time, Reid recognizes there were 'some differences, or perhaps changes in perception and emphasis, separating American constitutionalism from that of the mother country.' These differences, principally diverging theories of representation and consent, as well as a 'minor one' in the 'emerging colonial stress on the jury as a democratic institution', Reid does not see as having equally diverging legal implications. As will be suggested below, this point seems the most difficult to sustain. *Constitutional History of the American Republic* (Madison, 1986), p. 50–1.

11. Reid, *In Defiance of the Law*, pp. 31, 34; Greene, 'From the Perspective of Law', p. 74.

12. Roscoe Pound, *The Formative Era of American Law* (Boston, Mass., 1938), pp. 3, 6–7.

13. Some outstanding earlier proponents of the transit of ideas position have been Julius Goebel, Jr, *History of the Supreme Court of the United States*, vol. 1 (New York, 1971); Joseph H. Smith, *Colonial Justice in Western Massachusetts: The Pynchon Court Record* (Cambridge, Mass., 1961); and, to a somewhat more subtle extent, Zechariah Chafee, Jr, 'Colonial Courts and the Common Law', *Massachusetts Historical Society Proceedings*, vol. 68, 1952, pp. 132–59. A variant of this approach has found its way into the literature of political science through the 'fragment' theory of Louis Hartz and the interpretation of the colonial milieu by Samuel Huntington – a student of Hartz – as politically and institutionally one of 'Tudor polity'. See Samuel Huntington, 'New Society, Old State', in Edward Handler, ed., *The American Political Experience* (Lexington, 1968), pp. 90–103. The Tudor polity model interprets the ultimate revolutionary conflict between Britain and America as a disjunction and conflict in institutional modernization. Simply put, the argument is that while Britain moved forward with parliamentary sovereignty in the eighteenth century, an isolated America remained as a seventeenth-century fragment with regard to its political and institutional life. For an account of an historian's concern with the limitations of this approach, see Katz, 'Problem of Colonial Legal History', p. 459.

14. G. R. Elton, *The Tudor Constitution* (Cambridge, 1960), p. 344. Indeed, the very sovereignty of Parliament being claimed in England

during the eighteenth century was defended on the basis of the ancient constitution and the fundamental law. William Petyt, *The Ancient Right of the Commons of England Asserted* (London, 1680); also Petyt, *Jus Parliamentarium: Or, the Ancient Power, Jurisdiction, Rights and Liberties, of the most High Court of Parliament, revived and asserted* (London, 1739, but written in the 1680s); James Tyrell, *Bibliotheca Political: Or an Enquiry into the Ancient Constitution of English Government* (London, 1694); Humphrey Mackworth, *A Vindication of the Rights of the Commons of England* (London, 1701), p. 3. For an excellent discussion of this issue, see. H. T. Dickinson, 'The Eighteenth-Century Debate on the Sovereignty of Parliament', *Transactions of the Royal Historical Society*, vol. 26, 5th series (London, 1976). Edmund Burke would note later that whether one referred to an original contract, the ancient constitution, or the Revolution settlement, all were testimony to the fact that 'the people' retained no power which was distinct from the legislature representing them. Sovereignty rested explicitly and irremovably in the King, Lords, and Commons. See Burke, *Reflections on the Revolution in France* in *Writings and Speeches of Edmund Burke*, vol. III, pp. 287–308; also *An Appeal from the New to the Old Whigs*, in *Writings*, vol. IV, pp. 61–215. Dickinson suggests that precisely because fundamental references were technically useless in restraining Parliament, Americans chose to divide the exercise of sovereignty: 'The Eighteenth-Century Debate', p. 208.

15. Bernard Bailyn, *The Ideological Origins of the American Revolution* (Cambridge, Mass., 1967), p. 105; *Pamphlets of the American Revolution: 1750–1776* (Cambridge Mass., 1965), p. 66.

16. J. P. Reid, 'The Apparatus of Constitutional Advocacy and the American Revolution: A Review of Five Books', *New York University Law Review*, vol. 42, 1967, p. 194, cited in J. P. Greene, 'From the Perspective of Law', p. 66.

17. A failure to distinguish rhetoric from reality seems particularly at work in the 'Tudor polity' model. The deference to authority, the relative security of power removed from public view, the perception of law as unchallengeable, so essential to maintaining Tudor rule and its institutional balance, would seem to be wholly missing from American pre-revolutionary rhetoric. Recourse has most commonly been had either to anachronism, finding the seeds of judicial review in Coke and seventeenth-century fundamental law, or to the impositions of power politics of the Federalist party and its chief judicial spokesman, John Marshall. As I show below, however, they could not have retrieved the seeds of judicial review by looking back to Coke. The seeds were not there to be found. There are faults as well with the power politics explanation, which are discussed below in Chapter 7. See, for example, William Nelson, 'The Eighteenth-Century Background of John Marshall's Constitutional Jurisprudence', *Michigan Law Review*, vol. 76, 1978, pp. 893f.

18. Thomas Grey, 'Origins of the Unwritten Constitution', p. 869.

19. As will become clear later, this argument is concerned less to pinpoint

'sources' of fundamental law than to examine its functional relationship to general social and political processes and institutions. For a particularly enlightening examination of the need for colonial legal historians to examine this functional relationship, see Katz, 'The Problem of Colonial Legal History', in Greene and Pole, *Colonial British America*, pp. 457–489.

20. Stuart Prall, *The Agitation for Law Reform During the Puritan Revolution, 1640–60* (The Hague, 1966), p. 15. Margaret Judson, *The Crisis of the Constitution: An Essay in Constitutional and Political Thought in England, 1603–1645* (New Brunswick, 1949), pp. 55–6.

21. John Pym, *The speech or declaration of John Pym* (1641), in Andrew Sharp, ed., *Political Ideas of the English Civil Wars, 1641–49* (London, 1983), p. 34.

22. *Touching the Fundamental Lawes of This Kingdome, the King's Negative Voice, and the Power of Parliaments* (London, 1643), [S. L.: *Thomason Tracts*, E. 90(21), p. 1]. Also cited in Prall, *The Agitation for Law Reform*, p. 15. This tract termed Parliament itself as 'Fundamentall and Paramount', and 'not therefore to be circumscribed by any other laws which have their being from it, not it from them, but onely by that Law which at first gave it its being, to wit, Salus populi' (p.2). On such an account Parliament derived its origin from the natural law, reason, or the 'public good', but not necessarily with popular consent. This view effectively rendered Parliament supreme and limited by no law – fundamental law was simply identified with parliamentary supremacy and its pursuit of the 'salus populi'. Others defended parliamentary sovereignty on the grounds of fundamental law and its ancient origins. William Petyt, in particular, traced Parliament back to an Anglo-Saxon root, which made statute law superior not only to common law, but also to decisions by either kings or judges. *The Ancient Right of the Commons of England Asserted* (London, 1680); *Jus Parliamentarium* (London, 1739; written in the 1680s).

23.   For an interesting analysis of citations of legal and political authorities in eighteenth-century America, see Donald Lutz, 'The Relative Influence of European Writers on Late Eighteenth-Century American Political Thought', *American Political Science Review*, vol. 78, 1984, p. 193. A sampling of the Leveller discussion of fundamental law may be found in the following tracts: (Anon.) *The Fundamental Lawes and Liberties of England Claimed, asserted, and agreed unto, by severall Peaceable Persons of the City of London, Westminster, Southwark, Hamblets, and Places adjacent; . . .* (9 July 1653)[H. L.: *EC65 A100 653f]; John Lilburne, *The Legall Fundamentall Liberties of the People of England* (London, 8 June 1649) [H. L.: E. 560 (14)]; *England's New Chains Discovered* (London, 26 Feb. 1649), in Haller and Davies, eds, *The Leveller Tracts 1647–1653*, pp. 157–70, and *An Outcry of the Young-men and Apprentices of London . . . after the lost Fundamental Laws and Liberties of England*, cited in T. B. Howell, *A Complete Collection of State Trials* (London, 1816), vol. 4, p. 1326; John Jones, *Judges Judged Out of Their Own Mouthes* (London, 6 May 1650), [H. L.: E 1414 (1)]; *Jurors Judges of Law and Fact: Or,*

certain Observations of certain differences in points of Law between . . . Andr. Horn and (the author of) A Letter of due Censure . . . to . . . Lilburne (London: w.d., 1650), [H. L.: E 1414 (2)]; William Walwyn, *Juries Justified: Or, A Word of Correction to Mr. Henry Robinson; for His seven Objections against the Trial of Causes, by Juries of twelve men* (London: Robert Wood, 1651), [H. L.: *Ec65 W1798 651j]. As has been helpfully discussed by G. E. Aylmer, the term Leveller has been rather loosely applied to a number of thinkers who held disparate views on any number of specific religious, social, and economic issues. Aylmer, ed., *The Levellers in the English Revolution* (Ithaca, 1975), pp. 9–55. For obvious reasons, there should be an equal reluctance to impose a tighter unity of position on Leveller legal thought than the pamphlet and trial records will bear. However, my own conclusion is that perhaps a greater agreement among Leveller writers may be found on legal reform issues, and particularly on the question of the importance and scope of juries' lawfinding powers, than on any other issue. A similar though not identical conclusion is reached by Thomas A. Green, *Verdict According to Conscience: Perspectives on the English Criminal Trial Jury 1200–1800* (Chicago, 1985), p. 162.

24. While both the Levellers and Coke made reference to a fundamental law that pre-dated the Norman invasion, Coke argued that, legally, the Normans had done nothing to interrupt its historical continuity. From this legal perspective, no Conquest had taken place. The Levellers disagreed, attributing much of the corruption of England's 'fundamental laws' to the perverse legal practices they claimed were introduced under the 'Norman Yoke'. Before the Norman Conquest, ran one tract, 'the nation never knew or felt the charge, trouble, or intanglements of Judges, Lawyers, and Attorneys, Solicitors, Filors, and the rest of that sort of men . . .' (Anon.) *The Onely Right Rule for regulating the Lawes and Liberties of the People of England* (28 January 1652/3) [H. L.: E 684 (33); film A199, reel 105), p. 5. See also William Cole *A Rod for the Lawyers: Who are hereby declared to be the grand Robbers and Deceivers of the Nation . . .* (London, 1659) [H. L.: *EC65.C6766.659rb).

25. R. A. MacKay, 'Coke – Parliamentary Sovereignty or the Supremacy of the Law?' *Michigan Law Review*, vol. 22, 1923–4, p. 215. The discussions of Coke's jurisprudence are legion. It is useful to note those that remain among the more frequently cited. Samuel Thorne, 'Dr. Bonham's Case,' *Law Quarterly Review*, vol. 54, 1938, pp. 543–52. A. V. Dicey, *The Law of the Constitution* (London, 1959), p. 46; Charles H. McIlwain, *The High Court of Parliament and its Supremacy* (New Haven, 1910), pp. 139–48.

26. *English Reports* (London, 1912), vol. 8, p. 118, contains his dicta that 'in many cases the common law will control acts of Parliament, and sometimes adjudge them to be utterly void; for when an act is against Common right and reason, or repugnant, or impossible to be performed, the common law will controul it, and adjudge such an act to be void.' For a report of Coke's claim before James I that while 'God

had endowed his Majesty with excellent science and great endowments of nature; but His majesty was not learned in the law' which was 'not to be decided by natural reason but by artificial reason', see S. R. Gardiner, *History of England* (London, 1883), vol. 2, p. 38.

27. For the classic account of the deep fissure between the legal views of the Levellers and those of Sir Edward Coke with which this analysis takes at least partial issue, see J. G. A. Pocock, *The Ancient Constitution and the Feudal Law* (Cambridge, 1957, 1987), pp. 125–7. Pocock's position is to some degree shared by Christopher Hill in *Puritanism and Revolution* (London, 1958), pp. 75–82. However, for another critical view of the Pocock position, see Robert Seaburg, 'The Norman Conquest and the Common Law: the Levellers' Argument from Continuity', *Historical Journal*, vol. 24, 1981, pp. 791–806. For a helpful discussion of Leveller legal thought that shares Seaburg's perspective, see Green, *Verdict According to Conscience*, Ch. 5.

28. For perhaps the most strenuous critique of Coke's jurisprudence as suitable for a coherent historical continuity reading, see Holdsworth, *History of English Law* (London, 1922–32), vol. 5, pp. 475–9. See also MacKay, 'Coke', pp. 215–47; S. E. Thorne, *Sir Edward Coke, 1552–1952* (London, Selden Society, 1957). pp. 10–17.

29. Thorne, *Sir Edward Coke*, p. 17; see *Darcy v. Allein* (the Case of the Monopolies) 11 *English Reports*, 84 (44 Eliz., 1602), and the *Ipswich Tailors Case*, 11 *English Reports*, 53.

30. Thorne, *Sir Edward Coke*, p. 10. For a clear statement which suggests that he did not question the power of Parliament to set aside the common law, see 3 *English Reports*, XVIII; 4 *Reports* I, II, IX-XI. Cited in MacKay, 'Coke', pp. 217–21; J. W. A. Gough, *Fundamental Law In English Constitutional History* (Oxford, 1955), p. 206.

31. 4 *English Reports*, Preface, VI.

32. As both Maitland and Holdsworth have noted, Coke was, throughout his life, a strenuous advocate of one political cause or another. In terms of his legal advocacy, Holdsworth notes that 'whether he is reporting a case, or arguing for the supremacy of the common law in the state, or upholding the privileges of Parliament he does it with all his strength; and the result is that he talks and writes himself into a decided view of the subject. I doubt very much whether in all Coke's writings a passage could be found in which he admits he has left any uncertainty in the law. . . . His work therefore is disfigured by inconsistent statements. . . . And this readiness to accept anything in support of his view which he is defending, makes it easy for him to misrepresent his authorities by reading into them the sense which supports the conclusions he wishes to draw.' William Holdsworth, *A History of English Law* (Boston, 1927), vol. V. pp. 495–6.

33. Cited in Holdsworth, *History of English Law*, vol. III, p. 472.

34. Holdsworth, *History of English Law*, vol. V, p. 475.

35. One might easily suggest it was a primary concern of the age in which Coke lived. This overwhelming concern with certainty, particularly in regard to legal matters, is well brought out by Cynthia Herrup in 'Law and Morality in Seventeenth-Century England', *Past and Present*, no.

106, 1985, p. 108. As Herrup notes: 'A measured approach to law
and order might well have suited the social views and needs of the
eighteenth-century English gentry, but the religious intensity of the
early seventeenth century guided the social values of law enforcers in
a drastically different direction . . . ministers, gentlemen, and farmers
alike agreed that every moment of life, every task, was a new test of
character and resolve.' Far from being the complaint of Levellers and
radicals alone, legal reform oriented towards certainty was pressed in
pointed and colourful terms by representatives of order such as Henry
Robinson: '[England's laws] are such a forragenious piece of Intracac-
ies, such a vanity to become a Rule unto so famous a Nation; such a
Nose of Wax, lyable to be formed any way for the vexation of the
people; as that is the very memory thereof, and the Formalities of
their proceedings are quite extinct . . . and the nation forced to seek
out both new laws and Forms; wee could not happen upon so bad
again.' *Certain Considerations In order to a more speedy, cheap, and
equall distribution of Justice throughout the Nation* (London, Matthew
Simmons, 1651), epistle dedicatory.

36. (Anon.) *Certain Proposals for regulating the Law, to make the same
more plain and easy to be understood, and lesse chargeable and expens-
ive than heretofore*, n.d. (in the regin of Charles I), in Walter Scott,
ed., *The Somers Collection of Tracts* (London, 1812), vol. V, pp.
534–5. (Anon.), *The Law's Discovery: Or a brief Detection of sundry
notorious Errors and Abuses comtained in our English Laws, whereby
Thousands are annually stripped of their Estates, and some of their
Lives. By a Well-wisher to his Country* (London, 1653), in William
Oldys and Thomas Park, eds, *Harleian Miscellany* (London, 1909),
vol. II, p. 577. It should be noted that while the Revolution did
accomplish the rendering of statute law into English, existing case
reports were not translated until the *late* eighteenth century. This
should be noted with particular significance to the American colonies,
which also lacked their own domestic case reports until the 1830s.

37. *Certain Proposals for regulating the Law*, p. 535. The reduction of
the laws to a single handbook was a common proposal of the revolutionary era. William Shepard, perhaps Cromwell's principal law
reformer, proposed in 1656 that the entire law should be codified in
order to render it 'as short and as clear as may be.' Cited in Donald
Veall, *The Popular Movement for Law Reform, 1640–1660* (Oxford,
1970), p. 92.

38. Coke, *Institutes of the Laws of England, part 2* (1642) (London, 1809),
p. 179. Interestingly enough for those who press the non-historical
character of the Leveller legal position, Lilburne characterized the
fundamental law as that historical collection of charters, such as
Magna Carta, although in his second trial he added to this list quotations from Genesis, Deuteronomy, and the Acts of the Apostles.
See Christopher Hill, *Puritanism and Revolution*, p. 76.

39. The Leveller proposal that the law be rendered from Latin to English
was not put into effect until 1731 (4 George II, cap. 26). According
to D. B. Horn and Mary Ransome, the substitution in indictments

was opposed by lawyers and was deplored by Blackstone. *English Historical Documents* (New York, 1969), vol. x, p. 237. The act applied to all pleadings, rules, orders, indictments, informations, inquisitions, presentments, verdicts, etc. And, the stated purpose of the act was to prevent subjects from being 'ensnared or brought in danger by forms and proceedings in courts of justice, in an unknown language.' Importantly for Americans, however, the act specifically applied only to 'that part of Great Britain called England', and noted specifically that 'nothing in this act, nor any thing herein contained, shall extend to certifying beyond the seas any case or proceedings in the court of admirality, but that in such cases the commissions and proceedings may be certified in Latin as formerly they have been.' See *Statutes at Large*, vol. xvi, pp. 248–9.

40. The charge against Lilburne was that he 'didst maliciously, advisedly, and traitorously publish' 'false, poisonous, traitorous and scandolous' books such as *An Outcry of the Young-men and Apprentices of London, or an Inquisition after the lost Fundamental Laws and Liberties of England* which called the present government, among other things, 'tyrannous and usurped' and 'unlawful'. T. B. Howell, *State Trials* (London, 1816), vol. iv, pp. 1130, 1131, 1136. Although Lilburne's actual crime might be construed as seditious libel, he was charged with treason based on a number of statutes passed by the Rump in 1649 which extended the Treason Acts to the expression of opinion. Lilburne's opinions had been particularly sharply expressed in, for example, *England's New Chains Discovered* (London, 26 Feb. 1649) and *The Second Part of England's New Chains Discovered* (London, 24 March 1649). See W. Haller and G. Davies, eds, *Leveller Tracts, 1647–1653* (New York, 1944).

41. Howell, *State Trials*, vol. IV, pp. 1274–5.

42. Howell, *State Trials*, vol. IV, p. 1275.

43. Howell, *State Trials*, vol. V. pp. 407–19, 419–44. Lilburne's claim was again a technical one. See Thomas Green, *Verdict According to Conscience*, pp. 170–199, for a suggestion that the character of Lilburne's legal arguments grew more radical throughout his trials.

44. Howell, *State Trials*, vol. V, p. 416. In general, Lilburne made extensive use of quotations from Coke at his trials, as he did in his writings such as *The Legall Fundamentall Liberties of the People of England* (June 1649), in Haller and Davies, *Leveller Tracts*, p. 434.

45. *The Legall Fundamentall Liberties*, in Haller and Davies, *Leveller Tracts*, p. 434.

46. Howell, *State Trials*, vol. IV, p. 1381. Lilburne's case was not strengthened here by a mistake in incorrectly citing as support Coke's *Commentary on Plowden* instead of *Littleton*.

47. Howell, *State Trials*, vol. IV, p. 1381. Coke, *The First Part of the Institutes of the Laws of England: Or, A Commentarie upon Littleton* (1628; London, 1809), p. 366.

48. John Jones, *Jurors Judges of Law and Fact: Or certain Observations of certain differences in points of Law . . .* (London, w.d., 1650), p. 16. Despite Jones's attack on the claim that common men – 'mech-

anics, bred up illiterately in handicrafts' – were incapable of understanding the law, and his scathing criticism of lawyers (and judges) for having composed law in an 'uncouth Giberish of their own making', in a language of 'hotch-potch French and quelquechose latin', Jones still recognizes there will be cases which require 'men of social ability to interpret the laws' (pp. 47–50, 51–2, 78–9).

49. Howell, *State Trials*, vol. IV, pp. 1379, 1380.
50. Howell, *State Trials*, vol. IV, p. 1307.
51. Howell, *State Trials*, vol. V, p. 446.
52. Perhaps more importantly, despite Lilburne's acquittal of 1653, he remained a prisoner of state 'for the peace of this nation' until his death in 1657. See Pauline Gregg, *Free-Born John: A Biography of John Lilburne* (London, 1961), pp. 333–4.
53. Howell, *State Trials*, vol. VI, pp. 954f. Both Mead and Penn were charged with breach of the peace and unlawful assembly rather than directly breaching the recently renewed Conventicles Act. Penn and Mead published their own account of the trial as *The People's Antient and Just Liberties* (London, 1670), cited in Green, *Verdict According to Conscience*, p. 222. A sample of the tracts discussing the role of juries may be found in (Anon.), *The Jury-man charged: or, A Letter to a Citizen of London* (London, 1664), H. L.; William Smith, *Some Clear Truths* (London, 1664).
54. J. Gough, *Fundamental Law in English Constitutional History* (London, 1955), p. 206; Edward Corwin, 'Progress of Political Theory from the Revolution to the Founding', *American Historical Review*, vol. 30, 1924–25, p. 522.
55. Goebel, *History of the Supreme Court*, p. 92.
56. This was to remain true until the passage of Fox's Libel Act in 1792. See T. F. Plucknett, *A Concise History of the Common Law* (Boston, 1956), p. 501.
57. William Blackstone, *Commentaries*, IV, ch. II, pp. 150–1.
58. E. P. Thompson, *Whigs and Hunters* (London, 1975), pp. 158–69. On Thompson's account, Whig rulers were prisoners of their own rhetoric. '[T]hey played the game of power according to rules which suited them, but they could not break those rules or the whole game would be thrown away' (p. 263).
59. S. R. Gardiner, *History of England*, vol. VII, pp. 123, 361.
60. Stephen, *History of the Criminal Law* (London, 1883), pp. 382, 383. Stephen adds that 'the popular notions about the safeguards provided by the trial by jury, if only 'the good old laws of England' were observed, were, I think, as fallacious as the popular conception of those imaginary good old laws'. Stephen also called the ten years preceding 1688 'perhaps the most important in the judicial history of England'. It was not until an act of 1760 that it was provided for the continuance of judge's commissions on the death of the King (Geo. III, cap. 23). *Statutes at Large*, vol. XXIII, pp. 305–6.
61. Holdsworth, *History of English Law*, vol. V, p. 351.
62. See the trial of Algernon Sidney, in T. B. Howell, *State Trials*, vol. IX, pp. 815ff.

63. Holdsworth, *History of English Law*, vol. V. pp. 475–7.
64. G. W. Paton and D. P. Durham, eds, *Jurisprudence* (Oxford, 1982), p. 332. For example, Coke had earlier denied the right of habeas corpus in certain cases and had denied Parliament's authority to limit the royal prerogative.
65. Holdsworth, *History of English Law*, vol. V, pp. 474–5; Paton and Durham, *Jurisprudence*, p. 332.
66. Gordon Wood, *The Creation of the American Republic* (New York, 1969), p. 263.
67. Plucknett, *Concise History of the Common Law*, p. 248.
68. Rodney Barker, *Political Ideas in Modern Britain* (London, 1978), p. 260.
69. Holdsworth, *History of English Law*, vol I, p. 350.
70. See *Throckmorton's Case* (1554), *State Trials*, vol. II, p. 869.
71. *Floyd v. Barker* (1608), *Collected Reports*, vol. 12, pp. 23–4.
72. Holdsworth, *History of English Law*, vol. I, p. 345. While technically permissible, the practice of fining jurors was less common in the first half of the seventeenth century than in the 1660s, when judges attempted to enforce the unpopular Conventicles Act (1664) against Quakers. In fact, most Quakers were convicted, although not without considerable evidence of extreme pressure and harassment from the bench in several cases. See T. A. Green, 'The Jury, Seditious Libel and the Criminal Law', in R. H. Helmholz and T. A. Green, *Juries, Libel, and Justice: the Role of English Juries in Seventeenth- and Eighteenth-Century Trials for Libel and Slander* (Los Angeles, 1984), p. 80.
73. Holdsworth, *History of English Law*, p. 344.
74. Vaughan, 135 C.P. (Common Pleas). See *The English Reports* (Edinburgh, 1912), vol. 124, p. 1006. See also Holdsworth, *History of English Law*, vol. IX, p. 29; vol. I, p. 345.
75. *Bushell's Case, The English Reports*, vol. 124, p. 1010. This has also been the interpretation of at least one later historian examining the case. See Mark De Wolfe Howe, 'Juries as Judges of Criminal Law', *Harvard Law Review*, vol. 52, 1939, pp. 582–3. This case was somewhat unusual insofar as the Justices exchanged words with the jurors, particularly Bushell, about the basis of the verdict.
76. Even arguably the most influential pamphlet of the period, John Hawles' *The English-Men's Right* (1680), would require considerable stretching of interpretation by later generations of American colonists to suggest anything more than that juries must be allowed to determine the general issue of law and fact together in order to avoid becoming 'engines of oppression'. See also John Somers, *The Security of English-mens Lives or the Trust, Power, and Duty of the Grand Jury of England* (London, 1682), p. 2 (H. L.); [H. E.], *The Jury-man charged; or, A Letter to a Citizen of London. Wherein it is shewed the true meaning of the Statute, Entitled, An Act to prevent and Supress Seditious Conventicles* (London, 1664), p. 1 (H. L.). The tract refers to 'false Glosses and Interpretations detected', and accuses judges of having made 'a nose of Wax of the Law, and suffer the Law to be

baffled' (pp. 1, 15); John Hawles, *Remarks upon the Tryals of Edward Fitz harris . . . Colonel Sidney . . . and the Award of Execution against Sir Thomas Armstrong* (London, 1689) (H. L.), p. 47 Hawles notes that 'the Judges having been made by [the King], and it is in his Power to turn them out, punish, to prefer or reward them higher . . .' (pp. 76–9, 93, 101, 103); John Hawles, *The Grand-Jury-man's Oath and Office Explained: And the Rights of English-Men Asserted* (London, 1680) (H. L.), pp. 12–15; William Penn, *The People's Ancient and Just Liberties* (London, 1670) (H. L.); William Penn, *Truth Rescued From Imposture* (London, 1670) (H. L.); Henry Care, *English Liberties: Or, the Free-Born Subjects' Inheritance* (London, 1700, 1st ed., 1682), pp. 134–5; [John Tutchin], *The Observator*, vol. II, no. 40, 21–5 Aug. 1703; no. 41, 25–8 Aug. 1703 (H. L. Film SC8)

77. For a brief discussion of these trials, see Philip Hamburger, 'The Development of the Law of Seditious Libel and the Control of the Press', *Stanford Law Review*, vol. 37, 1985, pp. 698–700. *Trial of Dover, Brewster & Brooks* (1663), Howell, *State Trials*, vol. 6, p. 540; *Trial of John Pym* (1664), 82 *English Reports*, p. 1068; *Trial of Sir Samuel Barnadiston* (1684), *State Trials*, vol. IX, pp 1334–5; *Proceedings Against Richard Baxter*, *State Trials*, vol. XI (1685), p. 494: see Hamburger, pp. 698–9.

78. E. G. Henderson, 'The Background of the Seventh Amendment', *Harvard Law Review*, vol. 80, 1966, p. 333. While securing the right to juries to render a general verdict, the act clearly delineated the standard division between law and fact. It is a commonplace that in the years following passage of Fox's Libel Act, prosecution for seditious libel increased and juries convicted more often than previously. See Holdsworth, *History of English Law*, vol. X, p. 693; and D. A. Rubini, 'The Precarious Independence of the Judiciary, 1688–1701', *Law Quarterly Review*, vol. 83, 1967, pp. 343–55.

79. *Bushell's Case, The English Reports*, vol. 124, p. 1010. Even Robert Ferguson – considered by more recent accounts to have been the most politically radical of Whigs – remained conservative on this issue. See *The Second Part of No Protestant Plot* (London, 1682), pp. 20, 27, 28; (Anon.), *A Guide to Juries: Setting Forth their Antiquity, Power and Duty, From the Common-Law and Statutes . . . by a Person of Quality* (London, 1699; handwritten manuscript, 1689) (H. L.).

80. *Bushell's Case, The English Reports*, vol. 124, p. 1010.

81. Howell, *State Trials*, vol. IX, p. 817; John H. Langbein, 'The Criminal Trial before the Lawyers', *University of Chicago Law Review*, vol. 45, 1978, pp. 263ff.

82. Howell, *State Trials*, vol. XII, p. 183.

83. Hamburger, 'Development of the Law of Seditious Libel', p.699.

84. Hawles, *The English-Men's Right*, pp. 1–3.

85. (Anon.), *Of Tryals by a Jury* (1722), reprinted in *Justices and Juries in Colonial America* (New York, 1972), p. 297.

86. *English Reports*, vol. 124, p. 1010.

87. H. T. Dickinson, 'The Eighteenth-Century Debate on the Sovereignty of Parliament', pp. 192, 205; Dickinson, 'The Eighteenth Century

Debate on the "Glorious Revolution" ', *History*, vol. 61, 1976, pp. 29–45. J. A. W. Gunn, *Politics and the Public Interest in the Seventeenth Century* (London, 1969), p. 308. Gunn makes the very interesting suggestion that this expropriation of 'salus populi' by the Whigs under Walpole to justify 'reason of state' may explain the reluctance of later radicals, such as Wilkes, to employ it as a rallying cry for critics of government. Philip Hamburger has shown that the doctrine of seditious libel was substantially broadened in the aftermath of the Glorious Revolution to include 'seditious' criticisms of government generally, not just of particular officials, as had been the practice in Coke's time. Likewise the notion of treason was expanded to be used as a means of controlling a critical press. Hamburger, 'Development of the Law of Seditious Libel', p. 720.

88. Blackstone, *Commentaries*, IV, c. 33, s.5; Howell, *State Trials*, vol. VIII, p. 243.

89. Betty Kemp, *Kings and Commons: 1660–1732* (New York, 1957); J. H. Plumb, *The Growth of Political Stability in England, 1675–1725* (London, 1967).

90. See 'Some Remarks Upon Government and Particularly Upon the Establishment of the English Monarchy . . . in Two Letters Written by and To a member of the Great Convocation Holden at Westminster . . . the 22nd of Jan., 1688–89 by A.B.N.T', cited in Gunn, *Politics and the Public Interest*, p. 9. I owe the point concerning the restriction of the franchise in England after 1688 from a 40-shilling to a 200-pound freehold to Mr Alan Houston. For a discussion of the treatment of Catholic and Protestant dissenters, see E. P. Thompson, *Whigs and Hunters;* Douglas Hay *et al.* (eds), *Albion's Fatal Tree: Crime and Society in Eighteenth-Century England* (New York, 1975).

91. Helmholz and Green, *Juries, Libel, and Justice*, pp. viii, ix. Under the reforming guidance of Justice Holt, the Bench worked assiduously to eliminate altogether any jural space that might lead to acquittals in seditious libel cases. These modifications introduced by Holt, which in each case limited the ability of juries to avoid convictions, effectively structured the deferential attitude of English juries toward judges with regard to law, until passage of Fox's Libel Act in 1792. Indeed as late as 1783, Chief Justice Mansfield called the juries '(j)ealousy of leaving the law to the Court . . . puerile rant and declamation. The judges are totally independent of the ministers that may happen to be, and of the King himself.' Mansfield uttered this statement after having entered a verdict of conviction in the seditious libel prosecution of William Shipley, Dean of St Asaph (*State Trials*, vol. 21, p. 1040). The jury had found Shipley 'guilty of publishing only'. See Hamburger, 'Development of the Law of Seditious Libel', p. 756; Green, *Verdict According to Conscience*, p. 328.

92. Hamburger, 'Development of the Law of Seditious Libel', p. 752. Special juries, particularly those struck for seditious libel trials, tended to empanel groups of individuals – merchants, grocers, skilled craftesmen – from higher economic and social classes than ordinary juries. See Green, *Verdict According to Conscience*, p. 308.

93. See H. Mission, 'Memoirs and Observations in his Travels over England' (London, 1698, trans. 1719), p. 328. Cited in Green, *Verdict According to Conscience*, p. 278.
94. Leonard Levy, *Legacy of Supression: Freedom of Speech in Early American History* (Cambridge, Mass., 1960), p. 254; T. E. May, *Constitutional History of England*, vol. II, p. 142–50; *Rex v. Winterbottom*, in *State Trials*, vol. XXII, p. 875.

3 JURIES AND AMERICAN REVOLUTIONARY JURISPRUDENCE

1. Edmund Burke, 'Letter to the Sheriffs of Bristol', *Writings and Speeches of Edmund Burke* (London, n.d.), vol. 2, pp. 192–3. Julius Goebel, *The Law Practice of Alexander Hamilton* (New York, 1964–80), vol. I, p. 284. Attempts were made by British authorities to evade jury trials of colonial resisters to applications of the Docks Act (1772) and the Administration of Justice Act (1774). See Julius Goebel, Jr, *History of the Supreme Court*, pp. 87–8.
2. *Forsey v. Cunningham*, 1765, denied any right of appeal to a jury verdict beyond the writ of error. See also Herbert Johnson, *Essays on New York Colonial Legal History* (Westport, 1981), p. 154.
3. See Julius Goebel, Jr, *History of the Supreme Court*, p. 87.
4. Bernard Bailyn, *The Ideological Origins of the American Revolution* (Cambridge, Mass., 1967), p. 46. See also Bailyn's excellent introduction in his *Pamphlets of the American Revolution 1750–1776* (Cambridge, Mass., 1965), vol. I. The opposition writers, whose members sometimes referred to themselves as 'Whigs of the old stamp', have been characterized as a shifting coalition of Tories and dissident Whigs, who stressed the dangers to England's heritage of the loss of pristine virtue under the corruption of Walpole's 'Robinocracy'.
5. Bailyn, *Ideological Origins of the American Revolution*, p. 319.
6. John Rodney to Caesar Rodney, 3 March 1770. See G. H. Ryden, ed., *Letters to and from Caesar Rodney* (Philadelphia, 1933), p. 32.
7. See Sumner C. Powell, *Puritan Village: The Formation of a New England Town* (Garden City, 1965, pp. 179–82; John Demos, *A Little Commonwealth* (Oxford, 1970), pp. 48–50.
8. *Writings and Speeches of Edmund Burke*, vol. 2, pp. 128–9.
9. Gordon Wood, 'Conspiracy and the Paranoid Style', *William and Mary Quarterly*, vol. 32, July 1982, p. 407. The notion of the 'paranoid style' originated in the work of Richard Hofstadter, *The Paranoid Style in American Politics and Other Essays* (New York, 1965). However, Hofstadter employed the term pejoratively, and stopped short of characterizing the Revolution in such terms. Bailyn, on the other hand, is not attempting to reduce our understanding of the Revolution to mass psychosis. He characterizes the American revolutionaries as 'profoundly reasonable men, men of businesslike sanity', (*Ideological Origins*, pp. 18–19). Yet, to a complacent British government, the revolutionaries' fears of conspiratorial threats to liberty seemed irrational. See Bailyn, *The Ordeal of Thomas Hutchinson* (Cambridge,

Mass., 1974), pp. 2, 15. See also James H. Hutson, 'The Origins of "The Paranoid Style in American Politics": Public Jealousy from the Age of Walpole to the Age of Jackson', in J. H. Murrin *et al.*, eds, *Saints and Revolutionaries: Essays on Early American History* (New York, 1984), pp. 332–72.

10. See Richard Ashcraft, *Revolutionary Politics and Locke's Two Treatises of Government* (Princeton, 1986) for what now seems to be the definitive statement on Locke's active participation in the planning and financial support of Monmouth's Rebellion in 1685. My disagreement with this truly outstanding work is that in nesting Locke's philosophical and political writings so deeply in the historical context, one threatens to seriously underestimate Locke's profound originality as a thinker on an order wholly other than Shaftesbury and his ilk.

11. 'Speech on Conciliation with America', *Writings and Speeches of Edmund Burke*, vol. 2, p. 136.

12. Gordon Wood, *The Creation of the American Republic, 1776–1787* (New York, 1969), pp. 292, 625, 457. See also the now classic account of Edward Corwin, 'The Higher Law Background of American Constitutional Law', *Harvard Law Review*, vol. 42, 1928–9.

13. Wood, *Creation of the American Republic*, p. 457, fn. 43.

14. On this point, my own conclusions have profited greatly from discussions with Samuel H. Beer and from the important studies of Wilkite radicals by Pauline Maier and by John Brewer; see Pauline Maier, 'John Wilkes and American Disillusionment with Britain', *William and Mary Quarterly*, vol. 20, 1963, pp. 373–95; John Brewer, 'The Wilkites and the Law, 1763–74: a study of radical notions of governance', in John Brewer and John Styles, eds, *An Ungovernable People* (London, 1980), pp. 11–19, 128–71. See also an earlier but still helpful study of parliamentary reform by G. S. Veitch, *The Genesis of Parliamentary Reform* (London, 1965), p. 43.

15. John Trenchard and Thomas Gordon, *Cato's Letters or, Essays on Liberty, Civil and Religious, and Other Important Subjects* (New York, 1969), vol. 3, no. 85, p. 162. It should be noted that Trenchard and Gordon differed sharply in their confidence in the judgment of ordinary people: Trenchard harboured the greater elitist sentiments, and Gordon often sounded similar to Thomas Paine in his egalitarian expressions.

16. Burke, 'Speech on Conciliation with America', *Writings and Speeches*, vol. 2, pp. 124–5.

17. Donald Veall, *The Popular Movement for Law Reform: 1640–60* (Oxford, 1970), p. 100. Certainly, in Britain, barristers remained some of the most ardent critics of the colonial position. See (Anon.), *An Examination of the Rights of the Colonies upon Principles of Law. By a Gentleman at the Bar* (London: R. Dymott and J. Almon), 1776, pp. 6, 10, 11, 37.

18. Bailyn, *Ideological Origins of the American Revolution*, p. 28. The real effort to excise Locke's name from the 'discourse' of revolution in the eighteenth century has come not from Bailyn, but from J. G. A. Pocock. Pocock's somewhat justified early conclusion in 1971,

that 'the textbook account of Augustan political thought as *Locke et praeterea nihil* badly needs revision', swelled by 1972 to the claim that the predominant language of eighteenth-century politics was one in which Locke did not even figure. See 'Virtue and Commerce in the Eighteenth Century', *Journal of Interdisciplinary History*, vol. 3, 1972, p. 120. This much stronger view has been echoed by others, such as Robert Shalhope, 'Toward a Republican Synthesis: The Emergence of an Understanding in American Historiography', *William and Mary Quarterly*, vol. 29, 1972, pp. 49–80. However, this much stronger 'understanding' is not widely shared and, many have argued, not defensible. For a sample of these critics, see Herbert Storing, *The Complete Anti-Federalist* (Chicago, 1981), vol. I, pp. 4, 40, 83, 91, nt. 39, 41; Isaac Kramnick, 'Republican Revisionism Revisited', *American Historical Review*, vol. 87, June 1982, pp. 629–64; Joyce Appleby, 'What Is Still American in the Political Philosophy of Thomas Jefferson?', *William and Mary Quarterly*, vol. 39, 1982, pp. 283–309; Appleby, 'Republicanism in Old and New Contexts', *William and Mary Quarterly*, vol. 43, 1986, pp. 20–34; John P. Diggins, *The Lost Soul of American Politics* (New York, 1984). In addition to Bailyn's analysis, a more balanced assessment than Pocock's can be found in Donald S. Lutz, 'The Relative Influence of European Writers on Late Eighteenth-Century American Political Thought', *American Political Science Review*, vol. 78, 1984, pp. 189–97.

19. Bailyn, *The Origins of American Politics* (New York, 1968), p. 41. In Bailyn's edition of *Pamphlets of the American Revolution*, there are actually more recorded references made to Locke than to Trenchard and Gordon. Bailyn's work has been the focus of sharp criticism by at least one study of the importance of Locke's thought in the election sermons and writings of the revolutionary New England clergy. See Steven M. Dworetz, 'The Radical Side of American Constitutionalism: Locke and the New England Clergy, Revisited', a paper presented at the New England Political Science Association Annual Convention at Trinity College in Hartford, Connecticut, 5 April 1986.

20. Gilbert Ryle, *Critica*, 1967. Explicit presentations of the impact and importance of Locke's epistemological claims for the character and availability of human knowledge and moral certainty in judgment, and for evidence of the interrelatedness of this epistemology to theology and political theory, can be found in the election sermons cited and discussed by Alice Mary Baldwin, *The New England Clergy and the American Revolution* (Durham, N.C., 1928), and by Kenneth Murdoch in *Literature and Theology in Colonial New England* (New York, 1949). The importance of Lockean epistemology to early colonial religious and political thought has been further developed by Steven M. Dworetz, 'The Radical Side of American Constitutionalism: Locke and the New England Clergy, Revisited'. The importance of Locke's *Essay* to early eighteenth-century colonial literature has been emphasized by Cathy Davidson, *Revolution and the Word* (New York, 1986); by Emory Elliot, *Revolutionary Writers: Literature and Authority in the New Republic, 1725–1810* (New York, 1982); and

most explicitly by Robert Ferguson, *Law and Letters in American Culture* (Cambridge, Mass., 1984). For the impact of Locke's *Thoughts on Education*, see James Axtell, *The School Upon the Hill: Education and Society in Colonial New England* (New York, 1974), pp. 50, 51–2, 78–9, 85, 195, 245. That Locke's *Essay* was commonly used to teach reading in colonial America from as early as 1715 to as late as 1800, see Richard Ellis, *The New England Mind in Transition* (New Haven, 1973), pp. 34, 188–9, 198–9; Eugene P. Link, *The Democratic-Republican Societies: 1790–1800* (New York, 1965), p. 105.

21. John Dunn, 'The Politics of Locke in England and America in the Eighteenth Century', in John Yolton, ed., *John Locke: Problems and Perspectives* (Cambridge, 1969), p. 66. Dunn's effort fiercely to excise the relevance of Locke's ideas in colonial America is puzzling on several counts. Dunn offers a highly constrained framework for this claim – 'an outline history of the ways in which a single book [*Two Treatises*] was sensed to be relevant in England and America in the eighteenth century' (54). The method of establishing the insignificance of this work is to resort to the simplistic and inaccurate methodology of speculating about the actual number of copies in colonial libraries before the Revolution. Such a method is highly prone to error, as when Dunn claims that 'there is no evidence that the *Two Treatises* figured in the set curriculum of any American college before the revolution' (71). Dennis Thompson's own work in this area suggests otherwise. See 'The Education of a Founding Father: The Reading List for John Witherspoon's Course in Political Theory, as Taken by James Madison', *Political Theory*, vol. 4, 1976, p. 527. Dunn himself recognizes the obvious inadequacy of this method to 'demonstrate that few Americans read the *Two Treatises* before the revolutionary period.' Indeed, he provides some startling evidence of his own of the impressive use of 'the brilliant presentation of Locke's theory of government' by such radical religious critics of authority as Elisha Williams in 1744. In addition, by limiting the focus to the *Two Treatises* alone, Dunn sets up an unnecessary and invidious distinction between the relevance of the *Essay* and the *Two Treatises* to colonial thinking. This seems all the more surprising in light of Dunn's explicit concern with the relevance of Lock's epistemology to political thinking.

22. Bailyn, *Ideological Origins of the American Revolution*, p. 207. John Adams would later recall that Mayhew's *Discourse* was 'read by everybody, celebrated by friends, and abused by enemies', C. F. Adams, *The Works of John Adams* (Boston, 1850–56), vol. X, p. 288.

23. J. W. Thornton, ed., *The Pulpit of the American Revolution: Or the Political Sermons of the Period of 1776* (Boston, 1860), pp. 73–86. For an extensive discussion of the thoroughgoing influence of Locke on the election sermons of the New England clergy, see Steven M. Dworetz, 'The Radical Side of American Constitutionalism'. The present analysis differs from that of Professor Dworetz in focusing on

the explicit impact on colonial Americans of Locke's *Essay*, and his general epistemology, rather than his political or religious writings.

24. Mayhew claimed that the great modern teachers of liberty were 'Sidney, Milton, Locke and Hoadley'. Alden Bradford, *Memoir of the Life and Writings of Reverend Jonathan Mayhew* (Boston, 1838), pp. 96–97. See *Second Treatise*, sec. 168, pp. 426–7.

25. John Locke, *An Essay Concerning Human Understanding*, ed. P. H. Nidditch (Oxford, 1975), bk. I, ch. 3, p. 75.

26. Locke, *Essay Concerning Human Understanding*, bk. I, ch. 3, pp. 75, 82–3.

27. Locke, *Essay Concerning Human Understanding*, bk. I, ch. 3, p. 72.

28. Locke, *Essay Concerning Human Understanding*, bk. I, ch. 4, p. 99. Obviously, such a reading of Locke's epistemology throws out all efforts to understand him as a proponent of a hedonistic calculus and as a sceptic of natural law. I accept John Dunn's claim that Locke founded the legitimacy of political society upon the law of nature construed both as the reason and the will of God. I also agree with Dunn's argument that the best understanding of Locke's law of nature rests in the attempt to interpret his works within the broad social and psychological underpinning of the Calvinist world view. However, the extent to which colonial Americans, while accepting in its broadest terms both the politics of Locke and his perceptions of the epistemological foundations of the legal order, also accepted the reasons and rationale which Dunn claims alone made them acceptable to Locke is a separate issue, and one not to be addressed here. See John Dunn, *John Locke's Political Philosophy* (Oxford, 1973), pp. 87–95, 187–202, 237, 238.

29. Locke, *Essay Concerning Human Understanding*, bk. I, ch. 3, pp. 82–3.

30. Julian Franklin has recognized the innovation of Locke's argument for popular sovereignty, and effectively linked aspects of Locke's constitutional thought to that of one other contemporary cleric and writer, George Lawson. See *John Locke and the Theory of Sovereignty* (Cambridge, 1978).

31. *Two Treatises of Government*, II, sec. 3, p. 308.

32. *Two Treatises of Government*, intro., p. 94; *Essay Concerning Human Understanding*, bk. II, ch. 21, sec. 67, p. 278.

33. *Two Treatises of Government*, bk. II, sec. 124, p. 396; sec. 136, p. 404.

34. *Two Treatises of Government*, II, sec. 86, p. 367; sec. 149, p. 413.

35. Blackstone, *Commentaries on the Law of England*, vol. I, p. 161.

36. Blackstone, *Commentaries*, vol. I, pp. 51, 160.

37. Edmund Burke, 'Speech on Conciliation with America',*Writings and Speeches*, vol. 2, p. 137.

38. *Two Treatises of Government*, II, sec. 57, p. 348.

39. *Two Treatises of Government*, II, sec. 137, p. 406. Locke recognized that little of importance distinguished absolute from arbitrary power. Both reduced the rule of law to rule by law, that is by men. For this reason, the principle of restricting both the Crown and the Parliament

(both take part in the 'legislative' power of his theory) by fundamental law as the common lawyers understood it held little currency for him. He rejected the medieval authority for fundamental law adduced by Coke, and actual events had proven there simply were no legal limitations on Parliament.

40. Locke's critique of the 'pre-political' state of nature is that it is inappropriately structured juridically. First, it lacks an 'established and known law', and men – given the 'bias in their Interest, are not apt to allow of (the Law of Nature) as a law binding to them, in the application to their particular cases.' Second, it leaves every man to be judge in his own case, since there is no 'known and indifferent Judge'. Given the psychology of the *Essay*, this situation produces not a war of all against all – men are not psychologically so independent – but a degree of factionalism in which 'Men partial to themselves and their Friends' pursue their own interests to the detriment of others. However, man's natural situation is not one of chaotic disorderliness; rather each man has both the juridical and executive powers of the law of nature until government is instituted. Locke characterizes it as a state of men 'living together according to reason, without a common Superior on Earth, with Authority to judge between them.' It is also a state of equality in the only sense that is relevant to Locke: a jural equality in the common set of duties men owe to God. See *Two Treatises of Government*, II, sec. 46, property and money; sec. 77, family; sec. 56, religion; sec. 69, education; sec. 72, inheritance; and obviously, war; see also II, sec. 19, p. 321.

41. *Two Treatises of Government*, II, sec. 137, 406; sec. 142, p. 409.

42. With regard to the *Federalist*, the effort to excise Locke's influence seems particularly futile. It is the concepts, the categories, or, if one prefers, the discourse of Locke that informs the central questions addressed by Publius. Publius speaks the language of consent, of the natural rights of individuals, and above all he speaks the voice of the people's power to judge, rather than the language of virtuous rule.

43. Locke, *Essay Concerning Human Understanding*, bk. I, ch. 4, p. 101. Locke adds, 'What he believes only, and takes upon trust, are but shreds; which however well in the whole piece, make no considerable addition to his stock, who gathers them. Such borrowed Wealth, like Fairy-money, though it were Gold in the hand from which he received it, will be but Leaves and Dust when it comes to use.'

44. Thomas Jefferson to Thomas Priestly, 21 March 1801, in A. Koch and W. Peden, *The Life and Selected Writings of Thomas Jefferson* (New York, 1954), p. 562.

45. For a sampling of this argument in the pamphlet and sermon literature, see C. S. Hyneman and D. S. Lutz, *American Political Writing During the Founding Era, 1760–1805* (Indianapolis, 1983), vol. I, especially pieces by 'Aequus', pp. 62–6; Richard Bland, 'An Inquiry into the Rights of the Colonies', 1766, pp. 67–87; John Tucker, 'An Election Sermon', 1771, pp. 158–74; [John Perkins] A Well-Wisher to Mankind, 'Theory of Agency; Or, an Essay on the Nature, Source and extent of Moral Freedom', 1771, pp. 137–57. For a sampling of

newspaper articles, see articles in *The Massachusetts Spy*, by 'The Centinel', no. XXI, 14 November 1771, p. 1; by 'The Monitor', no. II, 5 December 1771, p. 2, which begins 'The heathen who know not the law are accursed'; 'To the British Nation', 5 December 1771, p. 2; 'The Centinel', no. XXV, 12 December 1771, p. 1; 'The Centinel', no. XXVI, 19 December 1771; 'A Political Dialogue between Sylvester and Philarchias', no. 22, 20 September 1770. For examples outside of Massachusetts, see articles in the *Virginia Gazette*, for 12 January 1769 [Rind]; 6 July 1769 [Rind]; 22 and 29 April 1773 [Rind]; 25 February 1773 [Purdie and Dixon]; 16 February 1775 [Pinckney]; 7 April 1775 [Purdie]. It is, of course, also a claim central to *Cato's Letters*, and one developed in explicitly Lockean terms. See no. 38 (22 July 1721), 'The Right and Capacity of the People to judge the Government'.

46. Alexis de Tocqueville, *Democracy in America* (New York, 1976), pp. 272–3. It is not insignificant that perhaps the first American reprint of an English lawbook may have been the radical jury tract by Sir John Hawles, *The Englishman's Right* (1693).

47. William Nelson, 'The Eighteenth-Century background of John Marshall's Jurisprudence', *Michigan Law Review*, vol. 76, 1978, p. 904. See also David Konig, *Law and Society in Puritan Massachusetts: Essex County, 1629–1692* (Chapel Hill, 1979).

48. Clinton Rossiter, ed., *The Federalist Papers* (New York, 1961), no. 82, p. 490.

49. Nelson, 'The Eighteenth-Century Background of John Marshall's Jurisprudence', pp. 917, 904; Nelson, *Americanization of the Common Law* (Cambridge, Mass., 1975), p. 21.

50. Amasa M. Eaton, 'The Development of the Judicial System in Rhode Island', *Yale Law Journal*, vol. 14, 1905, pp. 148, 153.

51. For an interesting study of the relative importance and difficulties of juries in colonial New York, see Douglas Greenberg, *Crime and Law Enforcement in the Colony of New York: 1691–1776* (Ithaca, 1974), pp. 172, 175–6.

52. William Nelson, 'The Legal Restraint on Power in Pre-Revolutionary America: Massachusetts as a Case Study, 1760–1775', *American Journal of Legal History*, vol. 18, 1974, p. 28.

53. Mark De Wolfe Howe, 'Juries as Judges of Criminal Law', *Harvard Law Review*, vol. 52, 1939, p. 584.

54. See Perry Miller, *The Life of the Mind in America* (New York, 1965), pp. 105f; Wood, *Creation of the American Republic*, p. 300, no. 68.

55. Burke, 'Speech on Conciliation with America', p. 166. Bailyn, *Ideological Origins of the American Revolution*, p. 105.

56. Adam Smith, *Lectures on Jurisprudence* (Indianapolis, 1982), pp. 286–7; Milton M. Klein, 'Prelude to Revolution in New York: Jury Trials and Judicial Tenure', *William and Mary Quarterly*, vol. 17, 1960, p. 452; Bailyn, *Ideological Origins of the American Revolution*, p. 105.

57. Cited in Klein, 'Prelude to Revolution', p. 455.

58. ibid.

59. Cited in Klein, 'Prelude to Revolution', p. 457.
60. ibid., p. 457.
61. Leonard Levy, *Emergence of a Free Press* (Oxford, 1985), pp. 63–4. In at least one of these successful prosecutions, *The Case of John Checkley* (1724), the judge was able to impose a special verdict. Levy's new work represents a remarkable rethinking and to some extent recantation of his powerful revisionist history, *Legacy of Suppression; Freedom of Speech in Early American History* (Cambridge, 1960). For example, Levy now asserts, he was wrong in claiming that the American experience with freedom of political expression was 'as slight as the conceptual and legal understanding was narrow' (p. x). Part of Levy's newer insight is that it *is* significant that while some colonies, such as New York, technically possessed a common law of seditious libel, colonial juries refused to find defendants guilty. On this basis, Levy quite correctly takes issue with the earlier claim by James Morton Smith that 'one method used to crush colonial opposition to ministerial policies was an accelerated use of the law of seditious libel.' *Freedom's Fetters: The Alien and Sedition Laws and American Civil Liberties* (Ithaca, 1956), pp. 426–7. Opposition was not crushed; the use of the seditious libel law was pointless in the face of jural intransigence. It would seem important to stress, however, that the argument developed here does not directly challenge Levy's work, nor suggest that expansive civil liberties were recognized and upheld by American colonials, but rather only that expansive jural powers were upheld.
62. *Rex v. Franklin*, Howell, *State Trials*, vol. 17, 1731, pp. 625–76.
63. Howell, *State Trials*, vol. 17, p. 628.
64. Howell, *State Trials*, vol. 17, p. 676.
65. Green, *Verdict According to Conscience*, p. 321.
66. As Levy notes, even prior to *Zenger*, in the trials for seditious libel of William Bradford (1693) and Thomas Maule (1696), juries were informed – to the consternation of judges – that they could render a general verdict and 'decide the law over the heads of the judges.' *Legacy of Suppression*, pp. 27, 33.
67. *The New York Weekly Journal*, no. 23, 8 April 1734; *The Trial of John Peter Zenger*, Howell (ed.), *State Trials*, vol. 17, 1735, p. 692. See also Stanley Katz, (ed.), *A Brief Narrative of the Case and Trial of John Peter Zenger, by James Alexander* (Cambridge, Mass., 1963), pp. 136, 4809, 58061, 133–8.
68. Milton Klein, 'The Rise of the New York Bar: The Legal Career of William Livingstone', *William and Mary Quarterly*, vol. XV, no. 2, pp. 335–6. Douglas Greenberg, *Law Enforcement in the Colony of New York 1691–1776* (Ithaca: Cornell U. Press, 1974), p. 33. Greenberg argues that the legal ignorance of New York's colonial judges before the revolution was nothing short of appalling (pp. 174–5). See also Bruce Mann's excellent study, *Neighbours and Strangers: Law and Community in Early Connecticut* (Chapel Hill: U. of North Carolina Press, 1987), pp. 83–4. Mann notes that common law pleading 'did not take root in New England, partly because of overt hostility

to it, but also because of the dearth of attorneys to use it. Pleading could hardly be more technical than the knowledge of the pleaders'. In his study, Mann distinguishes Connecticut from the rest of New England in order to demonstrate the former's general decline in the use of civil juries in eighteenth century. However, Mann also notes that while declining in use, Connecticut juries appeared to gain in strength through their ability (after 1715) to resist any judicial effort at overturning their verdicts. 'Juries retained their ability' Mann concludes, 'to voice their opinions – and through them, those of the community – forcefully'. (p. 78).

69. Greenberg, *Law Enforcement in the Colony of New York*, pp. 33–4, 185. Greenberg notes that New York was, in many ways, 'unique among the British colonies in North America'. It is unclear whether he intends in this uniqueness to include New York's lack of at least intentional innovation in its legal system. P. M. Hamlin, *Legal Education in Colonial New York* (New York: New York University Law Quarterly Review, 1939), pp. 71, ft. nts. 38, 335, 328, 320.

70. Joseph H. Smith and Leo Hershkowitz, 'Courts of Equity in the Province of New York: The Cosby Controversy, 1732–1736', *The American Journal of Legal History*, vol. 16, 1972, p. 31.

71. Katz, *Brief Narrative of the Case and Trial of John Peter Zenger*, p. 1.

72. Katz, *Brief Narrative of the Case and Trial of John Peter Zenger*, pp. 24–6.

73. Joseph H. Smith and Leo Hershkowitz, 'Courts of Equity in the Province of New York', p. 40. Smith and Hershkowitz note that Hamilton, who practiced largely in Philadelphia, was a friend and also an associate of Alexander in the latter's New Jersey practice. The apparent ease of mobility of lawyers' practices such as these between Pennsylvania, New Jersey and New York is interesting in itself.

74. See David M. Rabban, 'The Ahistorical Historian: Leonard Levy on Freedom of Expression in Early American History', *Stanford Law Review*, vol. 37, 1985, pp. 795ff; Katz, *Brief Narrative of the Case and Trial of John Peter Zenger*, p. 69. Interestingly enough, Coke argued that the truth of a libel only intensified the offence.

75. Katz, *Brief Narrative*, p. 67. Levy has noted that while many of the arguments presented by Hamilton could be thought to be 'derived from Cato', an essential element of the Zenger defence that could not have come from Cato was the 'appeal to the jury to decide for themselves rather than be bound by the court's instructions, whether the defendant's words were libellous.' *Legacy of Suppression*, pp. xxvii–xxviii.

76. 'Reflections on Libelling', *Cato's Letters*, vol. I, no. 32 (10 June 1721), p. 247.

77. *Anglo-Americanus' critique: Remarks on the Trial of John Peter Zenger, Printer*, reprinted in Katz, *Brief Narrative*, p. 172.

78. I deliberately paraphrase the words of William Nelson here because

he has argued that such legal activity did not take place until *after* the Revolution. See *Americanization of the Common Law*, p. 19.

79. From the *Pennsylvania Gazette*, no. 492, 1735, cited by Katz, *Brief Narrative*, p. 212.

80. See, for example, articles by 'Freeborn American', in the *Boston Gazette*, 9 March 1767; articles printed in *The Massachusetts Spy*, by 'Mucius Scaevola', no. 37, .14 Nov. 1771, and by 'The Centinel, no. xxiii,' no. 39, 28 Nov. 1771, and 'The Centinel, no. xxvi,' 19 Dec. 1771, who employs Locke's arguments to suggest free discussion is essential to government; see also 'A Son of Liberty', *The New-York Gazette; or Weekly post-boy*, no. 1423, 9 April 1770.

81. One of the 'scandalous' songs printed, by Zenger in the *New York Weekly Journal* explicitly defended 'their colonial law, which required legislative approval for the introduction of any new court, from Crown attempts to impose an exchequer court on the colony. The song ran 'Exchequer courts, as void by law, great grievances we call; Though great men do assert no flaw is in them; they shall fall, And be condemned by every man that's fond of liberty. Let them withstand it all they can, our laws we will stand by.' Reprinted in Katz, *Brief Narrative*, appendix, A, p. 111.

82. *Lyon v. Cobb*, Bris. C.P. 1769, in Robert T. Paine, *Minutes of Trials and Cases*, vol. I (Mss. Massachusetts Historical Society, Boston, Mass.), cited in Nelson, 'The Legal Restraint on Power', p. 23.

83. L. K. Wroth and H. B. Zobel, eds, *The Legal Papers of John Adams* (Cambridge, Mass., 1965), vol. I, p. 230.

84. Peter van Schaak to Robert Yates, 1786, reported in Richard B. Morris, ed., *Select Cases of the Mayor's Court of New York City, 1674–1784* (Washington, 1935), p. 56, cited in Wood, *Creation of the American Republic*, p. 296.

85. Elizabeth Brown, *British Statutes in American Law, 1776–1836* (Ann Arbor, 1964).

86. See Part II, ch. 6, art. 6, in Oscar and Mary Handlin, eds, *The Popular Sources of Political Authority: Documents on the Massachusetts Constitution of 1780* (Cambridge, Mass., 1966), p. 452.

87. Merrill Jensen, *Tracts of the American Revolution, 1763–76* (Indianapolis, 1978), p. 152; see also Wood, *Creation of the American Republic*, p. 107. Dickinson's 1768 discussion here casts doubt on the claim by Morton Horwitz of a sharp break between the character of court function (oracular) in the revolutionary era and its instrumental function in the early nineteenth century. As evidence of this sharp break, Horwitz claims 'one of the most dramatic manifestations of the new role of courts is a Pennsylvania statute of 1807 empowering the judges of the Supreme Court to decide which English statutes were in force in the Commonwealth.' *The Transformation of American Law, 1780–1860*, (Cambridge, Mass., 1977), pp. 23–4.

88. James Madison, *The Virginia Report of 1799–1800, Touching the Alien and Sedition Laws; Together with the Virginia Resolutions of Dec. 21, 1798* (Richmond, Va., 1850), p. 211.

89. Thomas Paine, *Common Sense*, in P. S. Foner, ed., *The Complete*

Writings of Thomas Paine (New York, 1945), vol. I, p. 6. For a discussion of this oral tradition in law, see Robert Ferguson, *Law and Letters in American Culture* (Cambridge, Mass., 1984), p. 16.

90. Wroth and Zobel, eds, *Legal Papers of John Adams*, vol. I, p. 230.
91. Nelson, 'The Eighteenth Century Background of John Marshall's Constitutional Jurisprudence', p. 919.
92. Wood, *Creation of the American Republic*, p. 296. The conclusion, largely attributable to Zechariah Chafee Jr and which still stands up well, has been called the 'synthetic rubber hypothesis'. It suggests that colonial law combined a selection of English common law precedents and principles, Parliamentary and local statutes, and local customs into an 'elastic conception' of the common law, the meaning of which in any particular case was likely to be uncertain, or at the very least contentious, rather than simply found or spoken.
93. Wood, *Creation of the American Republic*, p. 299. Wood notes that because of the very perplexities of colonial law, the judges were free, indeed were driven, to select and innovate so as to adjust continually to local circumstances. The problem of legal knowledge and its jurisprudential implications are evident here. Roscoe Pound notes that from 1692 to 1776 Massachusetts had ten chief justices and twenty-three associate justices. Of these, only one chief justice and two associate justices were lawyers. *The Formative Era of American Law* (Boston, 1938), p. 92.
94. Governor Henry Moore of New York, 26 Feb. 1768, quoted in Irving Mark, *Agrarian Conflicts in Colonial New York, 1711–1775* (New York, 1940), p. 77. Cited in Wood, *Creation of the American Republic*, p. 296, fn. 62.
95. Thomas Hutchinson to John Sullivan, 29 Mar. 1771, in Wroth and Zobel (eds), *Legal Papers of John Adams*, vol. I, p. xli, quoted in Wood, *Creation of the American Republic*, p. 297.
96. See, for example, David Flaherty, *Privacy in Colonial New England* (Charlottesville, 1967), p. 175.
97. Thomas Jefferson, *A Summary View of the Rights of British America (1774)*, in Julian Boyd, ed., *The Papers of Thomas Jefferson* (Princeton, 1950), vol. I, p. 134.
98. Miller, *Life of the Mind in America*, p. 66.
99. Wroth and Zobel, eds, *Legal Papers of John Adams*, vol. I, p. 230.
100. John Adams to Thomas Jefferson, 1815, and Adams to Hezekiah Niles, 1818, quoted in Bailyn, *Ideological Origins of the American Revolution*, pp. 1, 160.
101. Benjamin Rush, 1787, cited in Bailyn, *Ideological Origins of the American Revolution*, p. 230. See also J. Franklin Jameson, *The American Revolution Considered as a Social Movement* (Princeton, 1926), p. 20.
102. Nelson, 'The Eighteenth Century Background of John Marshall's Constitutional Jurisprudence', p. 914.
103. Forrest McDonald, *Novus Ordo Seclorum: The Intellectual Origins of the Constitution* (Lawrence, 1985), pp. 24, 41. William Nelson notes that juries were also used in Massachusetts to settle disputes over the

location of public roads. *Americanization of the Common Law*, p. 200, fn. 51.

104. McDonald, *Novus Ordo Seclorum*, pp. 24, 41.
105. Robert Treat Paine, 'Charges to Grand Juries, 1790–1804', MS, Massachusetts Historical Society, cited in Edith Henderson, 'Sources for the Study of Law in Colonial Massachusetts at the Harvard Law School, Cambridge, Massachusetts', in Daniel Coquillette (ed.), *Law in Colonial Massachusetts, 1630–1800* (Boston, 1984). In this volume, see also Charles McKirdy, 'Massachusette Lawyers on the Eve of the American Revolution: The State of the Profession', pp. 314–15.
106. Richard Ellis, *The Jeffersonian Crisis: Courts and Politics in the Young Republic* (New York, 1971), pp. 198, 161.
107. 'Camden', *The Pittsfield Sun*, 19 Dec. 1803; 'Zenas', *Pittsfield Sun*, 5 Dec. 1803. Cited in Ellis, *Jeffersonian Crisis*, pp. 198, 324.
108. 'Decius', *Independent Chronicle* (Boston), 10 Feb. 1806. Cited in Ellis, *Jeffersonian Crisis*, pp. 202, 324.
109. Nelson, 'The Eighteenth-Century Background of John Marshall's Constitutional Jurisprudence', p. 918. These early judicial challenges were just the beginning of a series of procedural changes restructuring the relationship between judges and juries in America over the course of the nineteenth century: the growth of the category of questions of law; the evolution of rules of evidence; the development of special notice and special interrogatories. According to one law journal note upon which I have drawn for evidence in this discussion, such procedural changes 'were the concrete manifestations of an underlying change, over the course of the century, in the way people conceived of the purpose and competence of the jury, and its role in the process of government.' See, 'The Changing Role of the Jury in the Nineteenth Century', *Yale Law Journal*, 1964, vol. 74, p. 170.
110. Nelson, *Americanization of the Common Law*, p. 165.
111. 'Decius', *Independent Chronicle*, 10 Feb. 1806. Cited in Ellis, *Jeffersonian Crisis*, pp. 202–3, 325.
112. 'Decius', *Independent Chronicle*, 31 Jan. 1804. Cited in Ellis, *Jeffersonian Crisis*, pp. 203, 325.
113. Wharton's *State Trials*, p. 688; see also *Sparf and Hanson v. U.S., U.S. Reports*, 1894, vol. 156, p. 70. For a discussion of the Callendar case, see Julius Goebel, Jr, *History of the Supreme Court*, pp. 648–51.
114. *The Virginia Report of 1799–1800, Touching the Alien and Sedition Laws; Together with the Virginia Resolutions of Dec. 21, 1798* (Richmond, Va., 1850), p. 211.
115. *Virginia Report of 1799–1800*, p. 212.
116. *Virginia Report of 1799–1800*, p. 211.
117. Wharton, *State Trials*, p. 144.
118. Samuel Chase, *Charge Book* (Maryland Historical Society), p. 15. Cited in Julius Goebel, Jr, *History of the Supreme Court*, p. 647.
119. Chase, *Charge Book*, p. 15, in Goebel, *History of the Supreme Court*, p. 647.
120. Julius Goebel, Jr, *History of the Supreme Court*, p. 651.
121. McDonald, *Novus Ordo Seclorum*, p. 291.

4 LOCATING THE 'VOICE OF THE PEOPLE'

1. Adams' statement of this position was recorded in 'Thomas Jefferson's notes on the debates and proceedings of The Virginia Resolution of Independence', (8, 10, June, July, 1776), in Merrill Jensen, ed., *English Historical Documents* (London, 1955), p. 870.
2. John Adams, 'Autobiography', in C. F. Adams (ed.), *The Works of John Adams* (Boston: 1850–56), 10 vols., vol III, p. 17.
3. Robert Taylor, *et al.*, eds. *The Papers of John Adams* (Cambridge, Mass., 1977), vol. 4, pp. 82–3.
4. C. F. Adams, ed., *The Works of John Adams*, vol. VI, p. 488.
5. While Montesquieu's position in *The Spirit of the Laws* on the complete separation of powers – particularly an independent judiciary – is often heralded as the guide for American thinking, and can be found explicitly reflected in the Massachusetts Constitution, it is too little and too infrequently recognized that what Montesquieu has in mind to exercise is not a permanent, independent court, but an impermanent, periodic jury. On Montesquieu's analysis – one which we have every reason to believe Adams understood quite well – the members of this jury – 'judges' – were to be periodically struck from and returned to the body of ordinary citizens. That the power of the people might rise up and judge offenders of the law and then recede back into the body of the citizenry is precisely what makes Montesquieu call this judicial function at once both 'terrible' in its power and yet 'next to nothing.' See Charles (Louis de Secondat, Baron de) Montesquieu, *The Spirit of the Laws*, trans. Thomas Nugent (New York, 1949), Bk. II, chap. 6, p. 153. For the only other discussion of which I am aware of Montesquieu's judiciary as a jury empowered, see Forrest McDonald, *Novus Ordo Seclorum* (Lawrence, 1985), p. 85.
6. *Papers of John Adams*, vol. IV, p. 89.
7. *Works of John Adams*, vol. III, p. 481.
8. *Sparf and Hanson v. U.S.*, *U.S. Reports*, vol. 156, Oct.
9. *Works of John Adams*, vol. III, pp. 481–2.
10. *Diary and Autobiography of John Adams*, vol. II, p. 3 (12 Feb. 1771).
11. *Diary and Autobiography of John Adams*, vol. II, p. 4.
12. See John Reid, *In a Defiant Stance: The Conditions of Law in Massachusetts Bay, the Irish Comparison, and the Coming of the American Revolution* (University Park, Pa., 1977), pp. 52–3.
13. Hendrik Hartog, ed., *Law in the Revolution and the Revolution in the Law* (New York, 1981) p. 185.
14. *Diary and Autobiography*, vol. III, p. 292 (1770), taken from Adams' notes on the Boston Massacre Trials. On the problem of jural omnipotence and the inability to grant new trials in criminal cases based on jural error, see *The Legal Papers of John Adams*, vol. II, pp. 407–8 (*Rex v. Richardson*). See also *Legal Papers*, vol. III, p. 18. The intractability of the colonial jury problem is recorded at the time of the Boston Massacre. The original statutory basis of jury selection in Massachusetts was a law of the early 1740s that replaced conventional

elections in the towns with a choice by lot. Under a later law (a Provincial Law, 'An Act for the Better Regulating the Choice of Petit Jurors', 29 March 1760, 4A&R 318 revised 20 March 1767, 4 *A & R* 920), a list of prospective jurors was made up by selectmen, and names of those to serve as jurors drawn at town meetings. Adams commented that '[t]he Method of Chusing them is the most fair and impartial that the wit of man could possibly devise'. However, at the time of the Boston Massacre Trial, the jury law had expired and, as one observer noted, 'the nomination of Jurors [was] now more in the hands of the people than ever before' (Dalrymple to Gage, 26 Aug. 1770), Adams, *New Light*, pp. 72, 73. As one contemporary source commented on the jury selection practices of the revolutionary period: 'This mode seems equitable, and it was unexceptionally practiced, untill [*sic*] the late Times of Confusion; but now, a new Form of Government had been instituted in this Province. They thought it necessary the new modes of law should coincide with them. Accordingly, the Select Men of Boston would draw out of the Lottery Box; and if any popular cause was to be before the Court, and that Juror was not like to serve the Cause, they would make some excuse for the absent Man, either he was sick or would not be well, or he was going [on] a Journey or Voyage; and so return his Name into the Box, and draw until they drew him who was for their purpose'. Peter Oliver, *Origin and Progress of the American Rebellion*, ed. D. Adair, J. Schultz, (San Marino, 1961), p. 85.

15. See *Rex v. Preston* and *Rex v. Wemms*, in *Adams Legal Papers*, vol. III, p. 309. It has been inaccurately charged that Adams conducted the defence in the Boston Massacre Trials so as to protect the Whigs of Boston, not his clients. (See Gary Wills, *Inventing America* (Garden City, 1978), p. 23.) In fact, Adams acted in the best interests of the defendants, as has been ably proven by John P. Reid, 'A Lawyer Acquitted: John Adams and the Boston Massacre Trials', *American Journal of Legal History*, vol. 18, 1974, pp. 189–207.

16. Adams seemed to feel it was the *duty* of the lawyer 'to proclaim the laws, the rights, the generous plan of power delivered from remote antiquity'. *Legal Papers*, vol. III, pp. 462–3.

17. It was the prosecution, nominally representing the Crown, but obviously in the *Wemms* case representing irate colonials, who attempted to employ local antagonism in order to convict, but calling on the jury to find a 'Verdict as the Laws of God, of Nature and your own Conscience will ever Approve.' *Legal Papers of John Adams*, vol. III, pp. 462–3.

18. *Legal Papers of John Adams*, vol. I, p. 230.

19. See Lysander Spooner, *An Essay on Trial by Jury* (Cleveland, 1852)

20. *Diary and Autobiography*, vol. II, p. 4. From 'Diary Notes on the Rights of Juries'. See also *Legal Papers*, vol. I, pp. 228–30. Lyman Butterfield, editor of the *Adams Diary*, suggests that this essay has every appearance of having been written for a newspaper. However, no printing has been found. It has been suggested that Adams did use some passages in preparation for his successful argument that a

jury can find against the instructions of a court in the case of *Wright & Gill v. Mein* (1771) discussed in the text. Adams' legal papers show a serious investigation of the issue of the scope of jury determinations.

21. *Diary and Autobiography*, vol. II, p. 4. This argument for observance of common law and common law adjudication in such cases is a lawyer's argument, wholly different from the Revolutionary argument of Adam's 'Clarendon' letters published in the *Boston Gazette* in January 1776, and basing the limited powers of Parliament in the Stamp Act issue on references to Coke and common law 'principle'. See *Legal Papers*, vol. I, p. lxxxv; *Works*, pp. 469–83; *Diary*, vol. I, pp. 265–8, 272–7, 286–92, 296–9.

22. *Legal Papers*, vol. I, p. 230. For a view opposing Adams, which insisted that 'when a jury will pertinaciously determine matters of law directly, against the opinion of the Court, a new trial should be given,' see A. Z. in *The Censor* (14 March 1772) cited in Wroth and Zobel, eds, *Legal Papers*, vol. II, p. 215. The author has seen no evidence to suggest such practice was followed in the colonies.

23. See Blackstone, *Commentaries*, vol. IV, p. 354; Hale, *Pleas of the Crown*, vol,. II, p. 310; Adams, *Legal Papers*, vol. I, p. 225.

24. *Diary of John Adams*, vol. I, p. 117.

25. The editors of Adams' *Legal Papers* have characterized the debate between Novanglus and the Tory, Massachusettensis (Daniel Leonard) as a set of lawyers' briefs which took the form of legal arguments presented to the jury of the public (vol. II, p. 219). While recognizing that Leonard presented his claims to the public in a style more easily digested by common listeners than did Adams, Leonard's argument nonetheless remains in all important respects but a paraphrase of criticisms raised by English common lawyers of the legal 'incompetency' of average colonials and their radical legal spokesmen such as Adams to judge the common law. For perhaps the best single expression of this attitude from the English Bar, see (Anon.), *An Examination of the Rights of the Colonies upon Principles of Law. By a Gentleman at the Bar* (London, R. Dymott and J. Almon, 1766). This barrister argues that 'it is widely provided by the Constitution of *England*, that the Necessities of the State, are to be judged of, by the representative Body of the People, not by the Individuals themselves. The common People have neither the means to know, nor Capacity to judge of the Public Wants. . . . An open, continued and avowed Resistance of the Law, is an open, continued, and avowed Resistance of the State' (p. 37).

26. *Papers of John Adams*, vol. II, pp. 230, 242.

27. Edward Handler, *America and Europe in the Political Thought of John Adams* (Cambridge, Mass., 1964), p. 5. It is Handler's position that Adams always exaggerated the uniqueness of America, and the disparity between American and European circumstances.

28. *Legal Papers*, vol. I, pp. 218–29, 228–30.

29. Coke, *Littleton*, p. 228a, cited in *Legal Papers*, vol. I, p. 220; Barrington, *Observations from the Statutes*, pp. 103–4, cited in *Legal Papers*, vol. I, p. 219; Blackstone's *Commentaries*, vol. III, p. 378, cited in

Legal Papers, vol. I, p. 219. See also *Junius' Letters to Chief Justice Mansfield* in *Letters of Junius*, vol. II, p. 159, cited in *Legal Papers*, vol. I, p. 219.

30. *Legal Papers*, vol. II, p. 219 (*Rex v. Baldwin*).
31. There are several accounts of the issues surrounding the trials for seditious libel of John Wilkes and his supporters. The best are, generally: L. W. Hanson, *Government and the Press, 1695–1763* (Oxford, 1936); R. R. Rea, *The English Press in Politics: 1760–1774* (Lincoln, 1963); George Rude, *Wilkes and Liberty: A Social Study of 1763–74* (Oxford, 1962). Particularly helpful in giving an account of the legal issues involved is John Brewer, 'The Wilkites and the Law, 1763–74: a study of radical notions of governance', in John Brewer and John Styles, eds, *An Ungovernable People* (London, 1980).
32. *Legal Papers*, vol. I, p. 207.
33. Rea, *English Press in Politics*, p. 82; Brewer, 'The Wilkites and the Law', p. 156.
34. Brewer, 'The Wilkites and the Law', p. 156; Hanson, *Government and the Press*, pp. 19–20.
35. Brewer, 'The Wilkites and the Law', p. 158.
36. Brewer, 'The Wilkites and the Law', p. 157, citing *North Briton*, nos. 64 (2 Sept. 1768), 176 (11 Aug. 1770); *Whisperer*, no. 24 (28 July 1770); and Hawles, *The Englishman's Right*, p. 32.
37. Brewer, 'The Wilkites and the Law', pp. 158–9.
38. See Rea, *English Press in Politics*, pp. 46–7; see also George Noble, *The North Briton: A Study in Political Propaganda* (New York, 1939), pp. 262–3; also Howell, *State Trials*, vol. XIX, pp. 1092–4.
39. Rea, *English Press in Politics*, p. 182.
40. Cited in Rea, *English Press in Politics*, p. 184.
41. Brewer also shares this conclusion in 'The Wilkites and the Law', p. 157.
42. (Anon.), *An Examination of the Rights of the Colonies upon Principles of Law. By a Gentleman at the Bar* (London: R. Dymott and J. Almon, 1766), pp. 9–10. [H.L.]
43. See Adams' comment on the origin of the case in *Novangulus: Works of John Adams*, vol. IV, pp. 29–30.
44. The jury issue was also present in another civil suit, *Cotton v. Nye*. See *Legal Papers*, vol. I, pp. 141–9.
45. *Legal Papers*, vol. II, pp. 173–210.
46. See the excellent discussion of the legally conservative arguments of James Otis in the *Writs of Assistance Cases* offered by M. H. Smith, *The Writs of Assistance Cases* (Berkeley, 1978).
47. *Legal Papers*, vol. II, pp. 188–9.
48. *Legal Papers*, vol. I, p. 207. The Massachusetts Superior Court had earlier let stand a jury verdict in *Erving v. Cradock* [Quincy *Reports*, 553 (1761)] which awarded to a colonial shipowner damages for trespass against a royal revenue officer. All five judges of the court instructed the jury against finding such a verdict – which would effectively nullify the Navigation Acts – yet the jury's decision was not set aside, as it most certainly would have been in England. As William

Nelson notes, 'in view of the fact that English judges would grant new trials when juries failed to follow their instructions, it is not surprising that English lawyers believed that juries had no power to determine questions of law.' *Americanization of the Common Law*, p. 193, fn. 165.

49. John Murrin has suggested that in the years immediately before the Revolution, Massachusetts lawyers became nearly obsessed with Anglicizing the law and the legal profession. While Murrin's evidence of jural resistance to any attempt to 'Anglicize' the law in this period is informative, the implication that increased knowledge of English law in the colonies meant increased appreciation, or that it provided a positive 'intellectual basis for unity until they could manufacture their own nationalism' seems undersupported. It leaves Murrin with the 'paradox' of why such an 'Anglicized' profession should not only participate in but lead a legal and constitutional revolution, and the difficult claim that somehow the Revolution 'utterly reversed the trend of the whole previous century.' The work of other, new legal historians such as William Nelson and Morton Horwitz provides evidence that the rise of genuine legal 'professionalism' and a concomitant attachment to Anglicizing the common law came generally late in the century, with the effort to legally (and nationally) consolidate the Revolution. See John Murrin, 'The Legal Transformation of the Bench and Bar of Eighteenth-Century Massachusetts', in Stanley Katz (ed.), *Colonial America* (Boston, 1971), pp. 415–49.

50. Judges in colonial Massachusetts have been described by historian William Nelson as men 'of substance who commanded the respect of the community', *Americanization of the Common Law*, p. 33. In contrast Douglas Greenberg has suggested that judges in colonial New York were 'on the whole, an ignorant lot, ill-suited to hold office, and often anxious to abuse the power which such office afforded them.' *Crime and Law Enforcement in the Colony of New York, 1691–1776*, p. 174.

51. *Legal Papers*, vol. I, p. 230; *Diary*, vol. II, p. 4.

52. Part of the sharp rejection of the Massachusetts Constitution of 1778 rested on the local 'returns' of townships such as Lenox, Ashfield, Pittsfield, and the Berkshires. In each case, a decisive rejection of any constitutional arrangement that would unselectively recognize the legitimacy of existing English common law was voiced by these towns, as well as the demand in all cases for a more explicit and expansive jury right. See Robert J. Taylor, *Massachusetts: Colony to Commonwealth* (New York, 1961), pp. 43, 93, 94, 67.

53. See the characterization of Alphons Beitzinger, in 'The Philosophy of Law of Four American Founding Fathers', *American Journal of Jurisprudence*, vol. 21, 1976.

54. Adams discusses in Novangulus what he terms the 'principles of nature and eternal reason'. They include: 'men by nature equal, that kings are but ministers of the people; that their authority is delegated to them by the people, for their good, and they have a right to resume

it, and place it in other hands, or keep it for themselves, whenever it is made to oppress them.' See *Works*, vol. IV, p. 15.

55. *Works of John Adams*, vol. III, pp. 862, 455, 462, *Dissertation on the Canon and Feudal Law*. Adams' approach to history is revealing. It was both critical and selective. As one historian notes, Adams 'sifted out' Whiggish views in support of American positions on the historic rights of Englishmen. For Adams, hsitory was by and large a record of human error. He drew his own conclusions about the causes of political collapses of the past. From history, the view of human nature he drew was not particularly sanguine: 'The first want of every man is for his dinner, his second is for his girl', and his third 'to usurp other men's rights'. (*Works*, vol. V I, p. 8). For a discussion of Adams as 'Political Scientist and Historian', see H. Trevor Colbourne, *The Lamp of Experience: Whig History and the Intellectual History of the American Republic* (Chapel Hill, 1965), p. 86.

56. *Works of John Adams*, vol. IV, p. 15; vol. VI, pp. 56, 114, 450, 453, 456. Adams wrote that 'although reason ought to always govern individuals, it certainly never did since the Fall, and never will till the Milleneum; and human nature must be taken as it is; as it ever will be' (*Works*, vol. VI, p. 115). He adds elsewhere '[a]ll we can do is guard and provide against this quality; we can not eradicate it' (*Works*, vol. V. p. 40). Thus while Gordon Wood considers Adams' *Defence of the Constitutions* the 'finest flowering of the American Enlightenment', Adams had little in common with the social/political views of many of his European Enlightenment counterparts. Peter Gay calls Adams 'probably the most caustic critic of the fatuous optimism that the age of Enlightenment produced.' See *The Enlightenment: An Interpretation*(New York, 1969), vol. II, p. 98. Perhaps Wood has in mind the opening lines of the *Defence* – which begins with encomiums for the advances and benefits of science, 'rendering Europe more and more like one community, or a single family' (*Works*, vol. IV, p. 283). In general, Adams' thought shows an uneasy balance between the optimism of technical advances of man as scientist (i.e., advances in natural philosophy, navigation, and commerce) and the pessimism of Puritan declension, with its original sin shaping his attitudes in political science, ethics, and moral development. Adams ridiculed Helvetius's and Rousseau's views of men, believing himself that the species was at best only possibly improvable. See L. J. Cappon, ed., *The Adams-Jefferson Letters* (Chapel Hill, 1959), vol. II, p. 435. Adams' own contemporaries saw nothing novel or 'enlightened' in the *Defence*. See Merrill Jensen (ed.), *Commentaries on the Constitution*, (Madison, 1981), vol. XIII, p. 84.

57. *Works of John Adams*, vol. III, pp. 449, 463.

58. It is in his private lament of the dissipating effects of men's lack of self-control, that Adams comes closest to aligning himself with those more public spokesmen of the American jeremiad. See Perry Miller, *The Life of the Mind in America* (New York, 1965), pp. 207–9; see also Sacvan Berkovitch, *The American Jeremiad* (Madison, 1978), pp. 4–11, 23.

59. *Diary of John Adams*, vol. I, p. 73.
60. Adams favoured proper political education for the very young and he believed that '[l]aws for the liberal education of youth, especially of the lower classes of people, are so extremely useful, that to a humane and generous mind, no expense for this purpose would be thought extravagant' (*Works*, vol. IV, p. 199).
61. *Works of John Adams*, vol. IV, p. 14. See Bernard Bailyn's discussion of the 'sensuous Adams', in 'Butterfield's Adams: Notes for a Sketch', *William and Mary Quarterly*, vol. 19, 1962, pp. 238f.
62. *Works of John Adams*, vol. VI, p. 64.
63. *Works of John Adams*, vol. IV, p. 82.
64. John R. Howe, *The Changing Political Thought of John Adams* (Princeton, 1966), p. 21.
65. Edward Handler, *American and Europe in the Political Thought of John Adams* (Cambridge, Mass., 1964), pp. 5, 26, 54–5.
66. Wood, *Creation of the American Republic*, pp. 585, 586, 592.
67. *Legal Papers*, vol. I, p. 138.
68. *Diary of John Adams*, vol. I, p. 299.
69. Colbourne, *The Lamp of Experience*, p. 105.
70. Wood, *Creation of the American Republic*, p. 588. See also Adams' diary entries of 29 Aug. and 24 Oct. 1774 in Paul H. Smith (ed.), *Letters of Delegates to Congress: 1774–1789* (Washington, 1976), vol. I, pp. 10–11.
71. Adams, 25 Sept. 1774 in *Letters of Delegates to Congress: 1774–1789*, vol. I, p. 99.
72. *Diary of John Adams*, vol. I, pp. 136–7. See also J. R. Pole, *Foundations of American Independence: 1763–1815* (Indianapolis, 1972), p. 80.
73. *Works of John Adams*, vol. IX, p. 429. See Ronald Peters, Jr, *The Massachusetts Constitution of 1780: A Social Compact* (Amherst, 1978), p. 177.
74. *Works of John Adams*, vol. VI, p. 488; vol. IV, pp. 194–5.
75. As Alan Heimert notes, 'Shortly after independence had been declared, John Adams, who for more than a decade had been arguing that the "people" need to be aroused as a "control" on arbitrary government, proposed that, so far as the constitutions of independent America were concerned, the first need was a check on the power of the multitude'. See *Religion and the American Mind, from the Great Awakening to the Revolution* (Cambridge, Mass., 1966), p. 518.
76. *Works of John Adams*, vol. III, p. 453; vol. IV, p. 195. See also Heimert, *Religion in America*, p. 518.
77. *Works of John Adams*, vol. IV, pp. 293–4, 579–80 (*Defence of the Constitutions*).
78. Madison to Jefferson, 1784, in R. A. Rutland and W. Rachal, eds, *The Papers of James Madison* (Chicago, 1977), vol. VIII, pp. 92–95.
79. John Adams to Benjamin Rush, 19 Sept. 1806. Cited in J. A. Schultz and D. Adair, eds, *The Spur of Fame: Dialogues of John Adams and Benjamin Rush, 1805–1813* (San Marino, 1966), p. 66. On Adams' conception of 'quasi or mixed government' and its lack of fit with the

demands of a national politics, see Douglas Adair, ' "Experience Must be Our Only Guide:" History, Democratic Theory, and the United States Constitution', in R. A. Billington, ed., *The Reinterpretation of Early American History* (San Marino, 1966), pp. 129–48.

5 LAW IN THE CONTEXT OF CONTINUOUS REVOLUTION

1. I owe this point to a comment made in discussion by Judith N. Shklar. See also Daniel J. Boorstin, *The Lost World of Thomas Jefferson* (New York, 1948), p. 132.
2. Jefferson wrote this in response to his daughter's expressed difficulties in translating Livy. Cited in Bernard Bailyn, 'Boyd's Jefferson: Notes for a Sketch', *New England Quarterly*, vol. 33, 1960, p. 390. Jefferson considered Hume (as well as Blackstone) as one of his 'favorite enemies'. He did so because he believed Hume's political and historical work had 'made Tories of all England, and are making Tories of those young Americans whose native feelings of independence do not place them above [Hume's] willy [*sic*] sophistries. . . .' See Jefferson's *Common Place Book*, ed. Gilbert Chinard (Baltimore, 1926), pp. 12, 52, 374; also Paul L. Ford, ed., *The Works of Jefferson* (Washington, 1904–5), vol. VI, p. 335. Jefferson did not recognize that the most fundamental difference separating himself and Hume was the latter's profound scepticism and his own profound lack of it. Hume's scepticism in epistemology and moral theory, as Hume recognized, could not provide the basis for an ordered polity. He therefore relied, in the absence of certain knowledge, on the experienced and time-tested patterns of political authority provided by tradition.
3. There is little question that between the two men lie stark differences in their degrees of optimism reflecting recognized differences in their epistemology, metaphysics, and moral theories. Adams wrote to Jefferson: 'I have a prejudice against what they call Metaphysicks because they pretend to fathom deeper than the human line extends. I know not very well what e'er the *to metaphusica* of Aristotle means, but I think I can form some idea of Investigations into the human mind . . . I would therefore propose this problem or Theorem for your consideration: whether it would not be advisable to institute in the Universities Professorships of the Philosophy of Human Understanding, whose object should be to ascertain the Limits of human knowledge already acquired . . . though I suppose you will have doubts of the propriety of setting any limits, or thinking of any limits of human Power, or human Wisdom, and human Virtue.' *The Adams-Jefferson Letters*: (Chapel Hill, 1959), vol. II, pp. 560–1 (21 Feb. 1820).
4. Boorstin, *Lost World of Thomas Jefferson*, p. 59.
5. *The Works of Jefferson* (Washington ed.), vol. VII, pp. 155–9.
6. *Adams/Jefferson Letters*, vol. II, p. 570.
7. Letter from Jefferson to Thomas Paine, 11 July 1789. In Julian Boyd, ed., *The Papers of Thomas Jefferson* (Princeton, 1950), vol. XV, p. 269.

8. *Papers of Thomas Jefferson*, vol. XV, p. 269; Albert Bergh, ed., *The Writings of Thomas Jefferson* (Washington, 1907), vol. II, p. 177. See also *The Works of Jefferson* (New York, 1904–5), ed. Paul L. Ford, vol. V, p. 224; vol. IX, p. 340.

9. *Writings of Thomas Jefferson*, vol. VII, p. 423 (19 July 1789).

10. *Writings of Thomas Jefferson*, vol. I, pp. 73–4.

11. *Writings of Thomas Jefferson*, vol. VII, pp. 423 (14 July 1789).

12. *Papers of Thomas Jefferson*, vol. XV, pp. 282–3.

13. *Papers of Thomas Jefferson*, vol. XV, p. 283.

14. *Papers of Thomas Jefferson*, vol. I, pp. 352, 362; for Jefferson's position on the need to include trial by jury in the Bill of Rights, see vol. XII, pp. 440, 558.

15. *Papers of Thomas Jefferson*, vol. XV, p. 269.

16. *Writings of Thomas Jefferson*, vol. II, p. 201.

17. *Writings of Thomas Jefferson*, vol. II, pp. 226, 206–7; vol. XV, p. 141.

18. P. L. Ford (ed.), *Works (Writings) of Jefferson*, vol. X, p. 376, vol. XVI, p. 156.

19. Jefferson to Madison, cited in Roy J. Honeywell, *The Educational Work of Thomas Jefferson* (Cambridge, Ma., 1939), pp. 121–2.

20. *Writings of Thomas Jefferson*, vol. XIII, pp. 280–1.

21. Boorstin, *Lost World of Thomas Jefferson*, pp. 53, 59.

22. *Writings of Thomas Jefferson*, vol. XVI, p. 45 (1812).

23. This is a view shared by Thomas Paine and one which Jefferson expressed early on. See Jefferson's letter to La Fayette, *Writings of Thomas Jefferson*, vol. VI, p. 108 (11 April 1787).

24. Revisionist historians such as Richard Matthews have also recognized the greater importance of Locke's *Essay* over the *Second Treatise*, in Jefferson's thought. However, the interpretation offered here departs on many points from Matthews' understanding of the *Essay*.

25. *Adams–Jefferson Letters*, vol. II, pp. 568–9. See also Gilbert Chinard, *Thomas Jefferson: Apostle of Americanism* (Ann Arbor, 1957), p. 519.

26. John Locke, *An Essay Concerning Human Understanding*, Bk. II, chap. XIII, secs. 12–14, pp. 302–5.

27. Locke, *Essay Concerning Human Understanding*, Epistle to the Reader, p. 9.

28. It is important to note that Jefferson himself interpreted Locke as a materialist, following the sensationalist reading given Locke by Destutt de Tracy and Dugald Stewart. Jefferson's materialism was also drawn, it appears, from Benjamin Rush and from early religious writers such as Origen, Tertullian, St Justin Martyr. See *Adams–Jefferson Letters*, vol. II, p. 568.

29. See Chinard, *Thomas Jefferson*, p. 524.

30. *Writings of Thomas Jefferson*, vol. XIII, p. 225 (to Rush); vol. X, pp. 85, 436 (to Rush). Again, Jefferson is glossing a claim by Locke that 'where the Mind judges that [a] Proposition has concernment in it; where the Assent, or not Assenting is thought to draw Consequences of Moment after it, and Good or Evil to depend on chusing . . . and

the Mind sets it self seriously to enquire, and examine the Probability: there, I think, it is not in our Choice to take which side we please, if manifest odds appear on either. The greater Probability . . . will determine the Assent: and a Man can no more avoid assenting . . . than he can avoid knowing it to be true' (*Essay*, bk. IV, chap. XX, sec. 16, p. 718). Note, however, that Locke is discussing the ability of reflective judgment and the rational weighing of argument and evidence to determine 'assent'.

31. *Adams-Jefferson Letters*, vol. II, p. 568.
32. *Writings of Jefferson*, vol. XV, p. 492 (4 Nov. 1823, to LaFayette); vol. XIII, p. 279. 'The same political parties which agitate the United States, have existed through all time.' See also vol. XVI, p. 74; vol. X, p. 75.
33. Bailyn, 'Boyd's Jefferson', p. 385.
34. *Writings of Jefferson*, vol. XIII, p. 177; vol. X, p. 404 (to Cabanis, 1803). Jefferson referred to Cabanis' *Rapports du physique et du moral de l'homme* as 'the most profound of all human compositions.'
35. Keith M. Baker, *Condorcet: From Natural Philosophy to Social Mathematics* (Chicago, 1975), pp. 225, 234–5. In a letter to Judge John Tyler (Gov. of Virginia) in 1812, Jefferson pointed out the undesirability of 'the civil code' (as in France), but added: 'I admit the superiority of the civil over the common law code, as a system of perfect justice' (*Works of Jefferson*, vol. VI, p. 66).
36. *Writings of Jefferson*, vol. XIII, pp. 279, 114–15 (to Rush). See Jefferson's interpretation of the motives of those castigating his governorship of Virginia in 1780 (vol. II, pp. 174, 177).
37. *Adams-Jefferson Letters*, vol. II, p. 565.
38. The two documents considered his major contributions to political thought – the *Declaration of Independence* and *A Summary View of the Rights of British America* – Jefferson readily recognized were neither single-author documents nor attempts to explore his own political theory in writing. The Declaration he described as an eclectic sampling of sentiments 'probably to be found in elementary books on public right, as Aristotle, Cicero, Locke, Sidney, etc.' He described the aim of this work as 'neither aiming at originality of principle or sentiment, nor yet copied from any particular and previous writing, it was intended to be an expression of the American mind.' See *Writings of Thomas Jefferson*, vol. XVI, p. 188. According to Julian Boyd, Jefferson's draft resolutions intended for presentation to the Virginia Convention of 1774 were – without his knowledge – edited, printed, and given the title, *A Summary View of the Rights of British America*, when illness prevented Jefferson's attendance at the Convention. Although it can be assumed that the basic, and for their time distinctive, views of this work to be Jefferson's, Boyd acknowledges that the manuscript draft of the *Summary View* contained both 'less and more' than the pamphlet edited by members of the Convention. Julian P. Boyd (ed.), *The Papers of Thomas Jefferson*, vol. I, p. 135.
39. Rush, quoted in Boorstin, *Lost World of Thomas Jefferson*, p. 233.

40. *Notes on the State of Virginia, Writings of Thomas Jefferson*, vol. II, p. 229.
41. *Autobiography, Writings of Thomas Jefferson*, vol. I; see also *Papers of Thomas Jefferson*, vol. II, pp. 305–24, for Jefferson's extensive proposals for legal reform.
42. *Writings of Thomas Jefferson*, vol. II, p. 185.
43. *Writings of Thomas Jefferson*, vol. XIV, p. 466; see also Chinard, ed., *Commonplace Book*, p. 260.
44. *Writings of Thomas Jefferson*, vol. II, pp. 120–1, 241.
45. Jefferson's comments on the attitude of the American Indian, his archetype of natural man, to government are useful here: 'It will be said, the great societies cannot exist without government. The savages therefore, break them into smaller ones' (*Writings of Thomas Jefferson*, vol. II, p. 129).
46. *Works of Jefferson*, vol. VII, p. 56 (16 Jan. 1817).
47. Jefferson, 12 Feb. 1790, cited in Noble Cunningham, Jr, *The Life of Thomas Jefferson* (Baton Rouge, La., 1987), p. vi. See also *Writings of Thomas Jefferson*, vol. II, p. 172; *Works of Jefferson*, vol. II, p. 496.
48. *Writings of Thomas Jefferson*, vol. II, pp. 168–9.
49. *Notes on the State of Virginia, Writings of Thomas Jefferson*, vol. II, pp. 168–9.
50. *Adams-Jefferson Letters*, vol. II, p. 562.
51. *Adams-Jefferson Letters*, vol. II, p. 561.
52. *Writings of Thomas Jefferson*, vol. II, p. 128; vol. XV, p. 76. Jefferson criticized what he believed was Tracy's position that 'justice was founded in contract only.'
53. *Summary View of the Rights of British America, Writings of Thomas Jefferson*, vol. II, pp. 209–10.
54. *Writings of Thomas Jefferson*, vol. VI, p. 85.
55. *Writings of Thomas Jefferson*, vol. II, p. 223. It is interesting that Jefferson did suggest reason and persuasion in the realm of religious differences. However, this practice did not carry over into the realm of politics, and it may say more about Jefferson's attitude toward the 'nature' of religion than anything else.
56. *Writings of Thomas Jefferson*, vol. II, p. 172.
57. *Writings of Thomas Jefferson*, vol. II, pp. 225, 162–3. See also James Hutson, 'The Paranoid Style in American Politics', in John Murrin *et al.*, eds, *Saints and Revolutionaries* (New York, 1984), p. 359.
58. *Writings of Thomas Jefferson*, vol. XV, p. 42; vol. XVI, p. 48; vol. XIV, p. 487.
59. *Writings of Thomas Jefferson*, vol. XVI, p. 48.
60. *Writings of Thomas Jefferson*, vol. XVI, p. 48.
61. *Writings of Thomas Jefferson*, vol,. XIV, p. 487.
62. *Writings of Thomas Jefferson*, vol. II, p. 207.
63. *Writings of Thomas Jefferson*, vol. XV, p. 42; vol. XVI, p. 48; vol. XIV, p. 487.
64. *Writings of Thomas Jefferson*, vol. II, p. 172; *Works of Jefferson*, vol. VII, p. 496.

65. Madison to Jefferson (4 Feb. 1790), cited in Marvin Meyers, *The Mind of the Founder* (Indianapolis, 1973), p. 233.
66. *Writings of Thomas Jefferson*, vol. XIV, p. 141. Jefferson took exception to the argument of Helvetius: 'What other motive than self-interest could determine a man to generous action? It is impossible for him to love what is good for the sake of the good, as it is to love evil for the sake of evil' (*De l'Esprit*: p. 142).
67. *Writings of Thomas Jefferson*, vol. XIV, p. 143.
68. This was true not only of Madison but of others, such as Joseph Hopkinson.
69. See Perry Miller, *The Life of the Mind in America* (New York, 1965), pp. 131–2.
70. See Meyers, *Mind of the Founder*, p. 232.
71. *Writings of Thomas Jefferson*, vol. II, pp. 162, 166–7.
72. *Writings of Thomas Jefferson*, vol. XV, p. 212.
73. *Papers of Thomas Jefferson*, vol. XI, p. 93 (30 Jan. 1787).
74. *Papers of Thomas Jefferson*, vol. XII, p. 356 (to William Smith, 13 Nov. 1787).
75. *Writings of Thomas Jefferson*, vol. XV, p. 24.
76. *Writings of Thomas Jefferson*, vol. XV, pp. 213–14.
77. ibid.
78. ibid.
79. *Writings of Thomas Jefferson*, vol. XV, p. 214 (to Roane, 1819). In his inaugural message to Congress in 1801, Jefferson apparently included but then suppressed his position that any of the three branches of government had the right 'to decide on the validity of an act according to its own judgment and uncontrolled by the opinions of any other department'. See A. J. Beveridge, *Life of John Marshall* (New York, 1916–19), vol. II, pp. 51–3 and appendix.
80. Jefferson noted that the character of states defied legal and political uniformity, since 'some states require a different regime from others.' 'What is done in one state very often shocks another, though where it is done it is wholesome.' *Works of Jefferson*, vol. IX, p. 283.
81. Boorstin, *Lost World of Thomas Jefferson*, p. 199.
82. *The Kentucky Resolutions of 1798*, *Works of Jefferson*, vol. VII, pp. 288–9.
83. *Works of Jefferson*, vol. VII, pp. 312–13.
84. In line with this project, Jefferson revived the notion of the 'wards' and 'hundreds' units of Germanic origin from which jurors would be drawn at local levels (*Writings of Thomas Jefferson*, vol. XV, pp. 70–1; vol. XII, p. 393). Adrienne Koch has recognized the somewhat original and political use to which Jefferson puts the 'wards'; *The Philosophy of Thomas Jefferson* (Gloucester, 1957), pp. 162–5. See also Morris Cohen, *Law: A Century of Progress* (New York, 1936), p. 270.
85. Madison to Jefferson, 29 December 1798. Draft. *Madison Papers*, Library of Congress. Cited in Adrienne Koch, *Jefferson and Madison* (New York, 1950), p. 193.
86. *Writings of Thomas Jefferson*, vol. XI, pp. 213–14; vol. X, pp. 410–11;

vol. XV, p. 214. See also Chinard, *Thomas Jefferson*, pp. 412–13, 417.

87. See Louis Hartz, *The Liberal Tradition in America* (New York, 1955), p. 128.

88. Julian Franklin, *John Locke and the Theory of Sovereignty* (Cambridge, Mass., 1978), p. 48.

89. 'The Republican Society of Newark, New Jersey', 1794, cited in Eugene P. Link, *The Democratic-Republican Societies: 1790–1800* (New York, 1965), p. 106.

90. Richard D. Brown, *Revolutionary Politics in Massachusetts: The Boston Committee of Correspondence and the Towns, 1772–74* (Cambridge, Mass., 1970), p. 134.

91. Hendrik Hartog, 'Losing the World of the Massachusetts Whig', in Hartog, ed., *Law in the Revolution and the Revolution in the Law* (New York, 1981), p. 163.

92. See 'Address of the Convention (March, 1780)' and 'The Return of the Town of Wilbraham on the Constitution of 1780', in Oscar and Mary Handlin, eds, *The Popular Sources of Political Authority* (Cambridge, Mass., 1966), pp. 439, 623.

93. For the most recent and informed discussion of the peculiar evolution of trial by jury in Virginia, see John M. Murrin and A. G. Roeber, 'Trial by Jury: The Virginia Paradox', in Jon Kukla (ed.), *The Bill of Rights: A Lively Heritage*, p. 109. I am particularly grateful to John Murrin for his valuable suggestions and comments on both Jefferson's jurisprudence and the character of Virginia's jural development. I do not wish to insinuate his agreement with the jural arguments developed here.

94. See, for example, Richard Beale Davis, *Intellectual Life in Jefferson's Virginia, 1790–1830* (Chapel Hill, 1964). See also Winthrop Jordan's review of Beale in *William and Mary Quarterly*, vol. 22, 1965, pp. 166–8. It is Jordan who suggests that 'when Jefferson died, Virginia was no longer Jefferson's.' As he notes: 'It was a long, long way from his *Notes on the State of Virginia* (1787) to John Robertson's (b. 1787) *Virginia, or the Fatal Patient: A Metrical Romance* (1828); from St George Tucker's (b. 1752) edition of *Blackstone's Commentaries* (1803) to George Tucker's (b. 1775) *Valley of the Shenendoah* (1824); from the elder Tucker's *Dissertation on Slavery* (1796) to the defence of slavery in 1832 by Thomas R. Dew (b. 1802). In 1787 Madison advocated national union; in 1822 George Tucker advocated dueling.'

6 THE POLITICS OF JUDICIAL SPACE

1. Although Hamilton is sometimes contrasted with other Founders as being an 'empire' theorist, it seems clear that Jefferson's reliance on locale or community as the source of law did not preclude his own commitment to building an American empire. Rather, as Gerald Stourzh and Joyce Appleby have shown, such an reliance simply shaped an agrarian and commercial farming 'empire' in contrast to

Hamilton's commercial manufacturing vision. See Gerald Stourzh,
Alexander Hamilton and the Idea of Republican Government (Stanford, 1970); Joyce Appleby, 'Commercial Farming and the "Agrarian
Myth" in the Early Republic', *Journal of American History*, vol. 68,
1982, pp. 833–49.

2. Hamilton to Gouverneur Morris, 19 May 1777, in H. C. Syrett, ed.,
The Papers of Alexander Hamilton (New York, 1962). vol. I, pp.
254–5.

3. David Hackett Fischer, *The Revolution of American Conservatism*
(New York, 1965), p. 197. On Fischer's assessment, 'the new realities
of American public life – enlarged popular participation, and the
emergence of parties – altered the structure of government as well as
the structure of politics' in post-revolutionary America. Hamilton's
political and jurisprudential thought is rooted in the recognition of
these altered circumstances.

4. Hamilton, Madison, Jay, *The Federalist Papers*, ed. Clinton Rossiter
(New York, 1961), no. 83, p. 499.

5. Consonant with their conception of expanding the area of jural competence, and the identification of the legal judgments of jurors with
the substance of political government, Jefferson's more 'radical republican' supporters argued for the power of juries to cross-examine
witnesses and lawyers. More important, they challenged in some cases
the modern concept of jural neutrality, and argued that 'the jury,
being of the neighborhood, may, and oftentimes do know something
of their own knowledge, as to the matter itself, the credit of the
evidence etc which may justly sway them in delivering their verdict.'
'Decius', *Independent Chronicle* (Boston, 24 Nov. 1806), cited in
Richard Ellis, *The Jeffersonian Crisis: Courts and Politics in the Young
Republic* (New York, 1971), p. 202. The term 'radical republican' is
taken from Ellis.

6. Hamilton's notes for arguments in *People v. Croswell* (N.Y. Sup. Ct.,
1803–04), reprinted in Julius Goebel, Jr and J. H. Smith (eds), *The
Law Practice of Alexander Hamilton* (New York, 1964–81), vol. I.
pp. 810–11.

7. 'The Law of Libel', in H. C. Lodge, ed., *The Works of Alexander
Hamilton* (New York, n.d.), vol. VIII, p. 386. Hamilton's manual
itself suggests confusion about the actual reception within New York
of the relative scope of the jury's power or right to determine law.
He cites support for the argument that on the one hand, 'the Proper
province of the Jury is to determine Matters of Fact and of Law; but
they may at their Peril determine both', making reference to outdated
threat of attaint. On the other hand, he notes that attaint had been
succeeded by new trials 'in all cases of Misbehavior of the Jury' or
'when the Jury have mistaken the Law'. In part, the apparent practical
contradiction here mirrors the confusion extant in New York that
evidence existed of a belief on the part of some 'judges and informed
commentators' prior to the Revolution that 'a court could grant a new
trial if the jury in a civil matter ignored he law'. Yet, as late as 1800
there remained no uniform agreement among judges on this within

the state. *Law Practice of Alexander Hamilton*, vol. I, pp. 118, 120; see Nelson, 'The Eighteenth Century Background', *Michigan Law Review*, p. 893, *Forsey v. Cunningham* (N.Y. Sup. Ct., 1763). See for example *Wilkie v. Roosevelt*, vol. 3, *Johns Cas.* 66 (N.Y. Sup. Ct., 1802). For Hamilton's argument in favour of truth as a defence in libel, see *People v. Croswell*, in *Law Practice of Alexander Hamilton*, vol. I, p. 808.

8. Alexander Hamilton, *Federalist Papers*, no. 83, p. 499.
9. ibid.
10. *Federalist Papers*, nos. 1, 6, 27; see Hamilton's speeches at the Constitutional Convention in Max Farrand, ed., *Records of the Constitutional Convention of 1787* (New Haven, 1911), 18, 22 June 1787.
11. See *Federalist Papers*, no. 27; Hamilton to John Jay, 1775, in H. C. Syrett, ed., *The Papers of Alexander Hamilton* (New York, 1962), vol. I, p. 176.
12. Farrand, *Record of the Constitutional Convention*, 18 June 1787.
13. See Hamilton, 'The Continentalist', 9 August 1781, in *Papers of Alexander Hamilton*, vol. II, p. 660; *Federalist*, no. 59, pp. 192–3.
14. Hamilton, 'Eulogium for Maj. General Greene, July 4, 1789', *Papers of Hamilton*, vol. V, p. 348.
15. *Federalist*, no. 27, p. 175. Hamilton's view is shared and enlarged upon in Madison's no. 10.
16. *Law Practice of Alexander Hamilton*, vol. I, p. 197.
17. ibid.
18. *Papers of Alexander Hamilton*, vol. III, p. 431.
19. *Papers of Alexander Hamilton*, vol. III, pp. 343–5.
20. 'A Letter from Phocion to the Considerate Citizens of New York', in *Papers of Alexander Hamilton*, vol. III, p. 484; Brief no. 2, *Rutgers v. Waddington, Law Practice of Hamilton*, vol. I, p. 339. The intense desire of the New York legislature to punish Tories was due in large measure to the considerable sufferings of that state's inhabitants during the war. New York was among the first states invaded, and a considerable part of it remained under British control during the entire war. Large numbers of inhabitants were driven off their farms and, with their property wasted, left exiled without support.
21. *Papers of Alexander Hamilton*, vol. I, pp. 176–7.
22. ibid.
23. However, its apparent legislative power was undermined by Article II, which not only lacked a 'necessary and proper' clause, but seemed to deny legislative supremacy to the Congress, even in matters of foreign affairs. 'Each state retains its sovereignty, freedom, and independence, and every Power, Jurisdiction and right, which is not by this confederation expressly delegated to the United States, in congress assembled.' See *Law Practice of Alexander Hamilton*, vol. I, p. 213.
24. *Papers of Alexander Hamilton*, vol. III, p. 485; *Law Practice*, vol. I, p. 296.
25. *Law Practice*, vol. I, pp. 11, 285.
26. New York Mayor's Court, 1784, removed by writ of error to N.Y. Supreme Court, 1784–85. Judicial review is here understood as the

claim that the judiciary has the exclusive and independent power of interpreting law, and that this power includes the review and voiding of legislative enactments which in the judgment of the judiciary are in conflict with a law of higher authority or legitimacy.

27. *Law Practice*, vol. I, p. 336.
28. *Law Practice*, vol. I, p. 354.
29. *Law Practice*, vol. I, p. 375.
30. *Law Practice*, vol. I, p. 358.
31. *Federalist* no. 22.
32. *Law Practice*, vol. I, p. 357.
33. *Law Practice*, vol. I, p. 415.
34. *New York Assembly Journal*, 8th assembly, 1st meeting (4 Oct.–29 Nov. 1784), cited in *Law Practice of Alexander Hamilton*, vol. I, p. 312.
35. J. B. Thayer, *Cases in Constitutional Law* (Cambridge, 1895), vol. I, pp. 78–79.
36. Julius Goebel, Jr, ed., *History of the Supreme Court*, vol. I, p. 139.
37. *Law Practice*, vol. I, p. 416.
38. ibid.
39. Farrand, *Records of the Constitutional Convention*, vol. II, pp. 73–74 (Roger Sherman); see also Madison, *Notes of Debates in the Federal Convention of 1787* (Athens, Ohio, 1966), p. 60. Both the New York and Virginia plans proposed Councils of Revision.
40. Madison, *Notes on Debates in the Federal Convention*, pp. 336–7.
41. ibid.
42. *Federalist*, no. 73, pp. 446–7.
43. Montesquieu, *The Spirit of the Laws* (New York, 1949), p. 181.
44. *Federalist*, no. 10, p. 80.
45. ibid.
46. Gaillard Hunt, ed., *The Writings of James Madison*, vol. V (New York, 1904), p. 320. See also Marvin Meyers, The Mind of the Founder (Indianapolis, 1973), p. xxxvii.
47. 'The Virginia Bill of Rights', 12 June 1776, reprinted in H. S. Commager, ed., *Documents of American History* (Englewood Cliffs, 1973), vol. I, p. 104.
48. *Federalist*, no. 49, p. 314.
49. *The Debates and Proceedings of the Congress of the United States* (Washington, 1834), vol. I, pp. 745, 775.
50. *Writings of James Madison*, vol. V, p. 320.
51. *Federalist*, no. 71, p. 433.
52. Notes for a Speech at the New York Ratifying Convention', July 1788, in *Papers of Alexander Hamilton*, vol. V, p. 151; *Federalist*, no. 15, p. 160.
53. Farrand, *Record of the Constitutional Convention*, vol. I, p. 299.
54. *Papers of Hamilton*, vol. I, p. 87.
55. *Works of Hamilton*, vol. V, p. 416; 'Farmer Refuted', *Papers of Hamilton*, vol. I, pp. 87–8.
56. *Papers of Hamilton*, vol. I, p. 90.
57. *Federalist*, no. 78, p. 467.

58. Hamilton, 'Speech to the Constitutional Convention', 18 June 1787. Several versions of this speech have been reported. The version used here is the one approved by Hamilton and reprinted in Saul Padover, *The Mind of Alexander Hamilton* (New York, 1958), p. 114; John Locke, *Essays on the Law of Nature*, ed. W. von Leyden (Oxford, 1958), p. 161.
59. For a discussion of the British judiciary's own understanding of judicial independence, past and present, see John Dawson, *Oracles of the Law* (Cambridge, 1958), pp. 1–99. See also Martin Shapiro, *Courts* (Chicago, 1981), pp. 32–5; Sir Ivor Jennings, *The Law and the Constitution* (London, 1959), pp. 239–54. It comes as no surprise that Walter Bagehot's nineteenth-century discussion of the 'efficient secret' of the British Constitution does not even discuss the British judiciary. Bagehot, *The British Constitution* (London, 1949).
60. Jonathan Elliot, *The Debates in the Several State Conventions on the Adoption of the Federal Constitution* (Philadelphia, 1907), vol. IV, p. 258.
61. 'The Brutus Letters', no. XI, in Cecilia Kenyon, *The Anti-Federalists* (Indianapolis, 1966), pp. 334–8.
62. *Federalist*, no. 78, p. 470.
63. *Federalist*, no. 78, p. 471.
64. *Federalist*, no. 83, p. 496.
65. Hannah Arendt, *On Revolution* (Harmondsworth, 1963), pp. 238, 235.
66. Robert C. McCloskey, ed., *The Works of James Wilson* (Cambridge, Mass., 1967), p. 770. McCloskey was the first to argue for the consistency of Wilson's democratic vision. Gordon Wood, however, has suggested the extent to which Wilson's attachments to strong national government led him to support Federalist arguments that the 'best' men in the community should be encouraged to participate in government. See Wood, *Creation of the American Republic*, pp. 492–3. However, to characterize such support as unqualified 'elitism', and consequently to label Wilson as antidemocratic in spirit, if not in practice, is to impose too stringent criteria for 'democratic' thought in the eighteenth century (or perhaps any other), and certainly requires us to set aside the greater number of Wilson's statements explicitly supporting popular sovereignty, proportional representation, the direct election of members, of both Houses of Congress and of the President. See Max Farrand, *Records of the Federal Convention of 1787*, vol. I, pp. 52, 69, 132–3, 179, 405–6, 483; II, p. 56. In particular, the conclusion of Hannah Arendt that Wilson was antidemocratic stems from a highly selective and acontextual reading of one quotation taken second-hand from William J. Carpenter's *The Development of American Political Thought* (Princeton, 1939), pp. 93–4. See Arendt, *On Revolution*, p. 236.
67. *Works of James Wilson*, pp. 77–8. Reid's revisions of, as well as indebtedness to, Lockean epistemoloy are well worth a study in itself. However, for a more detailed discussion of Wilson's explicit concerns with Locke's 'revolution principle' as well as his development of

elements of both Reid's and Locke's epistemologies, see S. C. Stimson, 'A Jury of the Country: Common Sense and the Jurisprudence of James Wilson', in Richard B. Sher, ed., *Scotland and America in the Age of Witherspoon* (Edinburgh, forthcoming).

68. *Works of James Wilson*, pp. 745, 374, 221, 103, 212.
69. *Works of James Wilson*, p. 723.
70. *Works of James Wilson*, pp. 735, 744, 105, 102, 738.
71. *Works of James Wilson*, p. 361.
72. *Works of James Wilson*, p. 362.
73. *Works of James Wilson*, p. 753.
74. Thomas Reid, *Works*, ed. Sir William Hamilton (Edinburgh, 1863), pp. 591, 641, 638.
75. Reid, *Works*, pp. 641, 941.
76. Farrand, *Records of the Federal Convention*, vol. I, p. 605) (13 July 1787).
77. *Works of James Wilson*, pp. 770, 771. See also Jennifer Nedelsky, *Property and the Framers of the U.S. Constitution: A Study of the Political Thought of James Madison, Gouverneur Morris, and James Wilson'*, *Ph.D dis.*, University of Chicago, 1977.
78. *Works of James Wilson*, p. 304; Farrand, *Records of the Federal Convention*, vol. I, pp. 132–3.
79. *Works of James Wilson*, pp. 387–8.
80. *Pennsylvania Gazette*, 24 March 1779.
81. *Philadelphia Pa. Journal*, 7 July 1784. Wilson won this argument in 1790.
82. *Works of James Wilson*, pp. 291–308; 318–19. See also Max Farrand (ed.), *The Records of the Federal Convention*, 4 vols. (New Haven, 1911), pp. 300–1.
83. *Works of James Wilson*, pp. 74, 72, 73.
84. *Works of James Wilson*, p. 74.
85. ibid.
86. *Works of James Wilson*, pp. 547, 74, 529.
87. *Works of James Wilson*, p. 546.
88. *Works of James Wilson*, p. 502.
89. Blackstone, *Commentaries of the Laws of England*, ch. 2, sec. V, p. 124.
90. *Works of James Wilson*, p. 324.
91. *Works of James Wilson*, p. 293.
92. *Works of James Wilson*, pp. 454, 450. The Trenton trial of 1782 is discussed in Julian Boyd, ed., *The Papers of Thomas Jefferson*, vol. VI, 1778–84, pp. 474ff.
93. Farrand, *Records of the Federal Convention*, vol.I, p. 98; *Works of James Wilson*, pp. 455–6.
94. At least seven others can be named: Elbridge Gerry, Rufus King, Roger Sherman, James Madison, Gouverneur Morris, Luther Martin, George Mason.
95. *Works of James Wilson*, pp. 330, 137, 138, 290, 291, 79, 80, 330.
96. *Works of James Wilson*, pp. 330–1.
97. 2 *Dallas* 419, 1793, pp. 454–5.

7 GOVERNMENT BY DISCUSSION: THE CONTINUING DEBATE OVER JUDICIAL SPACE

1. It was Edward Corwin's observation that, 'as a good Federalist, Chief Justice Marshall sought, naturally, to embody the point of view of his party' in constitutional law. See Corwin, *Court Over Constitution* (Princeton, 1938). It was, perhaps, Corwin's established brilliance as a constitutional scholar, as well as the period in which this claim was made, that explains the plausibility and longevity of this interpretation. See, however, William Nelson's effective critique of this position, in 'The Eighteenth-Century Background of John Marshall's Constitutional Jurisprudence', *Michigan Law Review*, vol. 76, 1978, pp. 894ff.

2. See Christopher G. Tiedeman, *The Unwritten Constitution of the United States* (New York, 1890), p. 163; Thomas Cooley, *A Treatise on The Constitutional Limitations Which Rest Upon the Legislative Power of the States of the American Union* (Boston, 1903), pp. 237–8; Raoul Berger, *Congress v. The Supreme Court* (Cambridge, Mass. 1969), pp. 335–6; Charles J. Cooper and Nelson Lund, 'Landmarks of Constitutional Interpretation', *Policy Review*, Spring 1987, pp. 10–24.

3. Nelson, 'The Eighteenth-Century Background', *Michigan Law Review*, p. 894.

4. 17 U.S. (4 Wheaton, 316, 1819); 11 U.S. (7 Cranch, 32, 1812); 27 U.S. (2 Peters, 245, 1829). Cited in Nelson, op. cit., p. 895.

5. Nelson, op. cit., pp. 895–6.

6. Nelson, op. cit., pp. 917, 901.

7. Nelson, op. cit., pp. 901–2.

8. Nelson, op. cit., p. 918.

9. Jonathan Elliot, ed., *The Debates in the Several State Conventions on the Adoption of the Federal Constitution* (Philadelphia, 1907), vol. III, p. 561. Perhaps nowhere were the problems of legal heterogeneity and uncertainty greater, and the lack of legal consensus more pressing, than in post-revolutionary New York – a state which even by 1775 could be accurately called a microcosm of the social, political, and legal diversity which would increasingly characterize the nation. In reviewing the failure of New York constitutional framers to consider explicitly the scope and powers of judicial and jural administration, commentators such as Julius Goebel Jr find 'inadvertent omission' an unlikely explanation, but suggest no alternative. However, the failure of the Articles of Confederation (1781) to include a national judiciary, the studied opacity of the judiciary power in the Federal Constitution, and the failure of the Judiciary Act of 1789 to confront directly either questions of judiciary versus jury control over the content of law or questions of the general reception of the common law, are powerful indices of a high level of disagreement and lack of consensus about jurisprudential questions which existed both within and certainly between the states. Governeur Morris, a member of the drafting committee at the Convention, explained the general looseness of the

Constitution's judiciary clause in terms of the lack of consensus: 'On that subject opinions had been maintained with so much professional astuteness that it became necessary to select phrases, which expressing my own notion would not alarm others.' Farrand, *Records of the Federal Convention*, vol. III, p. 420.

10. I owe this term and my understanding of its importance in American liberal political thought to discussions with Samuel H. Beer and Stephen T. Homes.

11. 6 *Wheaton*, 380, 1821.

12. Samuel Konefsky, *John Marshall and Alexander Hamilton* (New York, 1964), p. 109.

13. Robert Ferguson, *Law and Letters in American Culture* (Cambridge, Mass., 1984), p. 23. The relevant cases are *Marbury v. Madison* (1 Cranch 137, 1803); *Cohens v. Virginia* (6 Wheaton 264, 1821); *McCulloch v. Maryland* (4 Wheaton, 316, 1819); *Dartmouth College v. Woodward* (4 Wheaton, 518, 1819); *Sturgis v. Crowninshield* (4 Wheaton, 122, 1819).

14. 6 *Wheaton*, 418, 414, 384, 382, 393–4. Certainly, in not all cases will such 'persuasion' prove effective. Some historians suggest that Marshall's decision in *Cohens v. Virginia* 'precipitated widespread and bitter criticism [of the Court] that lasted for years.' George Haskins and Herbert Johnson, eds, *History of the Supreme Court of the United States* (New York, 1981), vol. II, p. 106; Konefsky, *John Marshall and Alexander Hamilton*, p. 95. The decision's unpopularity presents another difficulty for the claim that Marshall relied for the exercise of judicial review on a 'consensus' which inhered in the nation.

15. John Roche, *John Marshall: Major Opinions and Other Writings* (New York, 1967), pp. 121, 134.

16. 'A Friend to the Constitution', *Alexandria Gazette*, 30 June – 15 July 1819, in Gerald Gunther, ed., *John Marshall's Defense of McCulloch v. Maryland* (Stanford, 1969).

17. Louis Hartz, *The Liberal Tradition in America* (New York, 1955), pp. 10–11. This essay also takes issue which Hartz's rendering of the character of Locke's influence in American political thought. For Hartz, 'Lockianism' is a code word for an 'irrational' moral uniformity which may well characterize certain elements of the American perspective, but has little or nothing to do with Locke's own epistemology or politics.

18. For some of the most recent philosophical debates over which perspectives in fact do, or 'should', characterize American thought about politics and law, see Ronald Dworkin, *Taking Rights Seriously* (Cambridge, Mass., 1979); Dworkin, *A Matter of Principle* (Cambridge, Mass., 1985), ch. 2; Richard Rorty, 'Postmodernist Bourgeois Liberalism', *Journal of Philosophy*, vol. 80, 1983, *Consequences of Pragmatism: essays, 1972–1980* (Minneapolis: University of Minnesota Press, 1982), and *Philosophy and the Mirror of Nature* (Princeton, 1979); Richard J. Bernstein, 'One Step Forward. Two Steps Backward: Rorty on Liberal Democracy and Philosophy', *Political Theory*, vol. 15, no. 4, 1987.

19. Max Radin, *Handbook of Anglo-American Legal History* (St Paul, Minn., 1936), p. 217; James Willard Hurst, *The Growth of American Law: The Law Makers* (Boston, 1950), p. 351; 'The Changing Role of the Jury in the Nineteenth Century', *Yale Law Journal*, vol. 74, 1964, p. 179.
20. See *Debates and Proceedings in the State Convention of Massachusetts to Revise and Amend the Constitution*, vol. 3, 1853, pp. 44–52. Cited in 'Changing Role of the Jury', p. 178.
21. 'Changing Role of the Jury', p. 178.
22. Shaw's own jurisprudential thought has been strongly compared to that of Marshall. See G. Edward White, *The American Judicial Tradition* (Oxford, 1976). Shaw's problems with the issue of jury control over law, particularly in *Commonwealth v. Porter* 51 Mass. (10 Met.) 263 (1845), are briefly discussed in 'Changing Role of the Jury', *Yale Law Journal*, 1974, pp. 176–7.
23. White, *American Judicial Tradition*, p. 43.
24. White, *American Judicial Tradition*, p. 47.
25. See Joseph Story, *Commentaries on the Constitution of the United States* (Boston, 1891), vol. II, pp. 560–1.
26. 156 U.S. 51, 1895. This opinion is interesting not only because the dissent marshals as much case support and argument for the jury's right to decide the law as the majority does for the lack of one. More interesting, however, is the fact that the majority decision rests on a precedent, as Kent and Story would have it, but the precedent is Lemuel Shaw's argument in *Commonweath v. Athens*, which is argued not on the basis of precedent but by constitutional 'reasoning' and persuasion. 71 Mass. (5 Gray) 185 (1885).
27. Charles Fried, 'The Artificial Reason of Law or: What Lawyer's Know', *Texas Law Review*, vol. 60, 1981, p. 54. On this collapsed perspective of common and constitutional law, the constitutional question of a 'right to privacy in a public telephone booth' becomes a complex and knotty problem of 'professional' reasoning in which public arguments from either principles of political or constitutional thought can have no place.
28. Even the most profound critiques of American oracular theories of jurisprudence, such as John Chipman Gray's work, *The Nature and Sources of the Law* (New York, 1909), has been observed by H. L. A. Hart to resemble 'much more an English textbook on jurisprudence . . . than any other American book', and equally to acknowledge the influence of Bentham and Austin, whose work I would argue has little significance for American problems of constitutional adjudication. Indeed, Hart notes that Gray uses English thinkers and techniques 'to pursue a most un-English theme: that the law consists of rules laid down by the courts used to decide cases and that all else, statutes and past precedents included, are merely sources of law.' See Hart, *Essays in Jurisprudence and Philosophy* (Oxford, 1983), pp. 128–9. The more recent contribution of Ronald Dworkin to building a single, normative theory of how American judges may 'rightly' decide constitutionally controversial, 'hard cases', suggests

the confusions inherent in not more clearly separating English and American jurisprudential foundations and concerns. Dworkin takes as his principal opponent H. L. A. Hart and with him a tradition of English analytic, positivist, and utilitarian jurisprudence inspired by Bentham which has penetrated, if at all, only a very little way into American constitutional jurisprudence. (The notable exception is Richard Posner's work: see 'Utilitarianism, Economics, and Legal Theory', *Journal of Legal Studies*, vol. 8, 1979). Then, by employing a model for constitutional reasoning which most closely approximates English common law cases of product liability, Dworkin hopes to take the controversy out of disputed cases by squeezing the 'discretion' out of judicial 'interpretation'. However, judicial discretion is not the same thing as judicial space, as should be clear from the above analysis, and no amount of effort to eliminate the appearance of judicial choice (by showing that only one right answer exists) will lessen the American judiciary's controversial position.

29. H. L. A. Hart, 'American Jurisprudence Through English Eyes: The Nightmare and the noble Dream', in *Essays in Jurisprudence and Philosophy* (Oxford, 1983), p. 146.

30. The British Home Secretary has recently proposed a far-reaching and controversial shift in the conduct of British criminal justice, dispensing with a criminal suspect's right to silence by permitting juries to draw adverse inferences from such silence. For a public reaction to this proposal, see Malcolm Dean, 'The guilty sound of silence', *Guardian*, 30 November 1988, p. 25. The newly proposed Official Secrets Bill, which replaces section two of the Official Secrets Act of 1911, leaves the definition of alleged 'damage' open to wide legal interpretation and is considered a significant weakening of the 1911 Act's restrictions that the actual harm of such disclosure must be demonstrated, and those affected clearly identified. See Richard Morton-Taylor, 'Concessions leave "damage" definition unclear', *Guardian*, 1 December 1988, p. 3.

31. Sir Ivor Jennings, *The Law and the Constitution* (London, 1959), p. 254.

Bibliography

BIBLIOGRAPHIES

Adams, J. N., and Averley, G. *A Bibliography of Eighteenth Century Legal Literature*. Newcastle-upon-Tyne: Avers Publications, 1982.

Hall, Kermit. *A Comprehensive Bibliography of American Constitutional and Legal History, 1896–1979*. Millwood, N. Y.: Kraus International Pub., 1983.

Sweet, L. F., and Maxwell, W. H. *Sweet and Maxwell's Legal Bibliography*. London: Sweet and Maxwell, 1935–49.

Sweet, L. F. and Maxwell, W. H. *Sweet and Maxwell's Complete Law Books Catalogue*. London: Sweet and Maxwell, 1925.

Wing, Donald G., ed. *A Short Title Catalogue of Books Printed in England, Scotland, Ireland, Wales and British America and of English Books Printed in Other Countries, 1641–1700*. New York: Modern Language Association, 1967.

PAMPHLETS AND TRACTS

Sources

Aylmer, G. E. *The Levellers in the English Revolution*. Ithaca, New York: Cornell University Press, 1975.

Bailyn, Bernard, ed. *Pamphlets of the American Revolution 1750–1776*. Cambridge, Mass.: Harvard University Press, 1965.

Bodleian Library, Oxford University (Bd. L.)

British Library (B.L.)

Eaton, Daniel Isaac, and Paine, Thomas. *Five Tracts, 1793–1812*. New York: Garland Publishing, 1974.

Five Tracts on Libel Addressed to Charles Jones Fox, 1791–92. New York: Garland Publishing, 1974.

Freedom of the Press. Sir Roger L'Estrange's Tracts and Others 1660–1681. New York: Garland Publishing, 1974.

Freedom of the Press: Six Tracts 1698–1709. New York: Garland Publishing, 1974.

Freedom of the Press: Six Tracts, 1712–1730. New York: Garland Publishing, 1974.

Haller, William. *Tracts on Liberty in the Puritan Revolution 1638–1647*. 3 vols. New York: Columbia University Press, 1944.

Haller, William, and Davies, Godfrey, eds. *The Leveller Tracts 1647–1653*. New York: Columbia University Press, 1944.

Harleian Miscellany (H.M.)

Harvard Law School Library (Treasure Room) (H.L.S.)

Horace Walpole's Political Tracts 1747–1748, with Two by William Warbur-

ton on *Literary Property 1747 and 1762.* New York: Garland Publishing, 1974.

Houghton Library, Harvard University (H.L.)

Hyneman, Charles S., and Lutz, Donald S., eds. *American Political Writing During the Founding Era, 1760–1805.* 2 vols. Indianapolis: Liberty Press, 1983.

Justices and Juries in Colonial America: Two Accounts. New York: Arno Press, 1972.

Libels: Four Tracts, 1770. New York: Garland Publishing, 1974.

Libels, Warrants and Seizures: Three Tracts, 1764–1771. New York: Garland Publishing, 1974.

Moton, A. L. *Freedom in Arms.* New York: International Publishers, 1975.

The Extraordinary Case of William Bingley, Bookseller, 1770 and Robert Hall, *An Apology for the Freedom of the Press, 1793.* New York: Garland Publishing, 1974.

The Friends to the Liberty of the Press: Eight Tracts, 1792–1793. New York: Garland Publishing, 1974.

The Prosecution of Thomas Paine: Seven Tracts 1793–1798. New York: Garland Publishing, 1974.

Three Trials: John Peter Zenger, H. S. Woodfall, and John Lambert 1765–1794. New York: Garland Publishing, 1974.

Trenchard, John, and Gordon, T. *Cato's Letters or Essays on Liberty, Civil and Religious.* 4 vols. 3rd ed. New York: Russell and Russell, 1969.

Wilkes, John, and Churchill, C. *The North Briton.* 4 vols. London, 1772.

Wolfe, Don M., ed. *Leveller Manifestoes of the Puritan Revolution.* New York: Thomas Nelson and Sons, 1944.

Woodhouse, A. S. P. *Puritanism and Liberty.* Chicago: University of Chicago Press, 1951.

Selected Pamphlets and Tracts

A. B., N. T. *Some Remarks Upon Government and Particularly Upon the Establishment of the English Monarchy. In Two Letters Written by and to a Member of the Great Convocation Holden at Westminster the 22nd of January, 1688–89.* 1689. (B.T., 1675)

Almon, John. *The Trial of John Almon, Bookseller.* London, 1770.

An Agreement of the People For A Firme and Present Peace, upon grounds of common-right and freedome. 3 Nov. 1647. (Wolfe, pp. 225–34)

Anon. *The Fundamental Constitution of the English Government.* London, 1690.

Anon. *A Jury-mans Judgement upon the Case of Lieut. Col. John Lilburn.* June 1653. (H.L. E. 702 (6); film A199, reel 108)

Anon. *A Mirror for the Multitude; or Wilkes no Patriot.* 1770. (H.L.S.)

Anon. *A Mirror for the Rulers of the People.* London, 1761. (H.L.S.)

Anon. *A Second Postcript to a late Pamphlet entitled, A Letter to Mr. Almon in the Matter of Libel.* London, 1770.

Anon. *An Address to the Jurymen of London. By a citizen.* 2nd edition. London, 1775, originally 1752. (H.L.S.)

Anon. *Another Letter of Mr. Almon in Matter of Libel.* London, 1770. (H.L.S.)

Anon. *Sketch of an Answer to a Pamphlet Entitled 'Letter Concerning Libels, Warrants and Seizure of Papers'.* c. 1765. (B.L. Ms. Add. 35, 887, fols. 171 et seq.)

Anon. *The Doctrine of Libels and the Duties of Juries fairly stated.* London, 1752. (H.L.S.)

Anon. *The Fundamental Constitution of the English Government.* London, 1690. (H.L.S.)

Anon. *The Fundamental Lawes and Liberties of England Claimed, asserted, and agreed unto by severall Peaceable Persons of the City of London, Westminster, Southwark, Hamblets, and Places Adjacent . . .* 9 July 1653. (H.L. *EC65 A100 653f.)

Anon. *The Onely Right Rule for regulating the Lawes and Liberties of the People of England.* 28 Jan. 1652/3. (H.L. E 684 (33); film A199, reel 105)

Anon. *To the Supreme Authority, the Parliament of the Commonwealth of England. The humble petition of divers constant Adherers to this Parliament, and faithful Assertors of the fundamental Lawes and Liberties of the Commonwealth.* 29 June 1653. (H.L. 669f.16 (54); film A199, reel 246).

Ashurst, William. *Reasons Against Agreement with a late Printed Paper, intitled, Foundations of Freedome: Or, the Agreement of the People.* London, 1648. (H.L.)

(Billing, Edward.) *A Mite of Affection, manifested in 31. Proposals, Offered to all the Sober and Free-born People within this Commonwealth; Tending and tendred unto them for a Settlement in this day and hour of the Worlds Distraction and Confusion.* London: Giles Calvert. 1659. (H.L. *EC65.B4957.A659m)

Care, Henry. *English Liberties: or, the free-born subjects inheritance.* London, 1700. (H.L.S.)

Cole, William. *A Rod for the Lawyers: Who are hereby declared to be the grand Robbers and Deceivers of the Nation.* London: Giles Calver 1659. (H.L. *EC65.C6766.659rb)

Dyer, George. *An Address to the people of Great Britain, on the doctrine of libels, and the office of the juror.* 1799. (H.L.S.)

Erskine, Thomas. *The Speech of the Hon. Thomas Erskine at a Meeting of the Friends to the Liberty of the Press.* London, 1792.

Father of Candor (pseud.). *An Enquiry into the Doctrine Concerning Libels, Warrants, and the Seizure of Papers.* (Dublin, 1765) (New York: Garland Publishing, 1979.)

(Ferguson, Robert.) *The Second Part of No Protestant Plot.* London: R. Smith, 1682. (B.L.)

Hale, Matthew. *Pleas of the Crown.* London, Printed for Richard Tonson, 1678.

Hawles, John. *The English-Men's Right: A Dialogue Between a Barrister at Law and a Jury-Man: Plainly setting forth, 1. The Antiquity II. The excellent designed use III. The office and just Privileges of Juries, by the Law of England.* London: Richard Janeway, 1680. (H.L.S.)

Hawles, John. *Remarks Upon the Tryals of Edward Fitzharris, Stephen Colledge, Count Coningsmark, The Lord Russell, Collonel Sidney, Henry*

Cornish, and Charles Bateman. As also on the Earl of Shaftesbury's Grand Jury, Wilmore's Homine Replegiano, And the Award of Execution against Sir Thomas Armstrong . . . London: Jacob Tonson, 1689. (H.L.S.)

Hawles, John. *Of Tryals by a Jury* (1722).

(Jones, John.) *Juror Judges of Law and Fact. Or, certain Observations of certain differences in points of Law between* . . . *Adr. Horn and* . . . *(the author of) 'A Letter of due Censure and Redargution to Lieut. Col. John Lilburn'.* London: W. D., 1650. (H.L. E. 1414 (2): film A199, reel 182)

Jones, John. *Judges Judged Out of their Own Mouthes.* London, 1650. (H.L.S.)

Lilburne, John. *England's New Chains Discovered.* London, 1649. (Haller and Davies, pp. 157–70)

Lilburne, John. *The Second Part of England's New Chains Discovered.* London, 1649. (Haller and Davies, pp. 172–89)

Lilburne, John. *The Legall Fundamentall Liberties of the People of England* London, 8 June 1649. (B.L.: E. 560 (14); Haller and Davies, pp. 400–49, excerpts)

Lilburne, John. *England's Birthright Justified.* London, 1645. (H.L.S.; Haller, vol.3, pp. 258–307)

Lilburne, John. *A Worke of the Beast Or a Relation of a most unchristian Censure, Executed upon John Lilburne.* April 1638. (Haller, vol. 2, pp. 3–37)

Lilburne, John. *A Cry for Justice: or, An Epistle written by John Lilburne.* May 1639. (Haller and Davies, pp. 238–46)

Lilburne, John. *A Copie of a letter to Mr. William Prinne Esq.* 7 Jan. 1645. (Haller, vol. 3, pp. 181–7)

Minutes of the Extra-parliamentary Committee for Regulating the Law. (Hardwicke Papers; B.L. Add.M55,35,863)

Morris, Robert. *A Letter to Sir Richard Aston, Knt.* London, 1770. (H.L.S.)

(Overton, Richard?) *A Remonstrance of Many Thousand Citizens.* London: 7 July 1646. (Wolfe, p. 125)

Overton, Richard. *The Commoners' Complaint.* London: 10 Feb. 1646. (Haller, vol. 3, pp. 373–405)

Overton, Richard. *An Arrow against all Tyrants.* Nov. 1646. (Aylmer, pp. 68–70)

Penn, William. *The People's Ancient and Just Liberties.* London, 1670. (H.L.S.)

Penn, William. *Truth Rescued from Imposture.* London, 1671. (H.L.S.)

Pettingal, John. *Enquiry into the use and practice of Juries among the Greeks and Romans from whence the origin of the English jury may probably be deduced.* London, 1769. (H.L.S.)

The Putney Debates, 28, 29 Oct. 1647; 1 Nov. 1647. (Woodhouse, pp. 1–37, 38–95, 95–124)

The Resolutions of the First Meeting of the Friends to the Liberty of the Press. London, 19 Dec. 1792.

Robinson, Henry. *Certain Considerations In order to a more speedy, cheap, and equall distribution of Justice throughout the Nation.* London: Matthew Simmons, 1651. (H.L.)

(Somers, John.) *The Security of English-Mens Lives, Or The Trust, Power, and Duty of the Grand Jurys of England. Published for the Prevention of Popish Designs against the Lives of many Protestant Lords and Commoners* . . . London: T. Mitchel, 1681. (B.L.)

Starling, Sir William. *An Answer to the Seditious and Scandalous Pamphlet, entitled, The trial of W. Penn and W. Mead.* London, 1671. (H.L.S.) *Thomason Tracts.* (B.L., E. 541 (lb))

Towers, Joseph. *An Enquiry into the Question, Whether Juries are, or not, Judges of Law as well as fact; with a particular Reference to the Case of Libels.* London, 1764. (H.L.S.)

Walwyn, William. *Englands Lamentable Slaverie, Proceeding from the Arbitrarie will, severitie, and Injustices of Kings.* Oct 1645. (Haller, vol. 3, pp. 311–18)

Walwyn, William. *Juries Justified: Or, A word of Correction to Mr. Henry Robinson; for His seven Objections against the Trial of Causes, by Juries of twelve men.* London: Robert Wood, 1651. (H.L.)

(Walwyn, William.). *A Pearle in a Dounghill. Or Lieu. Col. John Lilburne in New-gate.* June 1646. (Morton, pp. 77–85)

Warr, John. *The Corruption and Deficiency of the Laws of England.* London, 1649. (H.L. (1745)III, pp. 240–2)

The Whitehall Debates. 8–11, 13 Jan. 1649. (Woodhouse, pp. 169–70, 171–8)

Wildman, John. *The Lawes Subversion.* London, 1648. (B.L. E. 431(2), 35).

NEWSPAPERS AND WEEKLIES

The Massachusetts Spy
The New York Gazette; or Weekly Post-boy

SELECTED BOOKS AND MONOGRAPHS

Aaron, Richard. *John Locke.* Oxford: Clarendon Press, 1971.

Adair, Douglas, and Schultz, John. *Peter Oliver's Origin and Progress of the American Rebellion.* San Marino: Huntington Library, 1961.

Adams, John. *The Legal Papers of John Adams.* ed. L. K. Wroth and H. B. Zobel. Cambridge, Mass.: Harvard University Press, 1965.

Adams, John. *The Political Writings of John Adams.* ed. George Peek. Indianapolis: Bobbs-Merrill, 1954.

Adams, John. *The Adams-Jefferson Letters.* ed. Lester J. Cappon. Chapel Hill: University of North Carolina Press, 1959.

Adams, John. *The Papers of John Adams.* ed. Robert J. Taylor, M. Kline, G. L. Lint. Cambridge, Mass.: Harvard University Press, 1977.

Adams, John. *Diary and Autobiography of John Adams.* ed. L.A. Butterfield. Cambridge, Mass.: Harvard University Press, 1961.

Adams, John. *The Works of John Adams.* ed. C. F. Adams. Boston: Little, Brown, 1850–56.

Adams, W. P. *The First American Constitutions: Republican Ideology and the Making of the State Constitution in the Revolutionary Era*. Chapel Hill: University of North Carolina, 1980.

Alexander, James. *A Brief Narrative of the Case and Trial of John Peter Zenger*. Cambridge, Mass.: Harvard University Press, 1963.

Allen, David G. *In English Ways; The Movement of Societies and the Transferal of English Local Law to Massachusetts Bay in the Seventeenth Century*. Chapel Hill: University of North Carolina Press, 1981.

Arendt, Hannah. *Crises of the Republic*. New York: Harcourt, Brace, Jovanovich, 1972.

Arendt, Hannah. *The Human Condition*. Chicago: University of Chicago Press, 1958.

Arendt, Hannah. *The Life of the Mind*. New York: Harcourt, Brace, Jovanovich, 1948.

Arendt, Hannah. *On Revolution*. Harmondsworth: Penguin, 1963.

Ashcraft, Richard. *Revolutionary Politics and Locke's Two Treatises of Government*. Princeton: Princeton University Press, 1986.

Austin, John. *The Province of Jurisprudence Determined*. New York: Noonday, 1954.

Aylmer, G. E., ed. *The Interregnum: The Search for a Settlement 1640–1660*. London: Macmillan, 1972.

Aylmer, G. E., *The Levellers in the English Revolution*. Ithaca: Cornell University Press, 1975.

Bacon, Sir Francis. *Novum Organum*. ed. F. H. Anderson. New York: Liberal Arts, 1960.

Bacon, Sir Francis. *Works and Life and Letters of Bacon*. ed. James Spedding, R. L. Ellis, D. D. Heath. London, 1862.

Bagehot, Walter. *The English Constitution*. London: Oxford University Press, 1949.

Bailyn, Bernard. *The Ordeal of Thomas Hutchinson*. Cambridge, Mass.: Harvard University Press, 1974.

Bailyn, Bernard. *The Ideological Origins of the American Revolution*. Cambridge, Mass.: Harvard University Press, 1967.

Bailyn, Bernard. ed. *Pamphlets of the American Revolution: 1750–1776*. Cambridge, Mass.: Harvard University Press, 1965.

Baker, Keith M. *Condorcet: From Natural Philosophy to Social Mathematics*. Chicago: University of Chicago Press, 1975.

Baldwin, Alice Mary. *The New England Clergy and the American Revolution*. Durham, N.C.: Duke University Press, 1928.

Barber, Benjamin. *Strong Democracy*. Berkeley: University of California Press, 1984.

Barker, Ernest. *Traditions of Civility*. Cambridge: Cambridge University Press, 1948.

Barker, Rodney. *Political Ideas in Modern Britain*. London: Methuen, 1978.

Beccaria, Cesare Bonesana. *An Essay on Crimes and Pubishments*. trans. Henry Paolucci. Indianapolis: Bobbs-Merrill, 1977.

Becker, Carl. *The Heavenly City of the Eighteenth-Century Philosophers*. New Haven: Yale University Press, 1932.

Beeman, Richard, Botein, Stephen, and Carter, Edward, eds. *Beyond Confederation*. Chapel Hill: University of North Carolina Press, 1987.

Beer, Samuel. *British Politics in the Collectivist Age.* New York: Vintage, 1969.

Beiner, Ronald. *Political Judgment.* Chicago: Chicago University Press, 1983.

Berger, Raoul. *Government by Judiciary.* Cambridge, Mass.: Harvard University Press, 1977.

Berger, Raoul. *Congress v. The Supreme Court.* Cambridge, Mass.: Harvard University Press, 1969.

Berlin, Isaiah. *Against the Current.* Harmondsworth: Penguin, 1982.

Berlin, Isaiah. *Two Concepts of Liberty.* Oxford: Oxford University Press, 1958.

Berlin, Isaiah. *Concepts and Categories.* New York: Viking Press, 1978.

Beveridge, A. J. *Life of John Marshall.* New York: Houghton, Mifflin, 1916–19.

Bickel, Alexander. *The Least Dangerous Branch.* New York: Bobbs-Merrill, 1962.

Bickel, Alexander. *The Supreme Court and the Idea of Progress.* New Haven: Yale University Press, 1978.

Bickel, Alexander. *The Morality of Consent.* New Haven: Yale University Press, 1975.

Billias, George A. *Law and Authority in Colonial America.* Barre, Mass.: Barre, 1965.

Billington, R. A., ed. *The Reinterpretation of Early American History.* San Marino: San Marino Press, 1966.

Blackstone, William. *Commentaries on the Laws of England.* ed. George Sharswood. Philadelphia: Lippincott, 1894.

Boorstin, Daniel J. *The Lost World of Thomas Jefferson.* New York: Holt, 1948.

Boorstin, Daniel J. *The Mysterious Science of the Law.* Boston: Beacon, 1958.

Bradsford, H. N. *The Levellers and the English Revolution.* London: Cresset Press, 1961.

Brewer, John, and Styles, John, eds. *An Ungovernable People.* London: Hutchinson, 1980.

Brown, Elizabeth. *British Statutes in American Law, 1776–1836.* Ann Arbor: University of Michigan Law School, 1964.

Brown, Richard D. *Revolutionary Politics in Massachusetts: The Boston Committee of Correspondence and the Towns, 1772–74.* Cambridge, Mass.: Harvard University Press, 1970.

Brown, Robert. *Middle-Class Democracy and Revolution in Massachusetts, 1690–1780.* Ithaca: Cornell University Press, 1955.

Burke, Edmund. *The Writings and Speeches of Edmund Burke.* 12 vols. London: Bickers & Son, n.d.

Burton, K. M., ed. *Milton's Prose Writings.* London: Dent, 1974.

Bryce, James. *Studies in History and Jurisprudence.* London: Oxford University Press, 1901.

Calabresi, Guido. *A Common Law for the Age of Statutes.* Cambridge, Mass.: Harvard University Press, 1982.

Cardoza, Benjamin. *The Nature of the Judicial Process*. New Haven: Yale University Press, 1921.

Carlyle, Thomas, ed. *Oliver Cromwell's Letters and Speeches*. 4 vols. Leipzig: Bernard Tauchnitz, 1861.

Chapin, Bradley. *The American Law of Treason*. Seattle: University of Washington Press, 1964.

Chinard, Gilbert. *Thomas Jefferson: Apostle of Americanism*. Ann Arbor: University of Michigan Press, 1957.

Chinard, Gilbert. *Jefferson et les idéologues d'après sa correspondence inédite avec Destutt de Tracy, Cabanis, J. B. Say, et Auguste Comte*. Baltimore: Johns Hopkins Press, 1925.

Cohen, Marshall. *Ronald Dworkin and Contemporary Jurisprudence*. Totowa, N.J.: Rowman & Allanheld, 1983.

Cohen, Morris. *Law: A Century of Progress*. New York: New York University Press, 1936.

Colbourne, H. Trevor. *The Lamp of Experience: Whig History and the Intellectual History of the American Republic*. Chapel Hill: University of North Carolina Press, 1965.

Coleman, John. *John Locke's Moral Philosophy*. Edinburgh: Edinburgh University Press, 1983.

Commager, Henry S. *Documents of American History*. Englewood Cliffs: Prentice Hall, 1973.

Cooley, Thomas. *A Treatise on The Constitutional Limitations Which Rest Upon the Legislative Power of the States of the American Union*. Boston: Little, Brown & Co., 1903.

Coquillette, Daniel, ed. *Law in Colonial Massachusetts: 1630–1800*. Boston: Colonial Society of Massachusetts, 1984.

Corwin, Edward. *The Doctrine of Judicial Review*. Gloucester: Peter Smith, 1914.

Corwin, Edward. *Court Over Constitution*. Princeton: Princeton University Press, 1938.

Countryman, Edward. *A People in Revolution; The American Revolution and Political Society in New York 1760–1790*. Baltimore: Johns Hopkins University Press, 1981.

Cragg, G. R. *Reason and Authority in the Eighteenth Century*. Cambridge: Cambridge University Press, 1964.

Crick, Bernard. *The American Science of Politics: Its Origins and Conditions*. Berkeley: University of California Press, 1959.

Croly, Herbert. *The Promise of American Life*. Cambridge, Mass.: Harvard University Press, 1965.

Cumming, Robert. *Human Nature and History*, vol. 2. Chicago: University of Chicago Press, 1969.

Davis, Richard Beale. *Intellectual Life in Jefferson's Virginia, 1790–1830*. Chapel Hill: University of North Carolina Press, 1964.

Dawson, John P. *Oracles of the Law*. Ann Arbor: University of Michigan Law School, 1968.

Dawson, John P. *A History of Lay Judges*. Cambridge, Mass.: Harvard University Press, 1960.

Dawson, John P. *Gifts and Promises*. New Haven: Yale University Press, 1980.

The Debates and Proceedings in the First Congress of the United States. Washington: 1834–56.

De Beer, E. S., ed. *The Correspondence of John Locke*. 8 vols. Oxford: Clarendon Press, 1976.

Demos, John. *A Little Commonwealth*. Oxford: Oxford University Press, 1970.

Dicey, A. V. *The Law of the Constitution*. London: Macmillan, 1959.

Dickens, A. J. *The English Reformation*. New York: Schocken, 1969.

Dietze, Eric. *Essays on the American Constitution*. Englewood Cliffs: Prentice Hall, 1964.

Dunn, John. *The Political Theory of John Locke*. Cambridge: Cambridge University Press, 1969.

Dworkin, Ronald. *Taking Rights Seriously*. Cambridge, Mass.: Harvard University Press, 1978.

Elliot, Jonathan, ed. *The Debates in the Several State Conventions on the Adoption of the Federal Constitution*. Philadelphia: Lippincott, 1907.

Ellis, Richard. *The Jeffersonian Crisis: Courts and Politics in the Young Republic*. New York: Norton, 1971.

Elton, G. R. *The Tudor Constitution*. Cambridge: Cambridge University Press, 1960.

Elton, G. R. *England Under the Tudors*. London: Methuen, 1955.

Ely, John Hart. *Democracy and Distrust*. Cambridge, Mass.: Harvard University Press, 1980.

Emerson, Ralph Waldo. *English Traits, Representative Men, Other Essays*. London: Dent, 1951.

The English Reports. (1307–1865) 176 vols. Edinburgh: William Green & Sons, 1900–30. Full Reprint.

Eusden, John. *Puritans, Lawyers and Politics in Early Seventeenth-Century America*. Hamden, Conn.: Archon, 1968.

Farrand, Max, ed. *The Records of the Federal Convention of 1787*. New Haven: Yale University Press, 1911.

Faulkner, Robert. *The Jurisprudence of John Marshall*. Princeton: Princeton University Press, 1968.

Ferguson, Robert. *Law and Letters in American Culture*. Cambridge, Mass.: Harvard University Press, 1984.

Finnis, John. *Natural Law and Natural Rights*. Oxford: Clarendon, 1980.

Fischer, David Hackett. *The Revolution of American Conservatism*. New York: Harper and Row, 1965.

Flaherty, David. *Privacy in Colonial New England*. Charlottesville: University of Virginia Press, 1967.

Flaherty, David. *Law and the Enforcement of Morals in Early America*. Chapel Hill: University of North Carolina Press, 1971.

Flaherty, David. *Essays in the History of Early American Law*. Chapel Hill: University of North Carolina Press, 1969.

Fliegelman, Jay. *Prodigals and Pilgrims: The American Revolution Against Patriarchal Authority*. Cambridge: Cambridge University Press, 1982.

Foner, Eric. *Tom Paine and Revolutionary America*. New York: Oxford University Press, 1976.

Ford, Paul L., ed. *Pamphlets on the Constitution of the United States*. New York: 1888.

Frank, Jerome. *Law and the Modern Mind*. New York: Tudor, 1936.

Franklin, Benjamin. *Autobiography and Selected Writings*. New York: Rinehart & Winston, 1959.

Franklin, Julian. *John Locke and the Theory of Sovereignty*. Cambridge: Cambridge University Press, 1978.

Friedman, L. J. *A History of American Law*. New York: Simon & Schuster, 1973.

Friedrich, Carl, and McCloskey, Robert, eds. *From the Declaration of Independence to the Constitution*. New York: Liberal Arts, 1954.

Gay, Peter. *The Enlightenment: An Interpretation*. New York: Knopf, 1969.

Geertz, Clifford. *The Interpretation of Cultures: Selected Essays*. New York: Basic Books, 1973.

Gilmore, Grant. *The Ages of American Law*. New Haven: Yale University Press, 1977.

Gardiner, S. R. *History of England*. London: Hurst, 1863.

Goebel, Julius, Jr. *History of the Supreme Court of the United States*. vol. I. *Antecedents and Beginnings to 1801*. New York: Macmillan, 1971.

Goebel, Julius, Jr, and Naughton, T. Raymond. *Law Enforcement in Colonial New York* New York: Commonwealth Fund, 1944.

Goodwin, Albert. *The Friends of Liberty*. Cambridge, Mass.: Harvard University Press, 1979.

Gough, J. W. A. *Fundamental Law in English Constitutional History*. Oxford: Clarendon Press, 1955.

Gough, J. W. A. *John Locke's Political Philosophy*. Oxford: Clarendon Press, 1973.

Gray, John C. *The Nature and Sources of the Law*. New York: Macmillan, 1921

Green, Thomas A. *Verdict According to Conscience: Perspectives on the English Criminal Trial Jury 1200–1800*. Chicago: University of Chicago Press, 1985.

Greenberg, Douglas. *Crime and Law Enforcement in the Colony of New York: 1691–1776*. Ithaca: Cornell University Press, 1974.

Greene, Jack P. *Peripheries and Center: Constitutional Development in the Extended Politics of the British Empire and the United States, 1607–1788*. Athens, Ga.: University of Georgia Press, 1986.

Greene, Jack P. ed. *The Reinterpretation of the American Revolution 1763–1789*. Westport: Greenwold Press, 1968.

Guest, A. G., ed. *Oxford Essays in Jurisprudence*. Oxford: Oxford University Press, 1961.

Guizot, F. *History of the English Revolution*. 2 vols. London: H. G. Bohn, 1856.

Gunn, J. A. W. *Politics and the Public Interest in the Seventeenth Century*. London: Routledge and Kegan Paul, 1969.

Hamilton, Alexander. *The Works of Alexander Hamilton*. ed. H. C. Lodge. New York: Putman's Sons, n.d.

Hamilton, Alexander. *The Papers of Alexander Hamilton.* ed. H. C. Syrett and J. E. Cooke. New York: Columbia University Press, 1962.

Hamilton, Alexander. *The Law Practice of Alexander Hamilton: Documents and Commentary.* Julius Goebel, Jr and Joseph H. Smith eds. New York: Columbia University Press, 1964–81.

Hanbury, H. G. *English Courts of Law.* Oxford: Oxford University Press, 1944.

Handler, Edward. *America and Europe in the Political Thought of John Adams.* Cambridge, Mass.: Harvard University Press, 1964.

Handlin, Oscar, and Handlin, Mary, eds. *The Popular Sources of Political Authority: Documents on the Massachusetts Constitution of 1780.* Cambridge, Mass.: Harvard University Press, 1966.

Hanham, H. J. *The Nineteenth Century Constitution.* Cambridge: Cambridge University Press, 1968.

Hanson, L. W. *Government and the Press, 1695–1763.* Oxford: Clarendon Press, 1936.

Hart, H. L. A. *The Concept of Law.* Oxford: Oxford University Press, 1961.

Hart, H. L. A. *Essays in Jurisprudence and Philosophy.* Oxford: Clarendon Press, 1983.

Hart H. L. A., and Honore, A. M. *Causation and the Law.* Oxford: Oxford University Press, 1959.

Hartog, Hendrik, ed. *Law in the Revolution and the Revolution in the Law.* New York: New York University Press, 1981.

Hartz, Louis. *The Liberal Tradition in America.* New York: Harcourt, Brace, Jovanovich, 1955.

Haskins, George, and Johnson, Herbert A., eds. *History of the Supreme Court of the United States.* vol. II. *Foundations of Power: John Marshall, 1801–1815.* New York: Macmillan, 1981.

Haskins, George. *Law and Authority in Early Massachusetts: A Study in Tradition and Design.* New York: Macmillan, 1960.

Hay, Douglas, *et al.*, eds. *Albion's Fatal Tree: Crime and Society in Eighteenth-Century England.* New York: Pantheon, 1975.

Hayek, F.A. *Law, Legislation, and Liberty.* 3 vols. Chicago: Chicago University Press, 1979.

Hazard, Paul. *European Thought in the Eighteenth Century.* New Haven: Yale University Press, 1954.

Heimert, Alan. *Religion and the American Mind, from the Great Awakening to the Revolution.* Cambridge, Mass.: Harvard University Press, 1966.

Helmholz, R. H. and Green, Thomas. *Juries, Libel, and Justice: the Role of English Juries in Seventeenth- and Eighteenth-Century Trials for Libel and Slander.* Los Angeles: Castle Press, 1984.

Hexter, J. H. *The Reign of King Pym.* Cambridge, Mass.: Harvard University Press, 1975.

Hill, Christopher. *Puritanism and Revolution.* London: Secker and Warburg, 1958.

Hobbes, Thomas. *The English Works of Thomas Hobbes of Malmesbury.* Sir William Molesworth (ed.), London: G. Bohn. 1839–45.

Hofstadter, Richard. *The Paranoid Style in American Politics and Other Essays.* New York: Knopf, 1965.

Hofstadter, Richard. *The American Political Tradition*. New York: Knopf, 1948.

Holdsworth, William. *A History of English Law*. Boston: Little, Brown, 1927.

Holmes, Stephen T. *Benjamin Constant and the Making of Modern Liberalism*. New Haven: Yale University Press, 1984.

Horwitz, Morton. *The Transformation of American Law, 1780–1860*. Cambridge, Mass.: Harvard University Press, 1977.

Howe, John R. *The Changing Political Thought of John Adams*. Princeton: Princeton University Press, 1966.

Howe, Mark DeWolfe. *The Garden and the Wilderness: Religion and Government in American Constitutional History*. Chicago: University of Chicago Press, 1967.

Howell, T. B., ed. *A Complete Collection of State Trials and Proceedings for High Treason and Other Crimes and Misdemeanors*. 20 vols. London: Hansard, 1814.

Hume, David. *A Treatise of Human Nature*. ed. L. A. Selby-Bigge. Oxford: Clarendon, 1955.

Hume, David. *Enquiry Concerning Human Understanding*. Oxford: Clarendon Press, 1966.

Hume, David. *Moral and Political Philosophy*. ed. Henry Aiken. New York: Hafner, 1968.

Huntington, Samuel. *Political Order in Changing Societies*. New Haven: Yale University Press, 1968.

Hurst, James Willard. *The Law of Treason in the United States*. Westport: Greenwood, 1971.

Hurst, James Willard. *Law and the Conditions of Freedom*. Madison: University of Wisconsin Press, 1956.

Hurst, James Willard. *The Growth of American Law: The Law Makers*. Boston: Little, Brown, 1950.

Hyneman, Charles S., and Lutz, Donald S. *American Political Writing During the Founding Era, 1760–1805*. 2 vols. Indianapolis: Liberty Press, 1983.

Jackson, R. M. *The Machinery of Justice in England*. Cambridge: Cambridge University Press, 1953.

Jaffe, Louis L. *English and American Judges as Lawmakers*. Oxford: Clarendon, 1969.

Jefferson, Thomas. *The Commonplace Book of Jefferson*. ed. Gilbert Chinard. Baltimore: Johns Hopkins Press, 1926.

Jefferson, Thomas. *The Portable Jefferson*. ed. Merrill Peterson. New York: Penguin, 1980.

Jefferson, Thomas. *The Writings of Jefferson*. ed. Albert Bergh. Washington: Thomas Jefferson Memorial Association, 1907.

Jefferson, Thomas. *The Papers of Thomas Jefferson*. ed. Julian Boyd. Princeton: Princeton University Press, 1950.

Jefferson, Thomas. *The Works of Jefferson*. ed. H. A. Washington. Washington: Taylor and Maury, 1853–54.

Jefferson, Thomas. *The Works (Writings) of Jefferson*. ed. Paul L. Ford. New York: Putnam's, 1904–05.

Jennings, Sir Ivor. *The Law and the Constitution*. London: Univ. of London Press, 1959.

Jenson, Merrill. *Tracts of the American Revolution, 1763–76*. Indianapolis: Bobbs-Merrill, 1978.

Jenson, Merrill. *The Documentary History of the Ratification of the Constitution*. Madison: State Historical Society of Wisconsin, 1976.

Johnson, Herbert. *Essays on New York Colonial Legal History*. Westport: Greenwood, 1981.

Johnson, Herbert. *Imported Eighteenth-Century Law Treatises in American Libraries, 1700–1799*. Knoxville: University of Tennessee, 1978.

Jones, J. R. *The Restored Monarchy 1660–1688*. Totowa: Rowman and Littlefield, 1979.

Jones, J. R. *The Revolution of 1688 in England*. New York: Norton, 1972.

Jones, Harry W. *Political Separation and Legal Continuity, Common Faith and Common Law*. Atlanta: American Bar Association Press, 1976.

Jordan, W. K. *Men of Substance: A Study of the Thought of Two English Revolutionaries, Henry Parker and Henry Robinson*. Chicago: University of Chicago Press, 1942.

Judson, M. A. *The Crisis of the Constitution: An Essay in Constitutional and Political Thought in England, 1603–1645*. New Brunswick: Rutgers University Press, 1949.

Kant, Immanuel. *The Critique of Pure Reason*. trans. Norman Kemp Smith. New York: St Martin's, 1965.

Kant, Immanuel. *Critique of Judgment*. trans. J. H. Bernard. New York: Hafner, 1966.

Kant, Immanuel. *The Philosophy of Law*. New York: Scribner, n.d.

Kelly, George A. *Politics and Religious Consciousness in America*. New Brunswick: Transaction Books, 1984.

Kemp, Betty. *King and Commons: 1660–1732*. New York: St Martin's Press, 1957.

Kent, James. *Commentaries on American Law*. Boston: Little, Brown, 1867.

Kenyon, Cecilia. *The Anti-Federalists*. Indianapolis: Bobbs-Merrill, 1966.

Kenyon, J. P. *Revolution Principles*. Cambridge: Cambridge University Press, 1977.

Kenyon, J. P. *The Stuart Constitution*. Cambridge: Cambridge University Press, 1966.

Kirchheimer, Otto. *Political Justice: The Use of Legal Procedures For Political Ends*. Princeton: Princeton University Press, 1961.

Kittrie, N. N., and Wedlock, E. D., Jr, eds. *The Tree of Liberty: A Documentary History of Rebellion and Political Crime in America*. Baltimore: Johns Hopkins University Press, 1986.

Knafla, Louis. *Law and Politics in Jacobean England*. Cambridge: Cambridge University Press, 1977.

Koch, Adrienne. *Jefferson and Madison*. New York: Knopf, 1950.

Koch, Adrienne. *The Philosophy of Thomas Jefferson*. Gloucester: Peter Smith, 1957.

Konefsky, Samuel. *John Marshall and Alexander Hamilton*. New York: Macmillan, 1964.

Konig, David. *Law and Society in Puritan Massachusetts: Essex County, 1629–1692*. Chapel Hill: University of North Carolina Press, 1979.

Landau, Norma. *The Justices of the Peace 1679–1760*. Berkeley: University of California Press, 1984.

Levy, Leonard. *Jefferson and Civil Liberties*. Cambridge, Mass.: Harvard University Press, 1963.

Levy, Leonard. *Legacy of Suppression: Freedom of Speech in Early American History*. Cambridge, Mass,: Harvard University Press, 1960.

Levy, Leonard. *Emergence of a Free Press*. Oxford: Oxford University Press, 1985.

Link, Eugene P. *The Democratic-Republican Societies: 1790–1800*. New York: Octagon Books, 1965.

Locke, John. *Two Treatises of Government*. intro. Peter Laslett. Cambridge: Cambridge University Press, 1960.

Locke, John. *A Common-Place-Book to the Holy Bible*. ed. William Dobb. William Baynes and Sons, 1824.

Locke, John. *The Works of John Locke*. 10 vols. London, Thomas Tegg *et al.*, 1823.

Locke, John. *An Essay Concerning Human Understanding*. ed. P. H. Nidditch. Oxford: Clarendon, 1979.

Locke, John. *A Letter Concerning Toleration*. Reprinted in *John Locke on Politics and Education*. ed. H. R. Penniman. New York: D. van Nostrand, 1947.

Locke, John. *Some Thoughts Concerning Education*. Reprinted in *The Educational Writings of John Locke*. ed. James Axtell. Cambridge: Cambridge University Press, 1960.

Locke, John. *Reasonableness of Christianity*. ed. T. Ramsey. Stanford: Stanford University Press, 1958.

Locke, John. *Essays on the Law of Nature*. ed. W. von Leyden. Oxford: Clarendon, 1954.

McCloskey, Robert. *The Modern Supreme Court*. Cambridge, Mass.: Harvard University Press, 1972.

McCory, Drew. *The Elusive Republic*. New York: W. W. Norton, 1980.

McDonald, Forrest. *Novus Ordo Seclorum: The Intellectual Origins of the Constitution*. Lawrence: University of Kansas Press, 1985.

McIlwain, Charles. *The American Revolution: A Constitutional Interpretation*. New York: Macmillan, 1924.

McIlwain, Charles. *Constitutionalism, Ancient and Modern*. Ithaca: Cornell University Press, 1947.

McIlwain, Charles. *The High Court of Parliament and Its Supremacy*. New Haven: Yale University Press, 1910.

McRee, G. J. *Life and Correspondence of James Iredell*. New York: D. Appleton and Co., 1857.

McWilliams, Wilson C. *The Idea of Fraternity in America*. Berkeley: University of California Press, 1973.

MacLean, Kenneth. *John Lock and English Literature of the Eighteenth Century*. New Haven: Yale University Press, 1936.

Macpherson, C. B. *The Political Theory of Possessive Individualism*. Oxford: Oxford University Press, 1962.

Madison, James. *Madison's Notes of Debates in the Federal Convention of 1787*. Athens, Ohio: Ohio University Press, 1966.

Madison, James. *The Papers of James Madison*. ed. R. A. Rutland and W. Rachal. Chicago: University of Chicago Press, 1977.

Madison, James. *The Writings of James Madison*. ed. Gaillard Hunt. New York: Putnam's Sons, 1900–10.

Maier, Pauline. *From Resistance to Revolution*. New York: Vintage, 1974.

Maitland, Frederick W. *The Constitutional History of England*. Cambridge: Cambridge University Press, 1908.

Marshall, John. *Major Opinions and Writings*. ed. John Roche. Indianapolis: Bobbs-Merrill, 1967.

Marshall, John. *The Papers of John Marshall*. ed. Charles T. Cullen and Herbert Johnson. Chapel Hill: University of North Carolina Press, 1977.

Matthews, Nancy L. *William Sheppard, Cromwell's Legal Reformer*. Cambridge: Cambridge University Press, 1984.

May, Henry. *The Enlightenment in America*. Oxford: Oxford University Press, 1976.

May, Sir Thomas E. *The Constitutional History of England: 1760–1860*. New York: A. C. Armstrong and Son, 1891.

Meyers, Marvin. *The Mind of the Founder*. Indianapolis: Bobbs-Merrill, 1973.

Meyers, Marvin. *The Jacksonian Persuasion; Politics and Belief*. New York: Vintage, 1960.

Montesquieu, Charles-Louis-Secondat, Baron de. *The Spirit of the Laws*. trans. T. Nugent. New York: Hafner, 1949.

Mill, John Stuart. *Auguste Comte and Positivism*. Ann Arbor: University of Michigan Press, 1973.

Mill, John Stuart. *Utilitarianism, Liberty and Representative Government*. New York: E. P. Dutton, 1951.

Miller, Arthur. *Social Change and Fundamental Law: America's Evolving Constitution*. Westport: Greenwood, 1979.

Miller, John. *The Federalist Era, 1789–1801*. New York: Harper & Brothers, 1960.

Miller, Perry. *The Legal Mind in America*. Garden City: Anchor Books, 1962.

Miller, Perry. *The Life of the Mind in America*. New York: Harcourt, Brace, World, 1965.

Morgan, Edmund. *Inventing the People: The Rise of Popular Sovereignty in England and America* . New York: W. W. Norton, 1988.

Murrin, John, *et al.*, eds. *Saints and Revolutionaries*. New York: W. W. Norton, 1984.

Nelson, William. *The Americanization of the Common Law: The Impact of Legal Change on Massachusetts Society, 1760–1830*. Cambridge: Harvard University Press, 1975.

Nelson, William. *Dispute and Conflict Resolution in Plymouth County, Massachusetts, 1725–1825*. Chapel Hill: University of North Carolina Press, 1981.

Nenner, Howard. *By Colour of Law: Legal Cultures and Constitutional Politics, 1660–1689*. Chicago: University of Chicago Press, 1977.

Newlin, Claude. *Philosophy and Religion in Colonial America.* New York: Philosophical Library, 1962.

Niehaus, C. R. *The Issue of Law Reform in the Puritan Revolution.* Ph.D. dissertation, Harvard University, 1978.

Noble, George. *The North Briton: A Study in Political Propaganda.* New York: Columbia University Press, 1939.

Norton, A. L. *The World of the Ranters.* London: Lawrence and Wishart, 1970.

Nozick, Robert. *Anarchy, State, and Utopia.* New York: Basic, 1974.

Padover, Saul. *The Mind of Alexander Hamilton.* New York: Harper & Brothers, 1958.

Paine, Thomas. *The Paine Reader.* ed. I. Kramnick. Harmondsworth: Penguin, 1987.

Paine, Thomas. *The Complete Writings of Thomas Paine.* ed. P. S. Foner. New York: Citadel Press, 1945.

Paton, G. W., and Durham, D. P., eds. *Jurisprudence.* Oxford: Clarendon Press, 1982.

Peters, Ronald, Jr. *The Massachusetts Constitution of 1780: A Social Compact.* Amherst: University of Massachusetts Press, 1978.

Peterson, Merrill D. *The Jeffersonian Image in the American Mind.* Oxford: Oxford University Press, 1962.

Phillips, O. Hood. *Principles of English Law and the Constitution.* London: Sweet and Maxwell, 1939.

Plucknett, T. F. *A Concise History of the Common Law.* Boston: Little, Brown, 1956.

Plumb, J. H. *The Growth of Political Stability in England, 1675–1725.* London: Macmillan, 1967.

Pocock, J. G. A. *The Ancient Constitution and the Feudal Law.* Cambridge: Cambridge University Press, 1957.

Pocock, J. G. A. *Politics, Language and Time.* New York: Atheneum, 1971.

Pocock, J. G. A. *The Machiavellian Moment.* Princeton: Princeton University Press, 1975.

Pocock, J. G. A. *Virtue, Commerce, and History.* Cambridge: Cambridge University Press, 1985.

Pole, J. R. *Foundations of American Independence: 1763–1815.* Indianapolis: Bobbs-Merrill, 1972.

Pole, J. R. *Political Representation in England and the Origins of the American Republic.* London: Macmillan, 1966.

Polin, R. *La Politique Morale de John Locke.* Paris, 1960.

Pollock, Frederick. *Essays in the Law.* London: Macmillan, 1922.

Popkin, Richard. *The History of Scepticism From Erasmus to Spinoza.* Berkeley: University of California Press, 1979.

Pound, Roscoe. *The Formative Era of American Law.* Boston: Little, Brown, 1938.

Presser, Stephan B., and Zainaldin, Jamil S., eds. *Law and American History: Cases and Materials.* St Paul: West Pub., 1980.

Purcell, Edward A., Jr. *The Crisis of Democratic Theory.* Kentucky: University Press of Kentucky, 1973.

Rawls, John. *A Theory of Justice.* Cambridge, Mass.: Harvard University Press, 1971.

Rea, R. R. *The English Press in Politics, 1760–1774.* Lincoln: University of Nebraska Press, 1963.

Reid, John. *In a Defiant Stance: The Conditions of Law in Massachusetts Bay, the Irish Comparison, and the Coming of the American Revolution.* University Park, Pa.: Pennsylvania State University, 1977.

Reid, John. *In Defiance of the Law: The Standing Army Controversy, the Two Constitutions, and the Coming of the American Revolution.* Chapel Hill: University of North Carolina Press, 1981.

Reid, John. *The Concept of Liberty in the Age of the American Revolution.* Chicago: University of Chicago Press, 1988.

Reid, Thomas. *Inquiry on the Human Mind on the Principles of Common Sense.* ed. K. Lehrer and R. E. Beanblossom. Indianapolis: Bobbs-Merrill, 1975.

Reports of the Supreme Court of the United States. ed. William E. Baldwin. New York: Baldwin Law Book Co., 1926-.

Rhys, Isaac. *The Transformation of Virginia, 1740–1790.* Chapel Hill: University of North Carolina Press, 1982.

Riley, Patrick. *Will and Political Legitimacy.* Cambridge, Mass.: Harvard University Press, 1982.

Robbins, Caroline. *The Eighteenth-Century Commonwealthman.* Cambridge, Mass.: Harvard University Press, 1959.

Roeber, A. G. *Faithful Magistrates and Republican Lawyers: Creators of Virginia Legal Culture, 1680–1810.* Chapel Hill: University of North Carolina Press, 1981.

Rorty, Richard. *Philosophy and the Mirror of Nature.* Princeton: Princeton University Press, 1979.

Rossiter, Clinton. *Alexander Hamilton and the Constitution.* New York: Harcourt, Brace, World, 1964.

Rossiter, Clinton., ed. *The Federalist Papers.* New York: Mentor, 1961.

Rousseau, Jean-Jacques. *Emile.* trans. Alan Bloom. New York: Basic, 1979.

Rousseau, Jean-Jacques. *On the Social Contract, with the Geneva Manuscript and Political Economy.* ed. Roger Masters. trans. Judith Masters. New York: St Martins, 1978.

Rude, George. *Wilkes and Liberty: A Social Study of 1763–74.* Oxford: Oxford University Press, 1962.

Ryden, G. H., ed. *Letters to and from Caesar Rodney.* Philadelphia: University of Pennsylvania Press, 1933.

Sabine, George, ed. *The Works of Gerrard Winstanley.* New York: Russell and Russell, 1965.

Say, Jean-Baptiste. *A Treatise on Political Economy.* trans. C. R. Prinsep. Philadelphia: Grigg and Elliot, 1832.

Seliger, Martin. *The Liberal Politics of John Locke.* London: George Allen, 1968.

Shapiro, Barbara J. *Probability and Certainty in Seventeenth Century England.* Princeton: Princeton University Press, 1983.

Shapiro, Martin. *Law and Politics in the Supreme Court.* New York: Free Press, 1964.

Shapiro, Martin. *Courts*. Chicago: University of Chicago Press, 1981.

Sharp, Andrew. *Political Ideas of the English Civil Wars: 1641–1649*. London: Longmans, 1983.

Shklar, Judith. *Montesquieu*. New York: Oxford University Press, 1987.

Shklar, Judith. *Legalism*. Cambridge, Mass.: Harvard University Press 1964.

Sieyès, Emmanuel-Joseph. *Qu'est-ce que le Tiers Etat?*. ed. and intro Roberto Zapperi. Geneva: Librairie Droz, 1970.

Skinner, Quentin. *The Foundations of Modern Political Thought*, 2 vols Cambridge: Cambridge University Press, 1978.

Smith, Adam. *The Wealth of Nations*. New York: Modern Library, 1937.

Smith, Adam. *The Theory of Moral Sentiments*. Indianapolis: Liberty Class ics, 1969.

Smith, Adam. *Lectures on Jurisprudence*. Indianapolis: Liberty Classics 1982.

Smith, James M., ed. *Seventeenth Century America: Essays in Colonia History*. Chapel Hill: University of North Carolina Press, 1959.

Smith, Joseph H. *Colonial Justice in Western Massachusetts: The Pynchor Court Record*. Cambridge, Mass.: Harvard University Press, 1961.

Smith, Morton H. *The Writs of Assistance Cases*. Berkeley: University o: California Press, 1978.

Smith, Paul H. (ed.), *Letters of Delegates to Congress: 1774–1789*. 15 vols Washington: Library of Congress, 1976.

Spooner, Lysander. *An Essay on Trial by Jury*. Cleveland: Jewett, Proctor. and Worthington, 1852.

Stephen, Sir James F. *A History of the Criminal Law of England*. London: Macmillan, 1883.

Storing, Herbert. *What the Antifederalists were For*. Chicago: University ol Chicago Press, 1981.

Story, Joseph. *Commentaries on the Constitution*. New York: Hillard, Grey and Co., 1833.

Story, Joseph. *The Miscellaneous Writings*. ed. William Story. Boston: Little. Brown, 1852.

Stourzh, Gerald. *Alexander Hamilton and the Idea of Republican Govern-ment*. Stanford: Stanford University Press, 1970.

Strauss, Leo. *Natural Right and History*. Chicago: University of Chicagc Press, 1953.

Taft, Barbara, ed. *Absolute Liberty: A Selection from the Articles and Papers of Caroline Robbins*. Hamden, Conn.: Aragon Books, 1982.

Tanner, J. R. *English Constitutional Conflicts of the Seventeenth Century*. Cambridge: Cambridge University Press, 1930.

Thayer, James B. *Cases in Constitutional Law*. Cambridge: George Kent. 1895.

Thompson, E. P. *Whigs and Hunters*. London: Allen Lane, 1975.

Thorne, Samuel E. *Sir Edward Coke, 1552–1952*. London: Selden Society. 1957.

Tiedeman, Christopher G. *The Unwritten Constitution of the United States*. New York: G. P. Putnam, 1890.

Tierney, Brian. *Religion, Law and the Growth of Constitutional Thought, 1150–1659.* Cambridge: Cambridge University Press, 1982.

Tocqueville, Alexis de. *Democracy in America.* New York: Doubleday, 1969.

Tuck, Richard. *Natural Rights Theories.* Cambridge: Cambridge University Press, 1979.

Ubbelohde, Carl. *The Vice-Admiralty Courts of the American Revolution.* Chapel Hill: University of North Carolina Press, 1960.

United States Supreme Court Reports Law. Ed. Rochester, N.Y.: Lawyers Co-operative Publishing Co., 1926- .

Van Alstyne, Richard. *Empire and Independence.* New York: John Wiley and Sons, 1965.

Van Leeuwen, Henry G. *The Problem of Certainty in English Thought, 1630–90.* The Hague: Martinus Nijhoff, 1963.

Vaughan, A. T., and Billias, George A. *Perspectives on Early American History: Essays in Honor of Richard B. Morris.* New York: Harper and Row, 1973.

Veall, Donald. *The Popular Movement for Law Reform: 1640–60.* Oxford: Clarendon Press, 1970.

Veitch, G. S. *The Genesis of Parliamentary Reform.* London: Constable, 1965.

Walker, Samuel. *Popular Justice: A History of American Criminal Justice.* Oxford: Oxford University Press, 1980.

Walzer, Michael. *The Revolution of the Saints.* New York: Atheneum, 1969.

Walzer, Michael. *Spheres of Justice.* New York: Basic Books, 1983.

Webb, R. K. *Modern England: From the Eighteenth Century to the Present.* New York: Dodd, Mead, 1973.

Weber, Max. *Law in Economy and Society.* ed. Max Rheinstein. Cambridge, Mass.: Harvard University Press, 1954.

Welch, Cheryl B. *Liberty and Utility: The French Idéologues and the Transformation of Liberalism.* New York: Columbia University Press, 1984.

Western, J. R. *Monarchy and Revolution.* Totowa, N.J.: Rownon and Littlefield, 1972.

Weston, Corinne. *English Constitutional Theory of the House of Lords: 1556–1832.* New York: Columbia University Press, 1965.

White, G. Edward. *The American Judicial Tradition.* Oxford: Oxford University Press, 1976.

Wilson, James. *Selected Political Essays of James Wilson.* ed. Ralph Adams. New York: Knopf, 1930.

Wilson, James. *The Works of James Wilson.* 2 vols. ed. Robert G. McCloskey. Cambridge: Harvard University Press, 1967.

Wills, Gary. *Inventing America.* Garden City: Doubleday, 1978.

Wolin, Sheldon. *Politics and Vision.* Boston: Little, Brown, 1960.

Wood, Gordon. *The Creation of the American Republic, 1776–1787.* New York: Norton, 1969.

Woodhouse, A. S. P. *Puritanism and Liberty.* London: Dent, 1986.

Worden, Blair. *The Rump Parliament 1648–1653.* Cambridge: Cambridge University Press, 1974.

Wright, Louis B. *The Cultural Life of the American Colonies*. New York: Harper & Row, 1957.

Yolton, John. *John Locke and the Compass of the Understanding*. Cambridge: Cambridge University Press, 1970.

Yolton, John. *John Locke and the Way of Ideas*. Oxford: Oxford University Press, 1956.

Yolton, John, ed. *John Locke: Problems and Perspectives*. Cambridge: Cambridge University Press, 1969.

Yolton, John. *Perceptual Acquaintance From Descartes to Reid*. Minneapolis: University of Minnesota Press, 1984.

Yolton, John. *Thinking Matter: Materialism in Eighteenth-Century Britain*. Minneapolis: University of Minnesota Press, 1983.

Zobel, Hiller. *The Boston Massacre*. New York: W. W. Norton, 1970.

SELECTED ARTICLES

Appleby, Joyce. 'What Is Still American in the Political Philosophy of Thomas Jefferson?' *William and Mary Quarterly*, vol. 39, April 1982.

Arnold, Morris S. 'Law and Fact in Medieval Jury Trials: Out of Sight, Out of Mind'. *American Journal of Legal History*, vol. XVIII, 1974.

Bailyn, Bernard. 'Political Experience and Enlightenment Ideas in Eighteenth Century America'. *American Historical Review*, vol. LXVIII, 1962.

Bailyn, Bernard. 'Boyd's Jefferson: Notes for a Sketch'. *New England Quarterly*, vol. 33, 1960.

Bailyn, Bernard. 'Butterfield's Adams: Notes for a Sketch'. *William and Mary Quarterly*, vol. 19, 1962.

Beitzinger, Alphons. 'The Philosophy of Law of Four American Founding Fathers'. *American Journal of Jurisprudence*, vol. 21, 1976.

Black, Barbara. 'The Constitution of Empire: The Case for the Colonists'. *University of Pennsylvania Law Review*, vol. 124, 1976.

Black, Stephen F. 'The Courts and Judges of Westminster Hall During the Great Rebellion, 1640–60'. *Journal of Legal History*, vol. 7, May 1986, pp. 23–52.

Brewer, John. 'The Wilkites and the Law, 1763–74: a study of radical notions of governance'. In *An Ungovernable People*. ed. John Brewer and John Styles. London: Hutchinson, 1980.

Brilmayer, R. L. 'Judicial Review, Justiciability and the Limits of the Common Law Method'. *Boston University Law Review*, vol. 57, 1977.

Cappelitti, Mauro. 'The Mighty Problem of Judicial Review', *Southern California Law Review*, vol. 53, 1980.

Chafee, Zechariah, Jr. 'Colonial Courts and the Common Law'. *Massachusetts Historical Society Proceedings*. 'vol. 68, 1952' on p. 21. vol. LXVIII, 1944.

'A Note on The Changing Role of the Jury in the Nineteenth Century'. *Yale Law Journal*, vol. 74, 1964.

Corwin, Edward. 'The Higher Law Background of American Constitutional Law', *Harvard Law Review*, vol. 42, 1928–29.

Corwin, Edward. 'Progress of Political Theory from the Revolution to the Founding'. *American Historical Review*, vol. 30, 1924–25.

Cotterell, Mary. 'Interregnum Law Reform: The Hale Commission of 1652'. *English Historical Review*, vol. 88, 1968.

Dunn, John. 'Consent in the Political Theory of John Locke'. *Historical Journal*, vol. 10, 1967.

Dunn, John. 'From Applied Theology to Social Analysis: the break between John Locke and the Scottish Enlightenment'. In *Wealth and Virtue*. ed. I. Hont and M. Ignatieff. Cambridge: Cambridge University Press, 1983.

Dunn, John. 'The Politics of John Locke in England and America in the Eighteenth Century'. In *John Locke: Problems and Perspectives*. ed. J. W. Yolton. Cambridge: Cambridge University Press, 1969.

Dworetz, Steven M. 'The Radical Side of American Constitutionalism: Locke and the New England Clergy Revisited'. A paper presented at the New England Political Science Association Annual Convention, Trinity College, Hartford, Connecticut, 5 April 1986.

Dworkin, Ronald. 'Law as Interpretation'. *Texas Law Review*, vol. 10, 1982.

Eaton, Amasa M. 'The Development of the Judicial System in Rhode Island'. *Yale Law Journal*, vol. 14, 1905.

Fish, Stanley. 'Working on the Chain Gang: Interpretation in Law and Literature'. *Texas Law Review*, vol. 60, 1982.

Fish, Stanley. 'Wrong Again'. *Texas Law Review*, vol. 62, 1983.

Fiss, Owen. 'Objectivity and Interpretation'. *Stanford Law Review*, vol. 34, 1982.

Flaherty, David. 'An Approach to American History: Willard Hurst as a Legal Historian'. *American Journal of Legal History*, vol. 14, 1970.

Foster, Herbert. 'International Calvinism Through Locke and the Revolution of 1688'. *American Historical Review*, vol. 32, 1926.

Frankfurter, Felix. 'John Marshall and the Judicial Function'. In *Of Law and Men*. ed. R. Elman. Hamden, Conn.: Archon Books, 1956.

Glazer, Nathan. 'Towards an Imperial Judiciary?' *The Public Interest*, vol. 41, Fall 1975.

Gordon, Robert W. 'J. Willard Hurst and the Common Law Tradition in American Legal Historiography'. *Law and Society Review*, vol. 10, 1976.

Greene, Jack. 'From the Perspective of Law: Context and Legitimacy in the Origins of the American Revolution'. *South Atlantic Quarterly*, vol. 85, no. 1, Winter 1986.

Grey, Thomas C. 'Origins of the Unwritten Constitution: Fundamental Law in American Revolutionary Thought'. *Stanford Law Review*, vol. 30, 1978.

Hart, H. L. A. 'Positivism and the Separation of Law and Morals'. *Harvard Law Review*, vol. 71, 1958.

Henderson, E. G. 'The Background of the Seventh Amendment'. *Harvard Law Review*, vol. 80, 1966.

Herrup, Cynthia. 'Law and Morality in Seventeenth-Century England'. *Past and Present*, no. 106, 1985.

Horwitz, Morton. 'Republicanism and Liberalism in American Constitutional Thought'. A paper presented for the Charles Warren Center for Studies in American History, 11 Feb. 1986.

Howe, Mark De Wolfe. 'Juries as Judges of Criminal Law'. *Harvard Law Review*, vol. 52, 1939.

Huntington, Samuel. 'New Society, Old State'. In *The American Political Experience*. ed. Edward Handler. Lexington: Heath, 1968.

Hutson, James H. 'The Origins of "The Paranoid Style in American Politics"': Public Jealousy from the Age of Walpole to the Age of Jackson'. In *Saints and Revolutionaries: Essays on Early American History*. ed. J. H. Murrin *et al*. New York: Norton, 1984.

Katz, Stanley. 'The Politics of Law in Colonial America'. In *Colonial America: Essays in Political and Social Development*. ed. Stanley Katz. Boston: Little, Brown; 2nd ed. 1976.

Katz, Stanley. 'Looking Backward: The Early History of American Law'. *University of Chicago Law Review*, vol. 32, 1966.

Kennedy, Duncan. 'The Structure of Blackstone's Commentaries'. *Buffalo Law Review*, vol. 28, 1979.

Kenyon, Cecilia. 'Alexander Hamilton: Rousseau of the Right'. *Political Science Quarterly*, vol. 73, 1958.

Klein, Milton M. 'Prelude to Revolution in New York: Jury Trials and Judicial Tenure'. *William and Mary Quarterly*, vol. 17, 1960.

Kloppenberg, James. 'The Virtues of Liberalism: Christianity, Republicanism, and Ethics in Early American Political Discourse'. *Journal of American History*, vol. 74, no. 1, June 1987.

Kramnick, Isaac. 'The "Great National Discussion": The Discourse of Politics in 1787'. *William and Mary Quarterly*, vol. 45, 1988.

Kramnick, Isaac. 'Republican Revisionism Revisited'. *American Historical Review*, vol. 87, June 1982.

Krasity, Kenneth A. 'The Role of the Judge in Jury Trials: The Elimination of Judicial Evaluation of Fact in American State Courts from 1795 to 1912'. *University of Detroit Law Review*, vol. 62, Summer 1985.

Levinson, Sanford. 'Law as Literature'. *Texas Law Review*, vol. 60, 1982.

Levinson, Sanford. 'On Dworkin, Kennedy and Ely: Decoding the Legal Past'. *Partisan Review*, vol. LI, 1984.

Lutz, Donald S. 'The Relative Influence of European Writers on Late Eighteenth-Century American Political Thought'. *American Political Science Review*, vol. 78, 1984.

MacKay, R. A. 'Coke – Parliamentary Sovereignty or the Supremacy of the Law?' *Michigan Law Review*, vol. 22, 1923–24.

Maier, Pauline. 'John Wilkes and American Disillusionment with Britain'. *William and Mary Quarterly*, vol. 20, 1963.

Mason, Alpheus T. 'The Federalist – A Split Personality'. *American Historical Review*, vol. 57, 1951–2.

McCloskey, Robert M. 'Deeds Without Doctrines'. *American Political Science Review*, vol. 56, 1962.

Morgan, Edmund. 'Colonial Ideas of Parliamentary Power, 1764–76'. *William and Mary Quarterly*, vol. 5, 1948.

Murphy, Walter. 'Who Shall Interpret? The Quest for the Ultimate Constitutional Interpreter'. *Review of Politics*, vol. 48, no. 3, Summer 1986.

Murrin, John. 'The Legal Transformation of the Bench and Bar of Eighteenth-Century Massachusetts'. In *Colonial America*. ed. Stanley Katz. Boston: Little Brown, 1971.

Nelson, William. 'The Legal Restraint on Power in Pre-Revolutionary America: Massachusetts as a Case Study, 1760–1775'. *American Journal of Legal History*, vol. 18, 1974.

Nelson, William. 'The Eighteenth-Century Background of John Marshall's Constitutional Jurisprudence'. *Michigan Law Review*, vol. 76, 1978.

Nelson, William. 'Changing Conceptions of Judicial Review: The Evolution of Constitutional Theory in the States 1790–1860'. *University of Pennsylvania Law Review*, vol. 120, 1972.

Parkin-Speer, Diane. 'John Lilburne: A Revolutionary Interprets Statutes and Common Law Due Process'. *Law and History Review*, vol. 1, Fall 1983.

Pole, J. R. 'Enlightenment and the Politics of American Nature'. In *The Enlightenment in Natural Context*. ed. R. Porter and M. Teich. Cambridge: Cambridge University Press, 1981.

Reid, John P. 'In Our Contracted Sphere'. *Columbia Law Review*, vol. 76, 1976.

Reid, John P. 'In a Defensive Rage: The Uses of the Mob, the Justification in Law, and the Coming of the American Revolution'. *New York University Law Review*, vol. 49, 1974.

Reid, John P. 'In Legitimate Stirps: The Concept of "Arbitrary", the Supremacy of Parliament and the Coming of the America Revolution'. *Hofstra Law Review*, vol. 5, 1977.

Reid, John P. 'A Lawyer Acquitted: John Adams and the Boston Massacre Trials'. *American Journal of Legal History*, vol. 18, 1974.

Resnick, David. 'Locke and the Ancient Constitution'. *Political Theory*, vol. 12, 1984.

Rhys, Isaac. 'Preachers and Patriots: Popular Culture and the Revolution in Virginia'. In *The American Revolution*. ed. Alfred F. Young. De Kalb, Illinois: Northern Illinois University Press, 1976.

Robbins, Caroline. 'Algernon Sidney's *Discourses Concerning Government*: Textbook of Revolution'. *William and Mary Quarterly*, vol. 4, July 1947.

Rubini, D. A. 'The Precarious Independence of the Judiciary, 1688–1701'. *Law Quarterly Review*, vol. 83, 1967.

Schreiber, Harry N. 'At the Borderline of Law and Economic History: the Contributions of Willard Hurst'. *American Historical Review*, vol. LXXV, 1970.

Schulz, Constance B. 'Of Bigotry in Politics and Religion: Jefferson's Religion, the Federalist Press, and the Syllabus'. *The Virginia Magazine of History and Biography*, vol. 91, 1983.

Shapiro, Barbara. 'Law and Science in Seventeenth Century England'. *Stanford Law Review*, vol. 21, 1969.

Shapiro, Barbara. 'Law Reform in Seventeenth Century England'. *American Journal of Legal History*, vol. 19, 1975.

Shapiro, Barbara. 'Latitudinarianism and Science in Seventeenth Century England'. *Past and Present*, no. 40, 1968.

Shklar, Judith N. 'Publius and the Science of the Past'. *Yale Law Journal*, vol. 86, 1977.

Shklar, Judith N. 'In Defense of Legalism'. *Journal of Legal Education*, vol. 19, 1966–67.

Smith, Joseph H. 'An Independent Judiciary: The Colonial Background'. *University of Pennsylvania Law Review*, vol. 124, 1976.

Snowiss, Sylvia. 'From Fundamental Law to the Supreme Law of the Land: A Reinterpretation of the Origin of Judicial Review'. In *Studies in American Political Development*, vol. 2. ed. Karen Orren and Stephen Skowronek. New Haven: Yale University Press, 1987.

Stimson, Shannon C. 'Interpreting the American Constitution: Beyond Dissidence and Orthodoxy'. *Revue Française de Science Politique*, vol. 38, 1988.

Storing, Herbert. 'The Constitution and the Bill of Rights'. Unpublished manuscript of a lecture delivered at Utah State University, 5 Dec. 1975.

Thayer, James B. 'The Jury and Its Development'. *Harvard Law Review*, vol. V, 1891–92.

Thayer, James B. ' "Law and Fact" in Jury Trials'. *Harvard Law Review*, vol. IV, 1890.

Thompson, Dennis. 'The Education of a Founding Father: The Reading List for John Witherspoon's Course in Political Theory, as Taken by James Madison'. *Political Theory*, vol. 4, no. 1, Feb. 1976.

Thompson, Martyn P. 'The History of Fundamental Law in Political Thought from the French Wars of Religion to the American Revolution'. *American Historical Review*, vol. 91, Dec. 1986.

Thompson, Martyn P. 'The Reception of Locke's Two Treatises of Government 1690–1705'. *Political Studies*, vol. 24, 1976.

Thompson, Martyn P. 'A Note on "Reason" and "History" in Late Seventeenth Century Political Thought'. *Political Theory*, vol. 4, no. 1, Feb. 1976.

Thorne, Samuel. 'Dr. Bonham's Case'. *Law Quarterly Review*, vol. 54, 1938.

Waldman, Theodore. 'Origins of the Doctrine of Reasonable Doubt'. *Journal of the History of Ideas*, vol. 20, 1959.

Willman, Robert. 'Blackstone and the "Theoretical Perfection" of English Law in the Reign of Charles II'. *Historical Journal*, vol. 26, no. 1, 1983.

Wood, Gordon. 'Conspiracy and the Paranoid Style'. *William and Mary Quarterly*, vol. 32, 1982.

Wood, Gordon. 'The Fundamentalists and the Constitution'. *New York Review of Books*, vol. 35, no. 2, 18 Feb. 1988.

Index

Act of Settlement (1701), 13, 25
Admiralty Courts, 34, 45, 78, 149
Adams, John (1735–1826), 48, 57,
    60, 131
  on debate over colonial
    government, 4
  on government, 90
  Jefferson and, 86, 104
  on juries, 55–6, 81–2
  jurisprudence of, 69–70, 71–4,
    81–5
  Thoughts on Government, 70
Alexander, James, 54
Allybone (Judge), 29
American Constitution
  Hamilton and, 106–7, 123
  Jefferson and, 101, 106
  juries and, 64
  Marshall and, 138, 139–40
  and participation, 9
  and the Supreme Court, 126–7
  see also Constitutional
    Convention
American court system, 56
  see also Supreme Court
American Revolution, 60
  Arendt on, 127
  Hamilton's view of, 110
  leaders of, 14
Anti-Federalists, 108, 120, 121
appeals
  to fundamental law, 22
  to jury verdicts, 50
Arendt, Hannah (1906–75), 8–9,
    127
Arnoux, Abbé, 87

Bailyn, Bernard, 35–6, 38, 163
  on Locke, 40–1
bicameralism, 130–1
Bickel, Alexander, 147
Bill of Rights, 120, 121
Blackstone, Sir William (1723–80),
    4, 32, 45, 128, 133

Boudinot, Elias, 134
Brewer, John, 76
British constitution, 10–11, 13
Burke, Edmund (1729–97), 34, 37,
    39, 45, 153
  on colonial judiciary, 49–50
  on use of criminal law to control
    opposition, 38
Bushell's Case, 26–7, 28

Callendar, James Thompson, 63, 64
'Camden', 61
Cartwright, Thomas, 4
Cato Letters, 39, 40–1, 54, 171
Chase, Samuel, 64
checks and balances, 70, 96–7, 131
Chisholm v. Georgia, 135
Citation Act, 111
citizenship, 30–1
civil law
  Adams on, 73–4
  Blackstone on, 45
  Locke on, 46, 73
civil society, 44
civil traverse jury, 71
codification of law, 18, 61
Cohens v. Virginia, 140
Coke, Sir Edward (1552–1634), 12,
    26, 114, 153, 156
  career of, 24
  and fundamental law, 15–17
Colden, Cadwallader, Lieutenant-
    Governor of New York, 50–1
colonial law, 12, 172, 173
  uncertainty in, 57–9
colonial legal thought, 12
colonial politics, 36, 37
colonial society, 59
Commissions of Oyer and
    Terminer, 19
common law, 76
  in the colonies, 56–7, 72–3, 129
  differences between English and

American, 77, 129, 141
  as fundamental law, 15–22
  inadequacy of for American
    jurisprudence, 144
  Locke on, 46
common man *see* people
community, Adams' theory of, 83–4
conditions of law, 10–11
Condorcet, Marie Jean Antoine,
    Marquis de (1743–94), 92
Confederation, 112, 114
Confiscation Act, 110, 111
conflict, 95, 119
Connecticut, 49, 171
consensus, 138, 140, 141
  see also local consensus
consent
  government by, 7, 46
  validity by, 128–9
constitution
  Jefferson on, 95, 98
  of man, 91, 93, 95
  see also American Constitution;
    British Constitution
constitutional amendments, 125
constitutional authority, 47
Constitutional Convention, 104, 134
constitutional jurisprudence, 103,
    143–5
constitutional law (American),
    123–4, 139–40, 145, 147
constitutionalism, 12–14, 152
  Locke and, 41, 44–5
contract, theories of, 7
corruption of judges, 109–10
Cosby, William, 52
Council of Revision, 117, 118, 134
courts
  as advisors to juries, 109
  colonial, 57
  as defenders of the system, 23
  different roles of, in England and
    America, 145–7
  in Hamilton's theory of state,
    106, 119
  independence of, 23
  see also Supreme Court
criminal law, 38, 63, 132
criminal traverse jury, 71

Crown
  control of, over judiciary, 49–50,
    76
  manipulation of law by, 28–9
  and rule of law, 23
crown prosecutors, 53
custom, and content of law, 12, 129

decision-making, 101
Declaration of Independence, 100,
    184
democratic politics, Jefferson's
    theory of, 100–3
Dickinson, John, 56–7, 60
diversity of opinions, 83, 94
Dr Bonham's Case, 16, 17
Duane, Mayor, 114–15, 117
Dunn, John, 41, 166
Dworkin, Ronald, 195–6

education, 80, 81, 129–30
  Adams on, 180–1
  Jefferson on, 88–9, 94
English Revolution, 4, 5, 31–2
equality, 90
*Essay Concerning Human
  Understanding* (Locke), 41, 42,
    44
Executive, and judiciary, 118–19

faith, 86, 122
fallibilism, 43, 141
fallibilty of man, 110, 122, 126
federalism, 9, 103
Federalist 22, 114
Federalist 73, 118
Federalist 83, 107–8, 109
Fliegelman, Jay, 8
Forsey v. Cunningham, 50–1
Fortescue, Sir John, 17
Franklin, Benjamin, 88
Franklin, Richard, 51, 52
freedom, 46, 47
  see also liberty
freedom of the press, 53
French, laws written in, 17–18
fundamental law, 14, 155
  appeals to, 22, 33
  Coke and, 15–17

fundamental law – *continued*
  as explanatory factor in American
    jurisprudence, 35
  as law of reason, 20–2
  and legal uncertainty, 17–22
  origins of, 15

Georgia, 60, 61
Gerry, Elbridge, 61
Ghorum, Nathaniel, 118
Gill v. Mein, 74, 77
Glorious Revolution *see* English
  Revolution
Glynn, Serjeant, 75
Gordon, Thomas, 41
government, 122
  checks and balances of, 96–7
  Jefferson's theory of, 97–8
  powers of, 47
  purpose of, 90, 130
  seventeenth-century challenges
    to, 23–4
grand jury, 71
greed, as a motivator, 111

habit, 99
Hamilton, Alexander (1755–1804),
  48, 54, 139
  on Council of Revision, 118–19
  on human nature, 110
  jurisprudence of, 106–14, 122
  on Supreme Court, 124–7
Hampden, John, 12
happiness, pursuit of, 90
Hart, H.L.A., 146, 150, 195
Hartz, Louis, 142, 194
Helvétius, Claude Adrien
  (1715–71), 92
hereditary institutions, 82
homogeneity, 94
Hopkins, Stephen, 149
House of Lords, 133
human knowledge, 31, 40, 59, 74,
  88, 143
  Adams on, 80–1
  Jefferson on, 91
  Locke on, 42–3
  see also knowledge of the law

human nature, Hamilton on, 110,
  122
human rights, 97–8, 120–1
Hume, David (1711–76), 182
Hutchinson, Thomas, 58

ideology, and revolutionary politics,
  37, 38, 40, 48
independent judiciary, 104
  Adams and, 69–70, 84
  colonial distrust of, 49–50
  Hamilton on, 107, 114
  Jefferson and, 102
innovation, 8
interpretation of law, 17, 18, 76
intrigue, perception of politics as,
  37

Jackson, Andrew, 142
James II, King of Great Britain, 24,
  28
Jefferies, George, Judge, 24
Jefferson, Thomas (1743–1826), 47,
  59, 65, 140
  political thought of, 86–9, 90–3,
    96–105
Jones, John, 15, 20, 159
judges (American), 60, 132, 144
  Hamilton on, 109
  and policy-making, 117–18
  power of, 142
judges (colonial), 48–50, 58–9
  appointment of, 13
  authority of, 73
  juries right to challenge direction
    of, 73
  knowledge of law of, 6, 78–9
  relationship of with juries, 59–60,
    81, 109
  royal control over, 55
judges (English)
  as censors of the administration,
    147
  control of, over ability to know
    law, 18, 76
  independence from politics of,
    23–4, 32
  relationship of with juries, 5, 26,
    28, 32–3

judges (English) – *continued*
  role of, 4, 24
  in seditious libel cases, 29–30
  tenure of, 25
judgement, 118–19, 139–42
  Adams on, 90
  at the centre of political
    considerations, 43
  by colonial juries, 60, 84, 85
  constitutional, 101
  independent, 100, 124
  Jefferson's views on, 87, 103
  by juries, 76, 87
  about law, 116
  Locke on, 44–5, 46
  by the people, 129–30
  see also judicial space
judicial control, 17, 18, 76
judicial discretion, 75–6
judicial independence, 6, 22–6, 76
  of judgment, 118–19
  lack of, 30
  Madison and, 119–20
  in revolutionary America, 48–55,
    58–9
judicial review, 6, 14, 39, 121–3, 189
  Adams and, 70
  Coke and, 15–16
  and fundamental law, 22
  Marshall and, 141–2
  and the Supreme Court, 141, 142,
    145–6
  Wilson and, 133–6
judicial space, 5, 6, 8, 26–9
  in colonial law, 59–60
  Hamilton on, 119
  Jefferson on, 100–5
  and judicial review, 141
  Supreme Court and, 145, 146–7
  see also judgment
juries *see also* jurors: trial by jury
juries (American)
  co-operation with judges, 132–3
  as a curb on the judiciary, 87–8
  Hamilton on, 107–9
  Jefferson on, 87–9
  powers of to determine the law,
    60–6, 104, 108–9, 132–3,
    142–3, 188

rights and duties of, 131–2
  role of, 107–9, 139
  Wilson on, 131–3
juries (colonial), 5, 6, 34–5, 48–51,
    59–60, 149
  Adams on, 71–4
  and judicial space, 56–60, 77
  powers of to determine the law,
    54–5, 72–9, 179
  relationship of with judges,
    59–60, 81, 109
juries (English)
  attempts to manipulate, 76
  and constitutional challenges, 26,
    27
  control over, in Stuart era, 31
  and dependent judges, 27
  exercise of power by, 5, 29
  function of, 5
  judgments of, 76–7
  and judicial space, 26–9, 30
  packing of, 28, 72
  penalties for, for finding against
    courts' direction, 26–7, 31
  powers of, 21, 29–33
  in seditious libel cases, 4–5, 29–30
jurisprudence
  colonial, 14, 39, 47, 57, 92
  English v. American, 3, 47, 48
jurors
  choice of, 176
  coercion of, 59, 160
  as judges of law, 20
  knowledge of law of, 57–8
  powers of, 12
  qualifications of, 31, 81

Keble, Justice, 20, 21
Kent, James, 143, 144
Kentucky Resolutions, 101–2
knowledge of the law, of common
    people, 131, 133

language, of law, 17–18, 83, 140,
    158
law
  criticism of application of, 27
  as defined by revolutionary
    colonials, 5

law – *continued*
  Hamilton on, 112
  interpretation of, 17, 18, 76
  Locke on, 43–4
  psychological force of, 112
  and revolution, 10
law of liability, 71
law of nations, 113, 114
law of reason, 20–1, 79–80
lawyers (colonial), 39, 77
legal certainty, 6, 17, 30, 99, 147
  see also legal uncertainty
legal reform
  in America, 61
  claims for, in England, 5, 30
legal uncertainty, 18–19, 30, 147–8
  Coke and, 17
  in colonial law, 10–12, 56–60, 78
  and language, 17–18
  Locke and, 41
  post-Revolution, 62, 126
  see also legal certainty
legislative powers, 70, 112, 116
legislative review, 70, 106
legislature, 113–16
  power of to judge content of laws,
    116–17
legitimacy
  of the Constitution, 123
  of law, 3, 45, 123–4
Letter from Phocion, 113
Levellers, 15, 155
  and challenge to the law, 22, 30
  and legal uncertainty, 17–18
Levy, Leonard, 51
Libel Act (1792), 27
libel law, 54
liberty, 126
  and an independent judiciary, 119
  threat to, 110
  and trial by jury, 34, 109
Lilburne, John (c. 1614–57), 15,
    157, 158, 159
  trial of, 18
local consensus, 104, 138–9
local government, 84, 138
  Adams on, 89, 90
localism
  Adams and, 82–3, 104

within federalism, 9
Jefferson's commitment to, 101–2
Locke, John (1632–1704), 37, 124,
    167, 168
  on civil law, 46
  on common law, 73
  on human knowledge and
    judgment, 42–4
  influence of on American
    revolutionary thought, 7, 41,
    40–8, 96, 166
Longman v. Mein, 74, 75, 77, 78

McCulloch v. Maryland, 138
Madison, James (1751–1836), 64,
    98–100, 102, 103, 117
  and Bill of Rights, 120, 121
  and Council of Revision, 134
  jurisprudence of, 119–20
Magna Carta (1215), 13, 22, 77
majority
  rule of, 127–8
  will of, 95, 98, 101, 103, 115
Mansfield, William Murray, Lord
    Justice (1705–93), 51, 74, 75,
    162
Marbury v. Madison, 140
Marshall, John (1755–1835), 69,
    147, 153
  jurisprudence of, 137–42
Massachusetts
  Court reports from, 57
  powers of juries in, 61
Massachusetts Constitutional
    Convention (1780), 56, 69, 104
Mayhew, Jonathan, 41–2
Mead, William, 21, 27, 159
Meal Tub Plot, 23
minority, needs of, 98–9, 103
'modes of discourse', 7
Monmouth's Rebellion, 23–4
moral certainty, 96, 147
Morris, Lewis, 11, 52
Murrin, John, 179

national government
  Adams on, 89, 90
  Hamilton on, 108
  Jefferson on, 89, 90, 96–7

national government – *continued*
  purpose of, 90
natural law
  Adams on, 79–80
  Hamilton on, 122
  Jefferson on, 99
  Locke on, 43–4
nature of man, 90–3, 96
Nelson, William, 49, 57, 138
New Jersey
  power of juries in, 60
New York
  common law in, 56
  threats to juries in, 53
New York Constitution (1777), 113, 116–17
New York Legislature, 112
New York Weekly Journal, 52, 53
North Briton, 75
North Carolina
  power of juries in, 61
'Novanglus' letters, 73–4, 79

'old constitutionalism', 12, 14
opinion *see* political opinions; public opinion
opposition writers, 163
  influence of on revolutionary ideology, 35–6, 38, 39
  see also pamphlet literature
Otis, James, 25, 78
Oyer and Terminer Commissions, 19

Paine, Thomas, 98
pamphlet literature, 27, 30, 33
  see also opposition writers
paranoia, 36, 37–8
Parliament, 45, 133, 154
  in comparison with Supreme Court, 146–7
  and fundamental law, 15, 25
parliamentary sovereignty, 13, 32, 38, 128–30
  v. 'old constitution', 152, 153
  and rule of law, 23, 45, 133
participation, 9, 130, 159
Penn, William, 21, 27, 159
Pennsylvania, 50

common law in, 56–7
power of juries in, 61
Pennsylvania Constitution (1776), 130
people
  ability of to judge right, 12, 88, 122, 123
  capability of to understand law, 6, 31, 40, 42, 59, 74, 143
  constitutent powers of, 44, 46
  see also majority, will of
physiology, Jefferson and, 91, 92
Pinkney, Charles, 124–5
Pocock, J.G.A., 40
political culture, and American revolution, 35, 39
political opinions, 94, 96
political power, Locke's definition of, 43–4
political utility, 99
Popish Plot, 23
popular sovereignty, 62, 119, 121
  and instability, 121–3
  juries as an expression of, 48, 81
  Wilson on, 130–1, 135–6
Pound, Roscoe, 13
power of attaint, 75
property rights, 12
psychology, and government, 122–3
public interest, and stability of government, 108, 122
public opinion, 130
  as expressed in juries' verdicts, 55
  Jefferson on, 96, 98
  power of, 31, 47
punitive laws, 112
Pym, John (1584–1643), 12, 15

reason, 9, 18, 30, 91, 130
  Adams on, 79–80, 179, 180
  and civil law, 73
  Jefferson on, 95
  law of, 20–2
  limitations of, 47, 122
  and will, 110, 112, 114
Reid, John, 10–11, 14, 151
Reid, Thomas, 92, 128
representation, 9, 129, 130
republican politics, 102–3

responsibility, of men for their political creeds, 92, 94
revolution
Jefferson on, 100
and scope of jural power, 4
revolutionary political ideology, 35–6, 37, 38
Rex v. Baldwin, 75
Rex v. Williams, 75
Rhode Island legislature, 49, 116
Richmond Syllogism, 64
Royal Prerogative, and rule of law, 23
rule of law, 23
Rump Parliament, legitimacy of, 19
Rush, Benjamin, 60, 93
Rutgers v. Waddington, 113, 114
Rye House Plot, 23, 37

scepticism, 128
science, Jefferson on progress on, 92
Scroggs, Judge, 24
Sedition Act (1794), 63–4, 103
seditious libel (treason), 4–5, 22, 23, 32, 51–2
in America, 108–9
in colonial cases, 5–6, 42, 52–6
juries in cases of, 26, 27, 29–30, 162
seditious libel trials
comparison of in England and America, 51–6
in Wilkite cases, 75–6
'self-evident principles', 140
self-government, 98, 103, 106, 108, 130
self-interest, 108, 119
separation of powers, 69–70, 83–4
Sewell v. Hancock, 78
Shaftesbury, Anthony Ashley Cooper, 1st Earl of (1621–83), trial of, 37
Shaw, Lemuel, 143, 144
Shay's Rebellion, 63
sovereignty, 3, 47
see also parliamentary sovereignty; popular sovereignty

Spooner, Lysander, 72
stability, 108, 121–2, 124, 140, 147
standards of justice, 123–4
state, Wilson's definition of, 135
states rights, 101–2, 135
Stephen, James, 24
Stewart, Dugald, 92
Story, Joseph, 143, 144
substantive law, 10, 27
Sugar Act (1764), 34
Supreme Court, 6, 9, 65–6, 124–7, 142
Jefferson and, 103
judicial review by, 102, 135
and judicial space, 144–8
Marshall and, 139, 140–1
Wilson on, 130–135

Tocqueville, Alexis de (1805–59), 9, 48, 81
townships, 9
tradition
authority of laws resting on, 43
as justification for reform, 13
'transit of ideas', 13, 22, 152
treason *see* seditious libel (treason)
Treaty of Peace (1783), 112, 113
Trenchard, John, 41, 51
Trenton Trial, 133
Trespass Act, 111, 113
Trevett v. Weeden, 116
trial by jury
Adams on, 78, 82
attack on, 50–1
in colonies, 34, 48, 78
in common law, 15
Hamilton on, 108, 109
Jefferson on, 87
in post-revolutionary America, 60–1, 116
Trial of the Seven Bishops (1688), 27, 28–9
truth, as a defence in libel, 54–5, 109
turbulent majorities, 86, 146
Two Treatises (Locke), 43, 44
tyranny, powers to resist, 42

unconstitutional acts, 129

*United States v. Hudson and
    Goodwin,* 138
utility, Jefferson's conception of,
    99, 101

Van Schaak, Peter, 56
Vaughan, Chief Justice, 27, 28, 31
verdicts
    directed, 51
    setting aside of, 51
    special, 54, 59, 72, 73
Virginia, 104–5
    Jefferson on, 93, 94
    trial by jury in, 149
    University of, 89
Virginia Bill of Rights (1776), 120
voice of the people, 123
    juries as, 71, 81

Walwyn, William, 15
Wemms, William, 72
whig and tory, 91
whigs, and constitutionalism, 32

Whiskey Rebellion, 63
Wildman, John, 39
Wilkes, John (1727–97), 75, 76
will
    of the people, 107, 112
    see also majority, will of
    and reason, 110, 112, 114
Wilson, James, 117, 141, 191
    on judicial review, 130–1, 133–6
    on majority rule, 127–8
    on parliamentary sovereignty,
        129–30
*Wilson v. Black Bird Creek Marsh
    Co.,* 138
Wirt, William, 64
Wood, Gordon, 35, 37, 38–9, 58,
    149
written case law, 57

Yates, Robert, 125

'Zenas', 61
Zenger, John Peter, 52
Zenger Case, 52–5, 59